Although Arnie Wilson comes from an artistic background (his father, Bernard, was a composer who met his wife Joan, a concert pianist, at London's Wigmore Hall where they were both featured in a concert) he has inherited few of their talents. 'I failed to learn the French horn, my favourite instrument, but did manage to play the flute in the Canterbury Youth Orchestra for a while,' he says. It was as a journalist rather than as a flautist that Wilson made his mark. He spent 15 years in television – on screen for 10 of them – and several years in Fleet Street, before becoming the *Financial Times* ski correspondent and skiing every day of the year in 1994 (thus entering the *Guinness Book of Records*). He also wrote regularly for the *FT*, occasionally interviewing celebrities for the paper's 'Lunch With The FT' feature. In 2001 he became editor of *Ski+board*, the Ski Club of Great Britain's magazine. Wilson, who has four skiing daughters from his first marriage, is the author of several books, but this is the first that is not about skiing. He and his Swedish wife, Vivianne – who were married on the mountain at Jackson Hole, Wyoming in 2000 – live in West Sussex, England.

Big name hunting

Confessions of a celebrity interviewer

Arnie Wilson

Revel Barker
Publishing

www.booksaboutjournalism.com

First published by Revel Barker Publishing, 2010

ISBN: 978-1-907841-01-9

Revel Barker Publishing
66 Florence Road, Brighton, England BN2 6DJ
revelbarker@gmail.com

CONTENTS

Guinness, Dudley Moore, Michael Winner, Michael Parkinson, Jane Birkin, Dirk Bogarde, Eric Clapton, Jacques Doillon, Serge Gainsbourg.

5   Paddy Milligan
Spike Milligan, Patricia Ridgeway (Paddy Milligan), David Whiting, Muriel Lady Dowding, Air Chief Marshal Lord Dowding.

6   Stars have sex too
Jilly Cooper, Edward Woodward, Jeffrey Archer, Ernie Wise, Tony Blackburn, Norman Parkinson, Denis Nordern, Michael Palin, Katie Boyle, Thora Hird, Desmond Morris.

7   Chutzpah
Nicholas Tomalin, Marmaduke Hussey, Sir Geoffrey and Lady Harrison, Clint Eastwood, Arnold Schwarzenegger, David and Iman Bowie, Princess Caroline of Monaco, Joseph Mallaun, Christie Brinkley, Franz Klammer, Roger Moore, Michael Caine, Fiona Fullerton, Anthony Perkins, Ringo Starr, Paul McCartney, Cliff Richard, Linda McCartney, Elvis Presley, Buddy Holly, Eddie Cochran, John Lennon, Henry Kissinger, Patrick McGoohan, Harry Fowler, Michael Winner, Mel Gibson, Sean Connery, Edward Heath, Lord Aldington.

8   TV and radio
David Hamilton, Sir Alastair Burnet, Brent Sadler, Tony Gubba, Terry Johnson, Peter Sissons, Reginald Bosanquet, Andrew Gardner, Leonard Parkin, Gordon Honeycombe, Sandy Gall, Ivor Mills, Robert Dougall, Richard Baker, Bob Verrall, the Queen, Jeffrey Archer, Norman St John Stevas, Terry Nation, Bernard Bosanquet, Dickie Davies, Fred Dinenage, Barry Westwood, Trevor 'The Weather' Baker, John Aspinall, Lord Lucan, Alan Clark, George Pellett, Charlie Drake, Dudley Moore, Gary Glitter, Christopher Lee, Bill Oddie, Ken Bruce, Barrie Humphries, Barry Manilow, Liza Minelli, Tom Jones, Lord Linley,

9   Wogan on Wogan
Sir Terry Wogan, Linda Johnson, Ned Sherrin, Robin Day, Bruce Forsythe, Andrew Gardner, Alan Bennett, the Queen.

10   Milligan madness
Spike Milligan, Richard Webb, A J Tew, Edmund Fisher, Michael Ayrton, Warren Mitchell, Paddy Milligan, David Watkins, David Whiting, Lady Dowding, Peter Sellers, Sheilagh Milligan, Sean Milligan, Bill Pertwee, Michael Bentine, Harry Secombe, Lynne Frederick, David Frost, Freddie Starr, Colin Cowdrey, Garrison Keillor.

11 Lean, Lawrence and Lara

Sir David Lean, Ken Russell, John Schlesinger, Alan Parker, Hugh Hudson, Michael Winner, Sam Spiegel, Peter O'Toole, Omar Sharif, Jack Hawkins, Sessue Hayakawa, Julie Christie, John Huston, Orson Welles, Billy Wilder, Lady Lean (Sandra Cooke), Terence Stamp, Sir Alec Guinness, James Fox, Sir John Mills, Rita Tushingham.

12 Actors galore

Andrew Faulds, Buzz Aldrin, Van Phillips, Jack Hawkins, Stanley Baker, Lord Mountbatten, Jackie Stewart, Shelley Winters, Peter Ustinov, David Suchet, George Chakiris, Peter Cushing, Oliver Reed, Charles Hawtrey, Billy Whitelaw, Barbara Windsor, George Best.

13 The royals

Prince of Wales, Diana Princess of Wales, Princess Caroline, ex-King Constantine of Greece, Lady Brabourne, Lord (Bill) Deedes, Denis Thatcher, Richard Kay, Nigel Dempster, Tony Coe, John Profumo, Christine Keeler, Prince Andrew, Peter Tory.

14 Stateside

Peter Tory, Tony Fisher, Robert and June Mintz, David Hemmings, William Shatner, Telly Savalas, Jimmy Stewart, Bo Derek, Dudley Moore, Robert 'Hoot' Gibson, Gene Roddenberry, Leonard Nimmoy, Brogan Lane, Rock Hudson, Liza Minnelli, John Derek, Rita Tushingham, Joan Collins.

15 Playing Politics

Harold Macmillan, President Jimmy Carter, Harold Wilson, Gerald Kaufman, Michael Green, Mandy Rice-Davies, Christine Keeler, Princess Royal (Princess Anne), Bill Deedes, Julius Deedes, Jeremy Deedes, Sir Alec Douglas-Home, Tony Blair, Alastair Campbell, Michael Foot, Neil Kinnock, Ramsay MacDonald, Margaret Thatcher, Denis Thatcher, Carol Thatcher, Peter Tory, Lord Carrington, Admiral Sir 'Sandy' Woodward, Sir Peter Hall, Cecil Parkinson, Sara Keays.

16 Explorers

Col John Blashford-Snell, Alf Leggatt, Prince of Wales, Sir Ranulph Twisleton-Wykeham Fiennes, Mikhail Gorbachev, Dr Armand Hammer, Franz Klammer, Dr Mike Stroud, Sir David Lean, Wilfred Thesiger, Sir Laurens van der Post, Lord Hunt, Sally Nesbitt, Edmund Hillary, Sherpa Tenzing Norgay, George Band.

17   The final frontier
Carl Sagan, Buzz Aldrin, Neil Armstrong, William Shatner, Yuri Gagarin, John Glenn, Konstantin Tsiolkovsky, Peter Tory, Robert 'Hoot' Gibson, Peter Fairley, Nigel Ryan, Mark Frary, Ed White, James McDivitt, Sir Patrick Moore, Orville Wright, Albert Einstein, Werner von Braun, David Whiting, Lord Dowding.

18   Eric Morecambe
Eric Morecambe, Ernie Wise, Peter Oakes, David Graves, George Burns, Tommy Cooper, Dean Martin, Jerry Lewis, Lord Lucan.

19   Music
The Beach Boys, Boy George, Frank Sinatra, Leonard Cohen, Dame Vera Lynn, Tony Coe, Spike and Paddy Milligan, Humphrey Lyttelton, John Dankworth, Stan Tracey, Stan Getz, Dizzy Gillespie, Count Basie, Ronnie Scott, John Horler, Cleo Laine, David Niven, Edward Rubarch, John Huston, James Ellis, Jeremy Kemp.

20   Back page stuff
Brian Clough, Stuart Imlach, Gary Imlach, Billy Wright, Ian St John, Jimmy Hill, Jimmy Greaves, Ron 'Chopper' Harris, Mike Yarwood, Graeme Johnston, Erica Roe, Roger Insall, Samantha Fox, Shirley Anne Field, Ian Ogilvy, Sir Terry Wogan, Colin Cowdrey, Rohan Kanhai, O'Neil Gordon 'Collie' Smith, Denis Compton, Sir Garfield Sobers, Franz Klammer, Sean Connery, Paul Chase-Gardner, Brian Johnston, John Arlott, Bill Frindall, Fred Truman, Graham Cowdrey, Harold Larwood, Sir Patrick Moore, David Whiting, Sir Stirling Moss, Damon Hill, Graham Hill, Felipe Massa, Kimi Raikonnen, Jimmy Clark, Peter Collins, Eugenio Castellotti, Gerhard Berger, Prince of Wales, the Queen.

21   Skiing
Arthur Sandles, Franz Klammer, Tommy Moe, Hermann Maier, Clint Eastwood, Princess Caroline, Arnold Schwarzenegger, Robert Redford, Dick Bass, Martin and Graham Bell, Cindy Crawford, Chrissie Evert, Andy Mill, Adam Faith, Susan Hampshire, Michael Edwards ('Eddie the Eagle'), John Dunn, Gloria Hunniford, Sandy Gall, Konrad Bartelski, David Vine, David Gower, Peter May, Allan Lamb, Heston Blumenthal.

22   Calm down, dears
Barbara Cartland, Michael Winner, Nigel Dempster, Paul Callan, Lord (Bill) Deedes, Sue Pollard, Peter Cook, Tony Blackburn, ex- King Constantine of Greece, ex-King Michael of Romania, Rico d'Ajou, Harry Fowler, Billy Fury, Dick Lester, Helen Shapiro, Ivor Mills, David Stein.

23 Old friends
Col John Blashford-Snell, Franz Klammer, Ken Bruce, Sir Terry Wogan, Kerith Coldham, Jimmy Young, Robert Sproul-Cran, John Gardner, Ian Fleming, Kingsley Amis, Peter Hall, Peter Brook, Paul Scofield, Richard Kay, Peter James, Paddy Milligan, Reginald Bosanquet, H E Bates.

24 Mentors acknowledged
Bob Friend, Paul Callan, Michael Hellicar, Peter Tory, Neil Mackwood, Peter McKay, Jeanette Bishop, Kenneth Branagh, Sir Geofroy Tory, Nigel Boonham, Archbishop of Canterbury (Robert Runcie), Nigel Dempster, Marquis of Bath, John Rydon, John Roberts, Arthur Firth, Lloyd Turner, Keith Waterhouse, Duncan Sandys, Tunku Abdul Rahman, Garth Gibbs, W W Soong, the Queen, Norman Hartnell, Seymour Heller, Frank Sinatra, Ava Gardner.

25 Last, but...
Eleanor Barry, Peter Tory, Duke of Athol, Maj-Gen Frank Richardson, Napoleon, Frederick the Great, Alexander the Great, Gen Kitchener, Gordon of Khartoum, Florence Nightingale, Bill Papas, John Ward, Diana Princess of Wales, Princess Royal, Duchess of Gloucester, Prince William, Prince Harry, the Queen, Prince of Wales, H E Bates, Laurie Lee, John Lennon, Harry Nilsson, Howard Jacobson, Rosie Boycott, Dame Barbara Cartland, Greta Scacchi, Jeremy Ashpool.

For my wife Vivianne,
and my daughters
Samantha, Lara, Amber and Melissa.

Wilson of Deal

TV News Quiz presenter: 'Who is this man?'
Nigel Dempster: 'That is Wilson of Deal, who makes four million pounds
a year out of gossip columns.'

When I accosted him at a World Wildlife Fund gathering, the Duke of Edinburgh turned to Prince Bernhard of the Netherlands (one of the organisation's founders) and said: 'This chap's not interested in wildlife – he's only interested in gossip.' Not quite right. I was interested in both – but had, indeed, tried to chat to both men about birthday presents. (It was Prince Bernhard's birthday.)

What I was also interested in (though less so today when 'celebrities' are ten a penny) was the cult of celebrity. Who are these people? Are they so different? They quarrel, flirt and cry (real tears, sometimes), they bleed when cut, they have children, and their hair thins and they age just like the rest of us. Yet strangely their fame, when emblazoned in glossy magazines, seems to make them different. And less real. They may seem immortal, and immune to suffering, but have you noticed how many of them – almost all, in fact, in the long run – disappear from the glossy pages and then from life itself? Sometimes you don't even notice when a famous actor or actress disappears from public life. It's only when you see a photo of them 10, 20 years later – perhaps in an obituary – that you say 'Good Lord – I wondered what had happened to him.' Or her. But you probably hadn't wondered. And while you weren't actually noticing their absence, they may have suffered the indignity of drifting helplessly into the stagnant backwaters of life. And just as a beautiful woman often finds it particularly hard to cope with losing her looks, the more famous a celebrity has been, the harder it is to adjust.

You could say my largely freelance journey through Fleet Street, television and radio has been eclectic. And my perambulations through some ten national newspapers and almost as many TV stations meant I was often bumping into celebrities. I was eager to write about them, even though at various stages of my career I was supposed to be working on news and current affairs rather than gossip or 'diary' stories. So often there seemed to be an irresistible diary angle. Although the celebrated diarist and columnist Peter McKay once told me that embarrassing stories were the key to gossip writing – and I can see his point – I think I managed to scratch a living from diaries without embarrassing the people I wrote about. Instead I went for the quirky or humorous angle, and it seemed to work just as well. What's more, my victims tended to trust me more that way, gave me several bites of the cherry, and often remained friends, or at least regular acquaintances.

For most of my career I either worked in newspapers while doing TV at weekends… or the other way round. Thus for more than 20 years I worked constantly in both media, with quite a lot of radio thrown in. This may explain the sometimes confusing timescale of some of the contents of this book. In any given week I might find myself a TV reporter Monday to Friday, then working on the news desk of the *Sunday People* on Saturdays, and writing for the diary pages on Sundays. In other periods I might be working from a freelance desk on a Fleet Street diary column somewhere, as well as doing two or three night shifts as a news reporter on the *Daily Mirror* – and working in TV at weekends. Confused? So was my young family. But not so confused that from time to time they dreaded my turning up at a function they happened to be at. My twins, Amber and Lara, were best friends with another set of twins, Sammy and Suzie Brown, whose father Steve just happened to be – at the time – Elton John's creative manager. He also helped manage Billy Connolly. Amber and Lara got to know Connolly quite well, and of course there were anecdotes about him and Elton that would have made excellent gossip stories. I wasn't allowed anywhere near them. And you should have seen my twins' faces when I turned up at Wembley Stadium to cover Wham!'s last concert… There in the audience were both sets of twins and certain members of Billy Connolly's family. I got the 'God, Dad, what are you doing here?' treatment. So while I busied myself interviewing various members of George Michael's family, plus a few other celebrities like Lulu, I wasn't allowed anywhere near my twins' entourage.

Amusingly, I have a similar situation today with Lara, who manages a rather smart dental practice in London which has some very big names as clients. Lara trusts me now, and tells me affectionate snippets about her famous clients, knowing that they will never appear in print.

There's one story I'm dying to tell (but I daren't ask), and I'm sure the celebrity involved wouldn't mind, because it shows him in a very good light. It's more than her job's worth of course, and in any case I would never betray a daughter's trust. The only time I slightly compromised Lara was not for a story but just a bit of mischief. I knew that Trevor Eve – the star of the BBC TV series *Waking The Dead* was a patient at her practice. So when I spotted him having a pre-match lunch a couple of tables away in one of the hospitality areas at Chelsea Football Club, I couldn't resist wandering across and quite shamelessly telling him a) how much I enjoyed his work and b) that Lara, another fan, had 'almost swooned' when she picked up the phone at work to find it was him booking an appointment. Eve did have a quiet chuckle at this. But Lara didn't when I texted her from the ground to tell her who I'd just met. 'Dad, I don't believe you did that,' she texted back.

One of the strangest feelings about my journalistically split personality was working for the *Star* or the *Mirror* one day and the *Financial Times* the next. I never did quite know who I was. It was a subject I once discussed briefly with Michael Parkinson. Briefly, because he unexpectedly got quite snotty when I mentioned one Sunday on the *Daily Mirror* that I worked for Southern Television during the week. I'd only rung him to wish him a happy birthday, but all he banged on about was whether Southern knew I was moonlighting at weekends, and what the National Union of Journalists would make of it. It was pointless continuing the conversation. Perhaps I caught him on a bad day. Not everyone, as I discovered when I rang Michael Winner for the first time, likes being rung on a Sunday… He did let me interview him eventually – but it certainly wasn't on a Sunday.

In 1986, skiing came along and took over my life. For the next 24 years I wrote about skiing for the *Financial Times* (and still do from time to time). But the shameless desire for celebrity interviews and diary stories remained manifest. Skiing brought me into contact with numerous big names, including Clint Eastwood, Robert Redford, Arnold Schwarzenegger, Jimmy Carter and many world class skiers like Franz Klammer, Jean-Claude Killy, Stein Eriksen, Hermann Maier and Tommy Moe.

Yet my only significant staff jobs apart from a few years learning my craft in various offices of the *Kent Messenger*, were ten years as an on-screen reporter with Southern Television and TVS, and 18 years as Saturday staff on the *Sunday People*. However, for many years I worked 'as staff' on the *Daily Mirror* diary in its many forms, as well as doing night shifts in the *Mirror* newsroom where my colleagues included Anne Robinson and Alastair Campbell.

My lengthiest diary experience was with Peter Tory who taught me an enormous amount about diary columns, first as the *Daily Express* William Hickey, to which I was a contributor, and more importantly on the *Daily Mirror*. Although my time with him on the *Mirror* was brief, it cemented our friendship and soon afterwards, when Peter started a new adventure on the *Daily Star*, he took me with him for four very happy summers (I had skiing commitments in the winter) on his eponymous gossip column. This included a memorable two weeks in the USA and interviews with Bo Derek, William Shatner, Dudley Moore, David Hemmings and an astronaut called Robert 'Hoot' Gibson. I also started writing a weekly limerick for him; in the end almost a hundred were published in the *Star* (and later in his *Sunday Express* diary). I loved writing them, and spent a lot of time trying to ensure they scanned. I feel a weakness with many limericks is that they don't (scan).

When Peter and I arrived in Los Angeles to do a series of columns for the *Star*, we received a friendly telegram (remember them?) from Jack Martin, one of Hollywood's most celebrated gossip writers, welcoming us to town and inviting us to a 'Look-alike party'. I took great delight in sending a telegram by return thanking

14

him for his kind invitation, but informing him rather cheekily that we were 'too busy with real thing'. Tory was tickled by that.

I seemed to be attached to Tory's coat-tails: when the *Star* was sold I followed him once again, this time to the *Sunday Express*. Here, still as a freelance, I was Peter's right-hand man on his diary page. We were a good team; he had superb writing skills, and I had the contacts he lacked. (The best compliment he ever paid me was one morning on the *Star* when he'd had the previous day off. 'Great column today, Arnie,' he said as he strode into the office. 'It was so good I thought I'd written it.')

Yet I never had a proper job in Fleet Street, largely because I turned down the only two ever offered me – as showbiz correspondent for the *Sunday People* (offered to me in 1976 at a salary of £6,750 – 'I think you should know that you faced formidable competition with high reputations and greater experience than you,' said the editor, Geoffrey Pinnington) – and, ten years later, the *Daily Star* (£25,000 a year and a company car). I turned down Pinnington. He was a nice man – old school – who had compassionately agreed to drop a story the actress Billie Whitelaw had given me about her son before she suddenly became concerned that his school friends might tease him, and asked very apologetically if we could 'kill' it.

My first decision was based on the fact that – flattered though I was to be offered a Fleet Street staff job – it would mean ending the on-screen TV work that I'd been doing for only a year. As it turned out, it was a good choice as I still had eight reasonably good on-screen years to go. It would also have meant giving up my life-time habit of selling diary stories to various other newspapers – perish the thought...

As for Lloyd Turner's equally flattering offer at the *Star*, I suppose the reason I rather ungraciously turned him down was that I didn't want my colours, such as they were, nailed to any one mast. And of course by then it would have rather interfered with my skiing career. Also – where would the fun be in simply being paid to churn out interviews with celebrities? Half the satisfaction of finding diary snippets – and occasional lead news stories – is never quite knowing which newspaper they may end up in. No good for the *Mail*? Try the *Sunday Express*. Or vice versa. Maybe this story will suit *Londoner's Diary*? As long as it ends up in print somewhere – mission accomplished.

The following chapters attempt to re-visit many if not all of the big names I have been lucky enough to interview. Some of them – like Oscar Peterson (who told me he liked chopping wood with those delicate, nimble jazz-pianist hands) and Noel Coward – who I interviewed in 1973 at London's Shaw Theatre where his god-daughter Mia Farrow was starring in *Mary Rose* – are missing, because I no longer have any record of what we talked about. So I can't vouch for the absolute accuracy of this delightful little vignette when Coward (pre knighthood) was approached thus by a reporter: 'Mr Coward, Mr Coward – have you got anything to say to the *Star*?'

Coward's answer, before ducking into his waiting limousine, was brief and simple.

'Twinkle,' he said.

Some extracts from *Big Name Hunting* have obviously been touched on before in the newspapers I was writing for. Many are garnered from tape recordings I made at the time. And by the very nature of passing time, some of the people I talk about in the following pages are, sadly but inevitably, no longer with us.

In many cases, for various reasons, only a fraction of the quotes from my recorded interviews appeared in print. My interview with Sir Terry Wogan, for example, was really only designed as a way of generating publicity for *Children in Need*, but while we were warming up for that, he generously answered many other questions that he must have known would never find their way into the original article. So most of what he told me has never been published before. This goes for Sir David Lean and Michael Winner too. It's been quite revealing to listen to them again. Because so many years have elapsed since I made these recordings, it's almost been like meeting them all over again, this time without having to buy them lunch – or vice versa. In fact during the weeks when I have worked on this book, it's also been a little like having lunch with myself every day.

Christopher Rieu, my headmaster at Simon Langton Grammar School, Canterbury, once wrote on my school report: 'Writes well and amusingly about nothing'. If ever there was a testament aimed at encouraging me to become a journalist that was it. (He also wrote, in other reports: 'We are wondering whether we made a mistake in taking him' and: 'Arnold is content to gravitate to the back of the class and there do nothing'). What a shrewd and observant man he was.

Nigel Dempster's remarks mentioned at the beginning of this introduction were deliberately flippant, but he got the basics right (apart from my earnings, which were several noughts adrift of the mark). At the time I had recently appeared on a BBC TV programme with my friend and ex-colleague Reginald Bosanquet (about whom more later), perhaps the most celebrated ITN newscaster of all time, to discuss gossip columns. The programme had tried to entice Dempster himself onto the screen but for whatever reason he had declined, so they took the easy option (as Bosanquet knew I was a willing hack) and went for me instead. The reference to 'Wilson of Deal' was based on a Fleet Street joke that Tony Arnold (an industrious news gatherer based at Deal) was sometimes confused with Arnold Wilson (me) although I was in fact 'Wilson of Ashford'. (For readers unfamiliar with the *modus operandi* of freelances, they traditionally collect the name of the area they purport to cover. And my official patch was Ashford, in Kent. In fact even to this day the cheques I occasionally receive from the *Daily Mail*'s Richard Kay – Nigel Dempster's 'heir' – are still addressed to Wilson of Ashford, even though I have not lived or worked in the Ashford area for more than 30 years.)

Chapter 1
Friends like Bob...

But how did my descent into celebrity journalism come about?

It was all thanks to the man I had gone to work for in Tunbridge Wells, Kent, more than ten years earlier. A man who would himself become something of a celebrity. He was called Bob Friend.

Bob Friend had seen some of my early scribblings in the *Kent Messenger* in Maidstone, where I had been given my own front page column – rather an honour for a cub reporter still wet behind the ears. He had hired me at the then not immodest wage of £15 a week. This wasn't too bad when I recall that the local Tiki Tonga restaurant served delicious business lunches for five shillings (25p in today's language). I moved in to a bed-sit in Upper Grosvenor Road, Southborough, while my new office 'home' in nearby Tunbridge Wells was christened 'the dungeon'.

Upstairs, Bob Friend – soon to become well-known as a BBC TV news correspondent in Tokyo, Sydney and the US, and then even more famous as a Sky Newscaster and bit-part actor (playing newscasters in movies like *Mission Impossible*) – was in constant touch from upstairs via a squawk box. Friend, who had employed me on a hunch, was about to change my life and steer me into a world I had never dreamed of visiting and scarcely knew was even there. It was the beginning of a 40-year flirtation with the heady world of celebrity.

At first I felt – as a raw 20-something local newspaperman – nervous, shy and embarrassed about talking to VIPs, particularly during 'cold calls'. But gradually, under Bob's pushy tutelage, I developed a habit – even a kick – from constantly chatting to lords and ladies, as well as to a handful of the biggest show-biz names of the day.

Sooner or later, it seems, if you work as a showbiz writer for any reasonable length of time, you end up meeting just about everyone.

And inevitably some actually become quite good friends. In the coming AF (After Friend) years I would meet or telephone – sometimes briefly, but others repeatedly, perhaps once a month, more than 200 celebrities – a whole chorus line of famous actors, some of whom were my childhood heroes; a handful of former prime ministers and cabinet ministers, newscasters and presenters galore, famous pop singers, cricketers, footballers and commentators, even an American president and other prominent US politicians. Some newscasters became colleagues and even friends. There was royalty too – chats (usually random encounters, I must admit) with Prince Charles, the Duke of Edinburgh, Countess Mountbatten, ex King Constantine of Greece, Lord Snowdon, and Princess Caroline – and stars of stage and screen, as well as illustrious film directors, authors and other writers, explorers, climbers, moguls (film, TV and otherwise), a whole gaggle of comedians, a handful of astronauts, musicians by the score, motor racing champions, and other sportsmen, glamour-girls (including three Miss Worlds), and even some hardened criminals.

But when I settled into the basement of Bob Friend's news agency in Tunbridge Wells, it was titled people – celebrities purely because of an accident of birth – rather than stars of stage, screen and radio who dominated the 'diary pages' (as gossip columns are referred to in the trade). The William Hickey page (in the then mighty *Daily Express*) included in its team the young Nigel Dempster. Charles Greville (in the then rather feeble *Daily Mail*) was a column that would eventually and famously morph into... Nigel Dempster's Diary.

I soon realised that my 'gossip' paragraphs (usually acquired with the full support of their subject) could perhaps be described as the 'soft under-belly' of Fleet Street. While news stories were hard to place because there was so much competition, diary stories were, by comparison, often money for old rope. Many hard-news reporters pooh-poohed the diaries, and thought them beneath their dignity, leaving those of us who understood gossip items to make hay. Whenever I went out to cover a news story, I always looked for a 'diary' angle too, so enhancing the financial rewards. The tiniest *bon mot* or quip was a candidate for someone's diary column. It was the way you told them that sometimes earned success.

Back in the mid 1960s, Bob Friend's VIP address book was full of Lord This, Lady That, Viscount This, and Sir So-and-so. My brief was to telephone the numbers in his book and talk about... god knows what. Why on earth, I wondered, would anyone, let alone a titled person, want to be rung out of the blue and subjected to inane questions from a pipsqueak who had been a journalist for only two or three years? But they did.

'They're used to it, Arnie,' Bob reassured me. 'They like being rung, and they like seeing their names in the gossip columns.' I wasn't convinced – but I soon would be. One of the first people I rang was called Lady Darlington. I didn't have a clue who she was, or whether she was married to a lord, a knight of the realm, a count, or even whether she was a widow.

I went downstairs to the dungeon, and timorously prepared to call her. It was a number in St Margaret's Bay, a spectacular cove not too far away, close to Dover on the Kent coast.

My mental preparations were rudely interrupted by Bob's rasping voice on the squawk-box. I jumped. 'Arnie?'

'Yes Bob?'

'Have you rung Lady Darlington yet? What did she say?'

Help. 'Just about to ring her Bob,' I said.

'Well get a move on because I've got a Southern Television news script I want you to write.'

I grabbed the phone and nervously dialled the number. It turned out that, at the age of 76, Lady Darlington was pushing a wheelbarrow around at her cliff-top home. And after a surprisingly pleasant chat ('I love hard work. I use a very light wheelbarrow – that's half the battle') I got the quote I wanted. 'I like to think I make a jolly good labourer!' That was the headline in John London, the *Evening News* diary column the next day. It was hardly earth-shattering, even by local newspaper standards. But good old Lady D...

I was off on the celebrity trail.

Chapter 2
Learning the ropes

I worked for Bob Friend for about a year before he fired me. Then he re-instated me. Then he fired me again. I never did quite work out what was going on in his mind. He certainly trained me well – equipping me not only to write diary stories, but also news scripts for the local TV station – both of which were to help me earn a decent living in the years to come.

'You're the best writer I've had,' he said one evening, shortly before telling me: 'I think perhaps you'd better go.'

It was certainly a roller-coaster experience. Bob had somehow broken his leg and I was quickly recruited to be his gofer. Back then he was doing regular broadcasts for BBC radio, some local, some national – gaining experience I would find useful in my own career, not only with various TV companies, but also with the Radio 4 travel programme *Breakaway* (alas, no more). But being deficient to the tune of one leg, to paraphrase Peter Cook in the celebrated TV sketch involving a one-legged Dudley Moore auditioning for the part of *Tarzan*, meant muggins had to hoick Bob's recording apparatus from interview to interview in the snows of 1966. In those days, just as early computers were outlandishly large and pretty unmanageable, the BBC's standard recording device was heavy and bulky.

In between assignments I shivered in the West Kent News Service dungeon in Vale Road, and continued my phone calls to the rich and titled, and wrote TV news scripts, and the occasional national news story. Most of my efforts ended up in the William Hickey column or, if they didn't make it there, John London in the *Evening News*. Those connections with the William Hickey team would lead me, rather tortuously, into a long-lasting friendship with the column's yet-to-be editor, Peter Tory, but that was all to come.

Many of my conversations with the Hickey team began with someone – often the then editor of the column, Richard Berens saying 'we're under a lot of pressure old boy!' (It was the Hickey leitmotif). Well so was I – from Bob Friend. But in spite of all this, it was extraordinarily exciting to see my material ending up in a national daily. Of course, back then everything had to be phoned over to a copy-taker (who usually sounded as bored as hell as he typed your golden words): 'Yeah… yeah… yeah,' he would intone lazily in between sentences, adding occasionally: 'is there much more of this, old boy?'

Still, life as a budding diarist was fun.

Bob Friend's rather more prominent counterpart in neighbouring Maidstone was an ex-Fleet Street character called Mike Borissow, ex-*Daily Mail* and then boss of the Kent News Agency. Although rivals, the two men were fairly relaxed about boundaries, and even on one occasion conspired to make their own news.

On a rather quiet and fruitless Sunday – an ideal day to try to sell anything half decent in the world of news or gossip as there was less competition from the hustle and bustle of weekday events – the two of them invented a 'small-traffic-accident, not-many-hurt' story. A paragraph duly found its way into a handful of the following morning's tabloids which told how two motorists had collided in a quiet Kentish lane after being distracted by a photo session involving a scantily clothed model. Taking their eyes off the road for a split second, the ensuing collision had dented their cars, but left the drivers uninjured. By a strange coincidence the names of the motorists that appeared in Monday's papers were Borissow and Friend.

Chapter 3
'Aristocracy is dead'

The word Aristocracy is from the Greek *aristokratia*, meaning 'the rule of the best'. Well that was fine for a few centuries, but then – shock, horror – in 2010 the Duke of Devonshire announced that 'aristocracy is dead.'

As the 12th duke in a line of noble ancestors stretching back three centuries, he had a £500million fortune and his home was Chatsworth House – with just three short of 300 rooms. But the Duke said he wanted to give up another inherited perk – his peerage. At 65 he said he would happily surrender his title if the government went ahead with proposals to remove all hereditary peers from the House of Lords. And he added that he would be content to go back to being called Peregrine Cavendish because he was 'only here by pure chance', adding: 'I haven't earned any of this. The aristocracy is not dying. It's dead. Coffin's nailed down, it's in the ground. It doesn't exist – except that people have titles.'

Back in the 1960s, however, although the last debutantes' coming out ball had been held in 1958, there was no shortage of interest in titled people. Or so the British newspapers assumed. The diary pages were full of them and in 1966, when I started to specialise in writing diary stories, it was almost entirely titled people – princes, dukes, lords, baronets and knights of the realm, along with their ladies, whose names seemed to fill these pages – often with faintly absurd or superficial stories and quotes. But as often as not, these people were fun – and usually extraordinarily co-operative. This was the bizarre, sometimes slightly freaky but often good-natured world I'd been plunged into.

Lady Darlington with her cliff-top travails as 'a jolly good labourer' was just the first of many titled people Bob Friend would ask me to interview by phone during the mid 60s. Looking back, it was a quite extraordinary existence for me to listen to the good-natured quips and quotes from a collection of people I otherwise would never expect to associate with, let alone find myself in company with at dinner.

The list of my good-natured 'contacts' was almost endless. Systematically, about once every month (depending on my initial reception and whether I thought they would tolerate regular calls), I would disturb their rural peace. Even sometimes on a Sunday.

So: 'Sorry to bother you on a Sunday, your grace/sir/ma'am...' was a regular opening gambit. The results were scarcely more than trivial – no front pages were ever held... But they paid my wages.

Lady Baker (then the wife of the Queen's former air aide-de-camp Air Chief Marshal Sir John Baker) told me about an unusual hobby: getting dinner guests to sign her tablecloth and then embroidering over the signatures; this worked well until she started to run out of space, meaning she could ask 'only really important guests' to sign... Sir Robert Cary (an animal-loving huntsman) informed me that he had imposed a speeding ban on himself to avoid running over foxes after giving one 'a proper and dignified burial'.

I called Prince and Princess Andrew Romanoff, whose habit of celebrating Christmas twice in quick succession at their home in Kent (their second celebration marking the Russian Orthodox date of January 7) was always a sure-fire candidate for the John London column in the old *Evening News*... Lady Cunningham, the honey-producing wife of the then unionist MP Sir Knox Cunningham, told me sadly she was lamenting the death of her queen bee... Viscount Hawarden's wife Susannah explained with glee that she had donated a valuable gold ring from the Sudan to Maidstone Museum, adding, with a huge sigh of relief: 'I won't have the creepy old thing in the house – it's come out of some old mummy's tomb'...

Poignantly, Sir Herbert Cohen, a retired barrister, by then in his early 90s, recounted how he'd planted some fir trees before the Great War and was now, from his wheelchair, watching them being chopped down for timber... Greta, Lady Oakes, a racing driver, described how the great Stirling Moss had once asked her whether she wanted to kill herself – 'and then proceeded to teach me how to drive properly'… Lady Nunburnholme admitted that trying to learn French by 'listening to 26 gramophone records' was viewed by his lordship (who she said relied on basic grammar and hand signs) as a 'bit of a joke'. She said French negatives were proving to be her downfall. 'I simply can't master the beastly things,' she told me. 'But I've galloped though one or two discs about shopping and how to order in restaurants'…

Lady Burrell was happy to tell me that having given the staff their customary Christmas break, she and Sir Walter would spend part of the festive season clearing out the ditches on their farm in Sussex. 'We don't mind mucky jobs,' she said cheerfully. 'I thoroughly enjoy sloshing about in the mud – it's glorious stuff. But I'm afraid we look like a couple of tramps!'… And Lady Davenport explained that while she and her Viscount husband were sunning themselves in Spain, they would seize the opportunity to have dry rot removed from their home in Sussex. 'After all, it would be unbearable trying to live in a house full of workmen'…

Sir William Garthwaite was offering a £50 reward (a princely sum in those days – almost equivalent to a month's wages for me) for the recapture of his mother-in-law's two-hundredweight oriental bronze tiger, stolen from the drive of his Kent home. 'I am very disturbed at losing it,' he said, 'especially as it doesn't belong to me. It would be crime if it were melted down'…

Lord Harris explained that most of his collection of around 200 clocks remained firmly on Greenwich Mean Time – even during the summer months (imagine having to change them all to British Summer Time and then back again). But he added: 'I suppose I must keep one or two in line with the rest of the country for my appointments'…

The then Lord Lieutenant of Kent, Lord Cornwallis, admitted candidly that a couple of glasses of Kentish cider had once knocked him flat on his back. 'A friend offered me a glass of the stuff,' he told me. 'I liked it very much. He said I ought to have one for the road. The next thing I remember is sitting *in* the road. My legs simply wouldn't work. Luckily my chauffeur picked me up in the car.'

But then, to my surprise and to a certain extent alarm, the whole emphasis of gossip columns changed. It was the beginning of the celebrity era. Lords and their Ladies were no longer centre stage.

I think the *Daily Mirror* Inside Page diary and the *Sunday Times'* Atticus column had a lot to do with changing the face of idle and banal gossip about the aristocracy to something rather more intelligent. We started to hear much more about real celebrities: people the readers had actually heard of... trade union leaders, movie stars, politicians, broadcasters and the like. I was in my element. And all went well until, little by little, then more and more, everyone wanted their five minutes of fame. It all went overboard eventually, with newspapers writing about so-called celebrities that we'd never really heard of – the TV weather-girls, *Big Brother* contestants, that sort of thing. 'Reality TV' didn't help. My own daughter, Samantha, was one of the producers on the very first *Big Brother* programme (mild by comparison with later versions in the series) and although she moved on after the first series I could say, a little tongue in cheek, that she has a lot to answer for.

But back in the late 1960s, when Sam was just a baby, it became apparent that I needed to repopulate my contacts book with real celebrities – and to ditch those known only for their titles. After all, when I was a child, a 'star' was somebody you would recognise in the street (though you'd probably never see them in the flesh, and they didn't open department stores). They had international fame. But where was I going to find them?

Chapter 4
Love from Joanna Lumley

The first serious 'non-aristocrat' contact I netted was an intriguing Australian author called Russell Braddon. I first met him at the Leas Cliff Hall, Folkestone (where I had washed up and cleared tables in the school holidays as a teenager). Braddon was on a TV panel for a programme being recorded by Southern Television, one of my future employers.

With my growing chutzpah for sidling up to celebrities, after the programme had been recorded I made contact. He was an intelligent, amiable guy and we soon struck up a rewarding friendship. Braddon had become famous after writing a book called *The Naked Island* about his ghastly experiences as a Japanese prisoner of war. He was imprisoned in Changi for four years: the book sold more than a million copies and made his name. It was illustrated by the prominent cartoonist Ronald Searle, a fellow POW. Braddon told me that the Japanese once asked Searle to sketch some pornographic drawings of women for them. He'd 'obliged' by drawing cartoons of his soon-to-be celebrated *Girls of St Trinian's* cartoons. The Japanese were not impressed.

It was such a refreshing change to be in regular contact with a genuine celebrity rather than someone who was just titled that I rang him on a regular basis and he would even ring me. I still have a telegram from him dated December 6, 1967, asking me to call him about a new book he had written. 'PLEASE PHONE EARLIEST CONVENIENCE AFTER 9 AM = RUSS.'

I wrote endless stories about his books for both the London evening papers – Londoner's Diary in the *Evening Standard*, and John London in the *Evening News*. While I have no doubt that I was very useful to him as an unpaid (by him, at least) ad hoc publicist, writing about his eclectic book subjects was fascinating. The book that sticks in my mind apart from the classic *Naked Island* was *The*

Inseparables – about the horrors of Dachau. It concerned a German youth who took a 'trip' to try to discover whether his parents were guilty of war crimes. Braddon wondered whether by his using the then highly controversial drug LSD to try to recreate the terrors of the concentration camp, it might help younger generations to comprehend the brutality and degradation inflicted upon the prisoners there. Being an author who did thorough hands-on research, Braddon decided he must try the hallucinogenic drug for himself. 'I have never written anything that has not been from first-hand experience,' he told me.

Before this experiment, Braddon had been relatively pragmatic about the prospect. 'I am absolutely against the taking of drugs,' he'd said. 'Frankly I'd rather have my appendix out than do what I am planning to do. But I have reached the point in my book where it is absolutely necessary for me to have a bad trip. It will be medically supervised. There will be nurses and doctors on hand, and before I can take the drug I have to have most stringent medical tests to see if I can cope with LSD.'

His trip was 'shattering'. Explaining this to me later, his theory was this: 'If you've had a pleasant, blameless life, taking LSD might be quite a pleasant experience. But if you have witnessed the horrors of a Japanese POW camp, or anything else which has traumatised you, your trip is likely to be horrendous. Mine was. Anyone who takes this stuff except under medical supervision is a maniac.'

By this time I'd left Bob Friend and his West Kent News Service operation and returned to the *Kent Messenger*, now in the Ashford office. I had learnt a few more tricks of the trade, and I set out to build up my own collection of contacts so that, in addition to routine work, I could augment my meagre salary with some freelance payments. Having 'recruited' Russell Braddon, I was keen to find more contacts so that a) Bob Friend would not accuse me of stealing his, and b) I could be in on the new vogue of writing more about film stars, authors and MPs and less about people whose only claim to fame was having some sort of title.

Ironically though, practically the first person I rang from my new desk was from an aristocratic background. And more so than I realised. It led to one of my more embarrassing moments in journalism. 'What would you like me to do?' I'd asked Bill Day, my new chief reporter. 'Oh, just ring around and make the usual calls,' he said cheerfully. That normally meant police, fire, and ambulance. It was a quiet Monday though, and disappointingly nothing much seemed to have happened over the weekend.

[Later in my *Kent Messenger* career I was assigned to the charming and genuinely leafy little town of Tenterden as office manager. Here I wrote a pastiche of the well known Christmas carol which I called 'Oh Little Town of Tenterden (How still we see thee lie)' – which was a friendly complaint that very little occurred in Tenterden for me to write about and I was rapped over the knuckles by the local police who thought I was encouraging crime.]

'Why don't you give a few regular names a call?' asked Bill, giving me a list. The first one on it was someone I didn't know called Lady Brabourne. Here we go again, I thought: ringing titled people…

I dialled; early telephone subscribers still had three-digit numbers. 'Hello,' said a deep, cultured voice – one of those wonderful women's voices that, in the nicest possible way, sounds almost half way to being a man's voice. 'Is that Lady Brabourne?' I asked, still not having a clue who she was and, moreover, fairly confident that, by now, having rung all kinds of Lady This and Lady That while working for Bob Friend, I could busk my way through a telephone conversation with any of them. 'Yes' purred the voice, rich as treacle.

'Ah, Lady Brabourne, it's the *Kent Messenger* here – just wondering what was happening in your neck of the woods…' I said casually.

'Well, nothing much, really. Lord Mountbatten's coming for the weekend – I don't suppose that's of any interest, is it?'

Suddenly excited by what sounded like a potential little scoop, I quickly scribbled 'Mountbatten!' in my new notebook, giving Bill a quick thumbs up. Page One, surely, awaited me. 'Have you known him long?' I asked. 'Is he a friend of the family?'

'My dear boy...' came the patient reply, 'he's my father.'

Ahem. No Front Page scoop then. Just an embarrassing silence. Many years later, when I had got to know the Countess (as she became) better (and had even helped her find her missing cat through a diary story when I was working for the *Daily Mirror*), I reminded her of this huge gaffe. 'I've been dining out for years on that story about not realising Lord Mountbatten was your father,' I said.

'Oh!' she boomed. 'That was you, was it? I've been dining out on it for years, too...'

The Countess once sent me (in her own fair hand) one of Lord Mountbatten's favourite poems:

> The codfish lays ten thousand eggs; the homely hen lays one;
> The codfish never cackles, to tell you when she's done;
> And so we scorn the codfish, while the humble hen we prize;
> Which only goes to show you that it pays to advertise.

There's a wonderful story about Mountbatten told to me by Colonel John Blashford-Snell, my long-serving explorer chum. Mountbatten was being driven by a uniformed Wren from London to Portsmouth for a Trafalgar Day dinner, and it seems Mountbatten had made it clear he was not struck with her driving. This had made her nervous, and en route she had to deal with the embarrassment of needing to spend a penny. She explained her intentions, stopped the vehicle, and rushed off to some nearby bushes. Finishing the task, she leapt back into the car and continued on her way. When the vehicle arrived and lackeys went to open the rear door, there was no-one there. It seems that Mountbatten had thought he might as well pop out of the car and follow suit, and when his driver rushed back in and drove off, she hadn't realised this because there was a partition in the vehicle and she couldn't see that he was no longer there. So there was Mountbatten in full dress regalia, with sword and medals, abandoned in a lay-by in the

Hampshire countryside. 'I think perhaps he completed the journey by bus,' said Blashers, perhaps not entirely convincingly.

It was the old Marlowe Theatre in Canterbury, near my then home at Old Wives Lees, near Chilham, which turned out to be my best source yet for new contacts – contacts who were much more interesting, and marketable, than all those lords and ladies. The Marlowe was a theatre that attracted numerous stars of stage, screen and radio, and it was an ideal hunting ground for my dog-eared notebook.

Here, in 1968, I met James Fox, whom I held in high esteem for his acting skills, but rather less so for his rather intense religious convictions. Strange as it may seem, once I had introduced myself, he regarded me with somewhat overzealous evangelism, and in his anxiety to convert me from my rather half-hearted Quaker convictions to his own brand of Christianity – a movement called The Navigators – he literally chased me round the backstage area of the theatre.

He had just finished work on a controversial film called *Performance*, in which he starred with Mick Jagger. Fox played the part of a sexual sadist, misogynist and professional 'performer,' who was a violent enforcer for an East London gang. After finishing work on the film, the combined trauma of taking a powerful psychedelic drug (shades of Russell Braddon) and his father's death, led Fox to suspend his film career, and it was around this time that he became an evangelist.

Apparently Fox, previously cast in rather upper crust roles, had spent several months in South London among the criminal underworld researching his role, and after making the film, suffered a nervous breakdown.

'My career has happened rather the wrong way round,' he told me. 'I was rather a novice when I made *The Servant*, which was a sort of crash course in acting. After that came a lot of film parts. But I've never really done much acting on the stage. I'm trying to rectify that, even though live performances terrify me.'

In spite of Fox's attempts to convert me to his cause, I remained, nominally at least, a Quaker. (Later, when working as a reporter with Southern Television, I interviewed his brother Edward in my home village of Smarden. He was filming Agatha Christie's *A Mirror Crack'd*, in which he played Inspector Delmot Craddock, alongside Angela Lansbury, Geraldine Chaplin, Tony Curtis, Rock Hudson, Kim Novak and Elizabeth Taylor. Nice chap, but – perhaps it was my limp questions – it was probably the most boring interview I ever did.)

It was at the Marlowe that I first bumped into the actress Imogen Hassall (most famous for her role as the gypsy's wife in the film *The Virgin and the Gypsy*). The so called 'countess of cleavage' confided in me that she wanted to have a breast reduction, and the next thing I knew, her then boyfriend wanted to beat me up for writing the story! Fortunately he failed to carry out this threat, and so did she. We remained friends.

Imogen also wanted a baby. Tragically, she never succeeded, and eventually took an overdose which killed her. 'I have lost three babies,' she had told me at her home in Putney, soon after her divorce from a TV director, Kenneth Ives . 'I'm 34 and not getting any younger. A baby would mean more to me than a thousand leading roles. I just want to have a family – even if it's as a single parent family – and be a mum. People must think I have queues of suitors. But the truth is I have no-one. I'm very lonely, really, and very poor. Sometimes I wish I had been born ugly. Perhaps when I get old I'll start getting decent parts. But first I must have my baby.' Sadly Imogen never did get old – nor have her child.

It was also at the Marlowe that I first met the delightful Joanna Lumley... a very different kind of actress and personality from Imogen. Her acting career was still in its embryonic stages and she was happy to talk to the likes of me. Indeed, I later took her down to the Dover studios of Southern Television and afterwards, driving her back to her home in Kent, managed to run out of petrol on a steep hill coming out of Dover. It must be the dream of every red-blooded male to run out of fuel on a country road with Joanna Lumley in the passenger seat...

But, far from being embarrassed, she leapt out of the car and helped me push it to the nearest garage (downhill, it should be stressed).

> 'Joanna!' I yelled, changing gear,
> 'We've run out of petrol I fear!'
> She said 'That's not fab
> 'But don't hail a cab –
> I'll get out and push, Arnie dear!'

Much later, people who realised that I specialised in writing about showbiz people started asking me to 'provide' celebrities to open fetes and other functions. I remember recruiting Rolf Harris (who sweetly autographed an original drawing of himself for my daughter Samantha, signing it to 'Sam Panther') along with Michael Bentine, Spike Milligan's delightful wife Paddy and others for this type of role. Others were persuaded to provide items of clothing for charity auctions. Eric Morecambe and Ernie Wise signed autographed photos and Peter O'Toole's daughter Pat rummaged in his sock drawer and sent me a pair of his socks.

Joanna Lumley sent me a wondrous white nightie with the words 'Lots of love from Joanna' scrawled on it in bright crimson lipstick. With it came a letter that said: 'I hope I haven't wrecked it by signing it!' I was very tempted to hang on to it, but in the end it fetched a pretty good price at auction. (Where is it now, I sometimes wonder – and has the lipstick faded?)

Joanna became the sort of friend who would come to our home for tea; but after the beauty came the beast (at least by reputation, although I found him strangely charming, in spite of his criminal record). I'd interviewed Walter 'Angel Face' Probyn while working as a Saturday 'casual' at the *Sunday People*. At one stage he'd been dubbed 'Britain's most wanted man' after opening fire on police officers in Scotland. I found him fascinating and I was naive enough to invite him home to meet my daughters. Don't ask me why – I have absolutely no idea, even today. He enjoyed the cucumber sandwiches and was as good as gold. It was me at my most Lord Longford-ish - what a chump!

In the early days of their careers, many actors and actresses who eventually became household names were initially keen to meet the Press. Later (inevitably), the boot was on the other foot, so to speak – when they no longer needed their services, they were not so keen to bump into journalists. I remember Michael Crawford (born with the unlikely name of Michael Patrick Dumbell-Smith) and his then young wife Gabrielle turning up at the digs I shared with three *Kent Messenger* colleagues and four spinsters (sounds more intriguing than it actually was) in West Malling, near Maidstone. Back then, Crawford's only real claim to fame was playing the character of Byron in the TV series *Not So Much a Programme, More a Way of Life*. Byron was a tough-talking 'Mod' biker. This part would lead to a string of film roles which secured his career, but it was interesting that someone with such a brilliant future should, early on, drag himself and his wife all the way to a small town in Kent simply to secure an interview with the local newspaper.

I hung on to Crawford's phone number – essential every time one met even a minor celebrity so that eventually, when I started freelancing, I'd have a good collection of contacts for repeat business (and to swap with fellow showbiz writers). I got quite a few phone numbers simply by trading ones I had already acquired – a little like a slightly more adult version of trading cigarette cards (for those who can remember that as a hobby).

That's what celebrity journalism was and is all about, really – making sure you kept phone numbers. However, I think I might have caught Daniel Day-Lewis a bit too early in his career. He was still a youngster of 13 when he used to answer the phone at the home of his famous poet-laureate father, Cecil Day-Lewis, or his mother, the actress Jill Balcon. If only I'd known how famous he was going to be in his own right… At this stage there was even talk about his becoming a poet like his father. After a public reading of two of his father's poems to fellow pupils at school in Sevenoaks, Day-Lewis Senior told me: 'His work is rather good. He wrote a poem about a fox being hunted which shows great empathy. But I don't feel he shows any compulsion to write poetry just because I do. It's entirely off his own bat.'

Few celebrities if any objected to being phoned. Most of them were as keen on publicity as I was keen on giving it to them. And somehow the true greats – at that time stars like Jack Hawkins, Alec Guinness and Dudley Moore – put up with calls with good grace even when they no longer needed the publicity. I almost always found that the bigger the name, the more gracious they were about being rung (with one or two exceptions – Michael Winner and Michael Parkinson spring to mind.)

Meanwhile I was getting to know the other Michael – Crawford – and Gabrielle quite well, and briefly even worked for them (the only time I ever did 'paid' PR for celebrities). Crawford faced a brief period of unemployment, in which he helped his wife stuff cushions for her shop. And I got paid in Indian cushions rather than cash. This was not a good time for Crawford. The man who on stage in productions like *Barnum* and *Billy* was so good at turning on a professional smile, was now depressed and unshaven, and sadly I was in on the fact that his marriage was failing. I knew they had virtually been living apart for 18 months.

Crawford, then 30, lived on his own in a London flat. But in spite of the temptation to sell the story, I realised this would be a betrayal of their friendship, so I tried a different tack – one that I would use again when celebrities I had become friendly with trusted me with details of personal problems. I said to Michael – and Gabrielle too – that their marriage break-up would inevitably find its way into one of the tabloids. My suggestion was that – in their own good time – they might as well keep control of the story by letting me write it, so that they would both have time to get the facts right, rather than being plunged into a sudden revelation with no time to influence or correct the story. In other words, since they had a 'tame reporter' working for them, I was arguably the best journalist to break the news.

I wrote the story exclusively for the *Sunday People*. 'It has been a terrible strain keeping quiet about it,' said Crawford. 'But I didn't want to jeopardise the chance of reconciliation by telling people.

Even now I haven't given up hope.' When he'd been offered the starring role in *No Sex Please, We're British* he was so determined to make it a success that he felt he had to get totally involved in the part. So he rented a hotel room near the theatre. The show was a big success, and he started going out to lunch with people and mixing a lot. Although he was basically a bit of a loner, it seemed to him necessary to circulate more, but this left very little time to be with his family. He said that when he later accepted the part of the White Rabbit in a film version of *Alice in Wonderland*, 'that's when the problems really started'.

He told me: 'I was getting only four and a half hours' sleep a night. I kept going by taking dozens of vitamin pills. The few hours I was sleeping led to enormous stress. I suppose that's when the friction between us started. It was rather like a nightmare except I was wide awake. I kept shouting at Gabrielle and frightening her. Suddenly we seemed unable to talk to each other. One day she took the children off to her parents and never came back. When I first moved to this flat I was close to despair. I love my family and there were so many hours when I kept thinking about them.'

But Gabrielle denied that it had been she who left him. 'I was living virtually alone for a year before we parted,' she told me.

Inevitably the rest of Fleet Street, which had heard rumours about a split but had nothing to back them up, followed up the story, but at least the original version had got the facts right.

The Crawfords seemed quite grateful that the story was now out in the open and had been dealt with in a sympathetic and accurate way. Divorce followed in 1975, even though Gabrielle had said earlier: 'What's the point of divorcing unless you plan to marry someone else?' But divorce they eventually did.

At the time of the split, Gabrielle had said: 'I don't think there is any prospect of a reconciliation as things are at the moment.' There wasn't. But, refreshingly, almost a decade later, Gabrielle told me she and Michael were friends again. Although not, as she explained, lovers: 'Both of us soon became involved with other people, and so you don't really make a great effort to heal the wound. I'm still his biggest fan – and his best friend,' she confided.

'I've an enormous amount of affection for him, and people do re-light flames. I don't know that it's possible for us because I think it's almost too good as friends – and you would worry that you might blow that by trying to get something back that wasn't there. It would be like marrying my brother! The concern for him and the sisterly love is there. But I don't think that's enough for us to get into bed together…'

She said: 'When we split up I was so bitter.' And she recalled a line in the film *The Shooting Party*: 'Unless you want to be lonely, don't get married.'

'When your husband is out filming from six in the morning and doing a play at night, it's tough. I think I was too immature to cope with it. I don't blame him. He was earning the money to give me and the children a very nice life. It would be very ungrateful of me to say that he was wrong to do it. But I certainly became very lonely. You think that when you don't see very much of someone, when you finally do see them, you'll have so much to talk about. But in fact you spend a lot of time breaking the ice again. Michael was on Broadway for six months. But he never really became a star until he didn't have to worry about me any more. I don't think he would have intentionally sacrificed his career for me, and I wouldn't have wanted him to. But it seems too much of a coincidence that, when suddenly he didn't have a young wife to worry about, he became a household name. I admire him tremendously because of the 100% he gives to his work. But I suppose you can't also give 100% to your marriage.'

Often being close to one celebrity led to contact with another. Gabrielle, realising that I could be trusted (very important for celebrity writers if they want to have a regular relationship with a star, and to be fed further stories), introduced me to Jane Birkin (she of the sexually charged song *Je t'aime*, the controversial film *Blow Up*, and the nude scene with Brigitte Bardot in the film *Don Juan 73*); Jane was one of her closest friends.

She was an unlikely sex-symbol, telling me: 'People have claimed I was the most flat-chested actress in Europe. But you don't want to develop anything (like breast implants) though. It'll all fall down in

37

the end.' At the time Jane had been working with Dirk Bogarde on his final film called *Daddy Nostalgie* (1990). Bogarde described her as 'the most under-rated actress' he'd ever worked with in his 75 films, lamenting the fact that she was 'only known in Britain for that 'boring record.'

Gabrielle had become a professional photographer, and she and I worked on a few stories together for the *Mail on Sunday*'s *You* magazine (including interviewing England cricketers about what they got up to in the winter if and when they weren't on tour. This, indirectly, had led to my one and only interview with Eric Clapton, who was playing in a charity cricket match. I have to say he was charming, although when I made a crass suggestion to Gabrielle that she might get an unusual shot of him getting into his cricket whites in the changing room, his mood changed quicker than his trousers...)

You magazine was hoping to use Birkin as a lure to attract Bogarde. The magazine thought that as Gabrielle had led me to Jane, Jane might lead me to him for an interview. The plan didn't quite work. Bogarde didn't take the bait, but he did talk to Gabrielle, on my behalf, about Jane's work on their film, and at least I secured dinner and an interview with Jane in Paris.

Jane and I were accompanied during the interview by her current boyfriend, the French film director Jacques Doillon, who – fortunately, perhaps – appeared to speak no English. In 1980 she had split up with her great amour Serge Gainsbourg, and replaced him in her affections with Doillon. During the interview there was a phone call from Serge. After she had put the phone down, I asked her how it was that she was still touch with him. She said: 'He is still part of the family. He is my daughter Charlotte's father. And in any case I have never un-loved anyone.'

One of my favourite quotes of all time.

Chapter 5
Paddy Milligan

Spike Milligan was on the phone from his home in Hertfordshire, and I could hardly believe my ears. He was pouring out his grief over the loss of his beautiful wife, the singer Patricia Ridgeway, at the cruelly early age of 43. And I didn't have a pen in my hand. Indeed, at first, as the sun sank towards the horizon, turning the lawn into a rich yellowy green hue almost reminiscent of the kind of sunset more familiar in a far-eastern paddy field, it seemed almost indecent even to think about taking notes. But in the end my journalist genes got the better of me. Not daring to break the spell by asking Spike to hang on while I found a pen – or alerting him to the fact that I was thinking of quoting him – I surreptitiously reached for a box of my daughter Lara's crayons. The first one my fingers closed around was a green one that seemed to echo the hues of the grass under the evening sun. I reached for some scrap paper and turned on the light. I felt it likely that if Spike kept talking it would soon be too dark to take notes, particularly scrawled in wax on inferior paper. And my shorthand was virtually non-existent.

What followed was perhaps the most poignant half hour in what would eventually be almost 40 years of writing about celebrities. Half an hour in which the privilege of being privy to the intimate thoughts of a household name would translate into an interview that actually had some real content, rather than the sometimes rather gratuitous and even vacuous posturings of interviewee and interviewer designed purely to fill some space in a gossip column. A tragic event – the early death of such a generous and glamorous spirit, who had become a personal friend – had for once produced a story no one could fail to be moved by. Few 'celebrity' stories these days seem to fulfil such criteria.

'I was madly in love with Paddy,' Spike was saying. I have no doubt he genuinely was but, unbeknown to me or anyone at the time, he had fathered a 'love child' during an affair while Paddy's health was already in decline. She had previously told me she'd had cancer five years earlier, when she was only 38.

Spike told me he had written a song for her. She would sing it, while he played the piano. 'The title is ironic now,' he said. 'It was called *This Goodbye*. There are lots of tapes of Paddy singing. I can't bring myself to listen to them just now. But I shall enjoy them again, later.'

As Spike unburdened his tortured heart, I scribbled away, still feeling guilty – almost as if he could actually see me in the sitting room of my cottage among the raspberry fields and farmhouses in a corner of the picture-postcard village of Smarden in Kent.

It was only two days since Patricia, or Paddy as she was known to most people, had finally given up her long battle with cancer. So why was Spike pouring his heart out to me? It was the result of a terrible dilemma that many writers will have experienced. If someone in the public eye dies – someone you've known for many years and built up a genuine friendship with – it's unrealistic not to write (nice things, if possible) about them straight away. Short of including this kind of material in an obituary, no newspaper is going to wait for anecdotes until after a 'suitable period' of time has elapsed. And it so happened that I had known Paddy for years – long before I had become close to Spike. Paddy and her daughter Jane had been guests in the very cottage where I was now listening to Spike's anguished outpourings. Jane had learnt the flute using the instrument that I played myself and had lent her. Paddy and Jane had looked after our red setter, Jemma, while we were on holiday. This was a real friendship – not just a casual showbiz relationship. I had met Paddy through David Whiting, whose mother Muriel, Lady Dowding (wife of Air Chief Marshal Lord Dowding of Battle of Britain fame), had founded Beauty Without Cruelty, an organisation dedicated to eliminating animal suffering in the cosmetics industry and banning the use of fur coats. Whiting, Lord Dowding's step-son, had been a key figure in a documentary I made about animal cruelty for Southern Television.

40

Paddy, the most warm-hearted and delightful woman you could wish to meet, had bravely ventured onto the ice floes off Newfoundland to try to publicise the annual slaughter of Canadian seals. I wrote about this for the *Evening Standard* Londoner's Diary, and Paddy and I became friends as a result. Soon I was receiving Christmas cards from 'Spike, Paddy and family', although I could see that they were written by Paddy. (Later, Spike used to sign the latest copies of his books for me, so I got to know the difference in their hand-writing.)

By the time Paddy died, she had shared with me some of the hilarious anecdotes that inevitably permeated life with Spike, both before and after their marriage. It was these stories – quirky, delightful and above all harmless – that I wanted to mention to Spike so that I could prepare him for their publication, very conscious of the fact that they would appear in print in a Sunday newspaper when he would barely have had time to begin to register the full trauma of his wife's death. But at least Spike understood that news was news, and waited for no man nor woman. But although – and because – I felt close to Spike by then, how could I possibly pick up the phone and confront him with such material, touching though it undoubtedly was, at such an awful time?

But I had plucked up the courage to do so, and had all 'my' material, passed on to me by Paddy, ready to read to him. And yet I worried that some of what Paddy had told me – however amusing and innocuous – might also be a touch too personal, and could easily prompt Milligan to tears. Like stories from their courtship – if you can call Spike's crazy one-man mission to marry her a courtship: after meeting her on a film set at Elstree, he insisted on dinner, and told her even before they'd finished the first course: 'Miss Ridgeway, one year from tonight we'll be married.'

He had followed this up with endless phone calls.

'I'm lying in the middle of the road and I could be run over at any moment,' had been one opening gambit.

'I've just tried to throw myself under a bus. And if you don't marry me, I'll do it again.' Paddy had smiled and replied, in her beautiful singer's voice: 'Spike, if you're lying in the middle of the road, how is it that you've managed to get to a phone?' (There were, of course, no mobile phones back then.) After a brief pause, Spike had said: 'Well I'm near the side of the road, and I just managed to get my arm into a phone box.'

Spike wouldn't take no for an answer, but Paddy told him to go away for six months, saying that if he still felt the same after not seeing her for all that time, she would think about it.

'The next six months were crazy,' Paddy had told me. 'He never stopped ringing me and writing letters. He kept saying he couldn't wait. But I made him. He used to ring up and say if I didn't marry him he'd go to bed with Hilda from Cheam. Finally, six months to the day, he turned up on my doorstep at dawn, white-faced, and asked for my answer. Well – you know what it was.'

Before I had a chance to remind Spike about those early days, and to see whether he was happy with my writing about them, he had started his torrent of anguish. I was completely unprepared for such an emotional outburst. What he said to me on the phone that February evening in 1978 soon eclipsed the material I initially had in mind to write about.

Spike focused on his daughter Jane, then 11, and the only one of his children he had with Paddy. The night after Paddy's death, Jane had hosted a dinner for all the family in her mother's favourite restaurant. One seat was left empty.

'We drank a toast' said Spike. 'To Mummy.

'Jane is being magnificent. That's because she's bloody brave. Like her Mum. After Paddy died, I said to the family: Right. Let's not mope around. Let's go out and have some dinner. Jane was so close to my wife that I let her choose where to go. She knew where Paddy liked to eat. I let her choose the food too.'

Jane had had no idea her mother was dying until almost the last moment. 'Some people thought I should tell her sooner,' said Spike. 'But I think my timing was perfect. Jane didn't know until the evening it happened. I never want to have to do anything like that again. It was appalling. Jane rushed into her mother's bedroom and kept crying out: I love you Mummy, I love you. And Paddy said: I love you too darling. They were about the last words she spoke. Jane went to bed that night cuddling the teddy bear that Paddy had as a little girl.'

Even Paddy herself didn't know she was dying until five days before it happened. 'Our doctor was marvellous, and kept it from her,' said Spike. 'She never suspected it was as bad as it was.'

Indeed, just days before she died, Paddy herself had told me: 'I'm not going to lose this battle, don't worry.' Tragically, she did, but what a fight.

'I knew she was dying,' Spike told me in that dramatic phone conversation. 'I could see it. She was gradually getting worse. But I told her she was going to recover. Then she asked someone outside the family whether she was dying. Apparently this person let it slip that she was. I went bonkers when I heard about it. Paddy seemed to lose a lot of hope. Five days later she was dead.

'She had refused painkillers because she believed passionately that anything which had been tested on animals was bad,' said Spike. 'She was very strongly against experiments on animals. She was so bloody brave: in such pain, I couldn't bear to watch. I kept breaking down in her room, so eventually I couldn't be with her when she was in pain, because seeing me cry only made things worse for her. In the end I lied to her. I put painkillers in her food without telling her.

'Paddy will be buried near our home, so we'll be able to visit her there. I like to think of her going back to the earth, and not being cremated. I planted a cherry tree outside her room, and I'd hoped she might last at least until spring. I hoped she might live to see the blossom.'

My phone conversation with Spike was billed as 'the year's most moving interview' in the *Sunday People*. It goes without saying, I hope, that he was not paid a penny for it. Yet soon after it was published, Spike was accused of 'selling his wife's story while she was still warm in the grave'. I found it hard to believe that anyone could be so insensitive as to jump to such a conclusion.

Almost ten years later Spike and I eventually fell out badly over another interview (a saga in which I have always felt almost as misjudged by him as he was by the man who thought he had been paid for the interview about Paddy). Until then Spike was almost always good company and generous in his dealings with me.

After we fell out, we never spoke again – or at least when we did, he wasn't aware that it was me on the phone. But that's another story.

Chapter 6
Stars have sex too

When I was covering the 1986 Tory Party Conference in Blackpool, security was so tight that some of the local prostitutes complained that access to those attending (not just MPs of course, but scallywags like me) was being restricted. I couldn't resist writing a limerick about this, but I was surprised to find it being banned by the *Star*. This was a first! I thought it was one of my better efforts, and always wanted to see it in print. I have a feeling that all these years on, the *Star* might feel differently about it. Anyway, here goes:

> When a hooker at Blackpool on sea
> Tried to visit a Tory MP
> The police said: 'Alas
> Since you haven't a pass,
> You can't enter – and neither can he!'

Sex, of course, sells newspapers. One of the tasks often requested of showbiz writers is to 'ring round' as many of their contacts as they can find and ask them all the same question. This often happened to me, but never in quite such embarrassing circumstances as when I was asked by a health magazine (many years ago it must be said) to discover the sex secrets of the stars... Specifically, the question was: is sex good for you?

You have got to have the cheek of the devil to ask this. I guess I had it. Here are some of the answers (in no particular order). Many are revealing, touching, funny and perhaps unexpectedly profound.

Author Jilly Cooper: 'Good sex is absolutely wonderful for you. Much better than, say, jogging, which is silly. But it's a bit of a chicken-and-egg situation because quite often – if you've got lots of lovers – you'll want to get slim in order to enjoy good sex, rather than getting slim as a result of sex. It's very important that it ends in orgasm though, because otherwise your mind won't benefit. Sex without an orgasm may be good exercise – especially if you're one of those *Kama Sutra* types and you go in for great sexual marathons. Women who get tired and avoid sex don't realise until they've had it again how good for them it is. They suddenly realise how desperately they needed it.'

Edward Woodward, star (among many roles) of ITV's *Callan*: 'It's fairly appropriate for me to talk about this because of my recent heart attack. You can assume I'm still indulging in sex because to have suspended it would have been to disable myself in an area which would have been most unfortunate. I think you can take it that sex is good for you – otherwise mankind and womankind would have died out millions of years ago. It's not just the exercise – you can get that playing golf! Of course I know that some people have actually died making love, so in a sense you have to pay your money – as it were – and take your choice on that. I'd rather die making love than in any other way. But seriously, making love when you are in love with someone – and not just fornication – is wonderfully beneficial for body and soul, I'm all for it. It's awfully good for you, I'm sure.'

Jeffrey Archer: 'Sorry – I wouldn't touch this with a barge pole.'

Ernie Wise: 'Making love is very very good for you, and definitely good for your health, but only when you're in love with someone. Not when you're just bonking. Two people being in love is the finest thing in the world – and expressing that love between you has got to be good. It's when you're doing it looking over your shoulder with a huge amount of guilt that it's bad. It's the difference between love and lust, you see.'

Tony Blackburn: 'I think I've said enough about sex already in the past – and the radio station I work for doesn't want that kind of publicity any more, so I think I'd rather not talk about it, thanks all the same.'

Norman Parkinson, celebrated portrait and fashion photographer: 'This is a very interesting topic. Everything we do in life is, I believe, generated by the three-letter word Sex. When we're at work, or shopping or sleeping, even though there are people who hide the truth from themselves – everything hinges, if we're honest, on sexual prowess. I think falling in love, and eventually – hopefully – making love is accepted by now as being a pretty enjoyable form of exercise. Over the years, of course, the frequency is less, whereas if you jog, the frequency can increase. But I don't think jogging is good for you. Gravity is the big enemy – we weren't designed to go pounding down the road. Jogging is bad for men and rotten for girls. But sex is the be-all of life.'

Denis Nordern: 'All I can say is that when I grew up I was taught that sex made you go blind. But I suppose that falling in love is better for your health than falling in anything else!'

Michael Palin: 'Of course sex is good for you. I've never had a moment's ill health within an hour of love making. Or even within two days of love making. (I've got to be careful what I say because I've been married 23 years.) Yes, love-making is very pleasant – on a good day – with the wind behind you – and with your clothes on of course… I don't want to get involved in any of that smutty stuff. They say making love is as good as a five-mile run. I don't think I move five miles when I'm making love, but we've got three bedrooms – make of that what you will…'

Katie Boyle: I can recommend it whole-heartedly – both as me and as an agony aunt. It's very important to be physically attracted to your partner. It makes your eyes sparkle, makes you breathe quickly, and gets everything going. But of course some of us are a bit past it. They say the Victorians didn't enjoy it, but I'm sure they did, you know. My mother certainly did. Queen Victoria did too, and she put it in writing. But I think monogamy is best – making love when you're watching the door or the curtains is not a good idea. I definitely think it should be in a double bed with your husband rather than on the chaise longue with a lover. It's certainly better for you than jogging – or skiing. There's not much danger of breaking a leg making love – or getting caught in an avalanche.

Thora Hird: 'I think I'm a bit long in the tooth to talk to you about sex, but I certainly haven't given it up. Sex is all very nice but it's much more important that you love the person. Only today I was coming home from the studios in a taxi and the sun was shining and I was thinking: How nice, Scotty [husband James] will be at home waiting for me, and it was a very cosy feeling. Loving someone is very good for you.'

Desmond Morris: 'Yes, sex is good for your health because it's fulfilling a natural drive rather than frustrating it, which is the thing that causes illness. It's puritans and fanatics who suffer from ill health because of the idea that pleasure is evil or because of some religious dictum that makes them bottle up inhibitions. They become aggressive and intolerant, which can result in mental or even physical damage. That doesn't mean of course that you should be completely uninhibited with a member of the opposite sex unless love comes into the equation. But two people acting out their love, and consummating it, is very beneficial.'

Chapter 7
Chutzpah

Like having an extra-marital affair, it's indefensible but tempting. Unlike an extra-marital affair, the chances are that you are the only one eager to proceed (although there are many examples of celebrities whose partners originally met them as newspaper or magazine interviewers). What I am talking about is the unforgivable but often rewarding habit of approaching celebrities while they are relaxing over a restaurant meal. You have to be thick skinned to do this, which I am not. Yet usually – although I have managed to restrain myself on odd occasions – I just can't help it.

Over the years I was prepared to risk rejection and embarrassment by approaching some unfortunate celebrity victim mid-forkful in the hope of getting a story. Cold calling someone is one thing – they can always put the phone down on you. And being 'armed' with a TV crew during a street interview gives you extra clout and is difficult for the victim to resist, especially as the TV crew give the ambush a more legitimate flavour.

The *Sunday Times* writer Nicholas Tomalin famously said the only qualities essential for real success in journalism were 'rat-like cunning, a plausible manner and a little literary ability'. He wasn't far off. The big secret of celebrity journalism, I believe, is a mix of charm and cheek that can't really be taught. I think working on screen for ten years in TV also helps you have the brass neck to approach celebrities without too much embarrassment about making a fool of yourself in public. (A tip: Sometimes, if the prospect of asking a prominent male personality a tricky question is daunting – try his wife!)

I recall being told that the then chairman of the BBC, Marmaduke Hussey, had fallen down the stairs at a function and his artificial leg had become detached during the fall. (He'd been severely injured during the war at Anzio, and had a leg amputated as a prisoner-of-war.) No laughing matter at all, but his wife, Lady Susan, a senior member of the Queen's household, seemed to trust my telephone voice, and told me what had happened. She must have known we were going to poke a little bit of fun at her husband, but she was utterly charming and filled in the gaps.

On another occasion, this time on a news desk, I was asked to try to get words with the unfortunate former ambassador in Moscow, Sir Geoffrey Harrison, after he'd been 'honey trapped' by 'a young and attractive' KGB agent posing as a chambermaid. It had all happened 13 years earlier, and the story had only now surfaced. It was, it had been said, 'an absolutely crazy aberration' on his part, and he had 'let his defences drop', after a long and distinguished career.

One of my colleagues had already tried to phone him at home in Sussex, and Sir Geoffrey had slammed the phone down. 'You try,' said the news editor, desperately. What a prospect – I was supposed to telephone a humiliated senior diplomat who had already given short shrift to a colleague. What were my chances? About as strong as Switzerland winning the World Cup. Still, I had no choice. To my huge relief – and perhaps predictably – his wife answered the phone this time. I played my trump card. 'Lady Harrison, I understand that you are standing by your husband.' How could she not comment? She did, and eventually, after I had laid on with the biggest trowel the thickest charm in my repertoire, she handed me over to her husband, who reluctantly gave me the interview I wanted. He said he felt 'very embarrassed' about it all.

'It seemed reasonable to think that after 13 years what happened would not be revealed,' he said. 'At the time I made a full confession both to the Foreign Office and to my wife. She has known all about it all these years and she is standing by me.'

It was the *Sunday People* lead story the following day, with the headline: Our ex-man in Moscow confesses: ENVOY AND THE SEXY CHAMBERMAID.

On another occasion, when I was covering the miners' strike for Southern Television in Kent, I found myself in a room with about 14 miners. While I was chatting to them off-camera, the youngest of them said something that was electrifyingly controversial – he was quite desperate for the strike to end – and I was eager to get his quote on film. Rather than risk frightening him into silence by interviewing him alone, with the others all looking on, I decided to ask every miner in the room a similar question in private, knowing full well that his answer was the only one that would be aired that night – if only I could get him to repeat what he had rather naively said to me earlier.

A friend labelled this kind of interviewing technique the 'bum steer questions' concept, in that all the brief interviews I did that day were just for show – to avoid drawing too much attention to the young miner and getting him into trouble... At least until his colleagues saw his sound-bite that night and realised that their own quotes were on the cutting room floor. Rat-like cunning...?

On the ski slopes, a spontaneous approach to a celebrity can be nipped in the bud by the 'victim' more easily, although even the likes of Clint Eastwood and Arnold Schwarzenegger played ball. (I once had lunch 'with' Clint Eastwood in Sun Valley when he was unlucky enough to have a table next to mine, and I slithered into a seat next to him – with his reluctant blessing.) And in the same resort I persuaded Arnold Schwarzenegger to ski with me after spotting him three chairs ahead on a ski lift. He even agreed to an interview for the *Financial Times* although he kept quiet about the fact that the following day he was going into hospital for heart surgery. What a scoop that would have been...

Approaching subjects in a restaurant brings a far greater risk of rejection. However, over the years I have generally got away with it. The most notable example was my meeting with David Bowie and his second wife-to-be, Iman. It happened in a London restaurant where I had joined ski-writing colleagues for a brochure launch – a routine annual function in which a ski tour operator entertains specialist ski writers with details of their up-coming winter projects. Such functions are often held in smart restaurants.

I spotted Bowie and Iman as soon as I sat down – reflected in a mirror above our table. I resisted the urge to introduce myself for at least half an hour. And then I could refrain no longer – even though

I was fully aware that the eyes of my peers were on me, no doubt disapprovingly, as I made my way across to the Bowie table. To their great credit, both of them took my arrival in their stride. I did my usual grovelling apology, and explained that I was a ski writer attending a brochure launch. A little dishonest, that, but I felt if I asked them only about skiing I would have more success with getting at least a skiing story than if I said I was diary writer (I certainly would never have called myself a gossip writer.)

To my amazement both Bowie and Iman leapt to their feet – as if the meeting had been scheduled – and shook hands with me. And just as I did when I found myself sitting next to Princess Caroline of Monaco at an outside restaurant table in the Austrian ski resort of Zürs, I restricted my questions to those concerning skiing. Additionally, the Princess was unaware that I was a writer (and for that matter I was unaware who she was until my ski guide and friend Joseph Mallaun kicked me under the table and whispered 'Caroline'), so in fairness to her, there would be no sly questions about her domestic life. But I did write about her excellent skiing, and threw in some quotes from her ski instructor saying it was he who had a job keeping up with her on the mountain.

I can be good and equally bad at faces: I once met Christie Brinkley, the model who provided much of the inspiration for her former husband Billy Joel's big hit *Uptown Girl*, at a party for Franz Klammer in the Colorado ski resort of Telluride. I chatted to her for half an hour before I realised who she was.

David Bowie served up what to me is the perfect story – a 'gossip' paragraph about skiing, which duly appeared in Nigel Dempster's column in the *Daily Mail*. He said his son Duncan (then known as Zowie) and he had put together some music for a new album, based on ski pistes. Such runs are graded green or blue (easy), red (intermediate) and black (difficult). The music for each ski run reflected the degree of difficulty. Clever idea. Nice little story. Graciously delivered.

Other victims of my mid-prandial interruptus, as it were, include Roger Moore and Michael Caine, both of whom I pounced on in the

VIP tent near the racecourse at the Derby. Both were charming, and even signed autographs for my twin daughters Amber and Lara.

It was at the Derby that I bumped into the actress Fiona Fullerton. She was disarmingly candid about an offer she'd received from *Playboy* magazine: 'I made it quite clear that I would not pose full-frontally,' she said. 'But I thought I would meet them anyway to see whether there was any chance of a compromise involving my being clothed – or at least partly covered up. At the meeting, one of them came up to me and said: Good god, what a wonderful pair of tits you've got – how much did they cost? Typical Los Angeles mentality,' said Fiona.

After these initial meetings, Roger Moore was agreeably approachable whenever I spotted him – sometimes in the Swiss mountains. Caine was a tougher nut to crack. I nagged him gently for a proper interview and finally, after many months, he capitulated.

Of course pouncing on celebrities inevitably means rejection from time to time. It's a little like asking several pretty girls if they would like to have dinner – or even come to bed. A few will say yes, and many will turn you down or even maybe slap your face. The whole idea, of course, is that if you get some positive response it will have all been worthwhile. You could say nine slapped faces and one 'OK, why not?' is a result…

In Los Angeles Anthony Perkins of *Psycho* fame gave me the cold shoulder when I accosted him during a break in a night shoot. I almost got away with it when I met Ringo Starr at Piñons, one of the poshest restaurants in Aspen, Colorado. I was on my way out and made a glib remark to the maître d' that I'd been disappointed not to find any celebrities in the restaurant. 'Well sir, you've been sitting with your back to Mr Richard Starkey for the last half hour…'

And sure enough, I had. Ringo had been sitting right next to me, back to back, and my bottle of wine had even shared the same ice-bucket as that of his dinner companions, though Ringo himself was on the wagon at the time. Half kneeling on the floor next to him, I introduced myself as a ski writer (a legitimate claim since I was in fact skiing in Aspen) and it turned out it was his first visit to the slopes of Colorado. However the 'interview' fell apart pretty much immediately when he said, rather cuttingly: 'Would you mind if I have my dinner now?'

Quite right Ringo. I had the cheek of the devil to interrupt your evening. But that's show business, as they say.

I did rather better with Paul McCartney. Working at Southern Television at its Southampton HQ enabled me to cosy-up to all manner of stars who came to take part in its programmes. Wearing my newspaper hat rather than my official TV one, I had a few chats with Cliff Richard, and when Paul brought Linda to the studios he was quite happy to let me conduct a newspaper interview for the *Evening Standard* Londoner's Diary. The next time I met him was for an interview for *Day by Day*, the TV programme I officially worked for.

McCartney, rehearsing with his then band Wings in a barn at Tenterden, was in good form. Strumming his guitar off and on throughout the interview and making amiably sarcastic remarks about why we had spent so much time interviewing Kevin Keegan on the previous night's show, he took over the interview to such an extent that I had to remind him that I was supposed to be asking the questions. I remember mentioning that some pop singers had become extra famous by dying young, including Elvis Presley, Buddy Holly and Eddie Cochran. Paul, rather sensibly, said he'd rather not die young even if it meant less fame. And pointed an imaginary gun at his head saying in spite of that he might die young anyway. John Lennon was still alive when I interviewed Paul, but when he was killed I knew that the interview about rock stars' shortened lives would have been like gold dust. Incredibly, the studio library had lost the tapes of the unused material...

You could say I got what I deserved when I approached Henry Kissinger who was dining alone at El Padrino's restaurant in Los Angeles during its last year of operation in 1987 and asked rather gormlessly for a quick chat. I got a fairly polite 'no' which was marginally better than the reception I got from the urbane Patrick McGoohan, the star of the mysterious TV series *The Prisoner*. I'd had his phone number for months after swapping some numbers with another writer. I'd occasionally looked at his number in my contacts book and knew that sooner or later, when I was in a confident mood, I'd give it a whirl. My call was not welcome, I could tell straight away. I made it easy for him. When I heard his brusque tone of voice, I said: 'Sounds like you'd like me to get lost.'

'Yes,' he said. And put the phone down.

The amiable cockney actor Harry Fowler (whose face was so linked with the shady characters he often played that he told me he was sometimes asked 'weren't you in the nick with me?') set me up for an unpleasant exchange with Michael Winner. 'You know, you should interview him some time,' he said, encouragingly. 'Here's his number. You'll get him on a Sunday – that's when he likes to get calls.' Like a mug, I fell for it. It was obvious Winner was angry from the first (and only!) outburst. 'What the hell are you doing ringing me on a Sunday?' he said. 'Don't you ever call me here again.' I never did find out what was behind this set-up by Fowler, but when I reminded Winner only recently, he told me: 'Harry always pulled gags like that.'

There were times when even I chickened out of ambushing celebrities and attempting to interview them. I once spotted Mel Gibson in a smart LA restaurant, and was sorely tempted, but managed to resist... And I had a wigless Sean Connery in my sights at Dover Car Ferry Terminal on the set of a scene in *Diamonds Are Forever*, Connery's one-off return to the role of Bond. I flunked that too.

On another occasion, I was working with an ITN film crew and had instructions to interview Ted Heath, the Prime Minister. Heath was in Kent paying a visit to his friend Lord Aldington, a prominent Tory, and a former deputy chairman of the party. I had a choice: ambush him as he arrived and perhaps get nothing. Or arrange to do it properly, later. I rather weakly chose the latter, only to find that Heath, having dangled the prospect of an interview if I waited, changed his tune once safely inside the Aldington residence and refused to do it. Needless to say, ITN were not best pleased. My cocktail of charm and chutzpah never even got a look in.

Chapter 8
TV and radio

The TV presenter 'Diddy' David Hamilton once admitted that while doing continuity announcing at Thames TV, he asked the people in make-up to repair a split in his trousers. No-one knew he was broadcasting in his underpants because his legs were hidden by the desk. As a sort of follow-up, we once wondered, in Peter Tory's column on the *Star*, whether anybody would be any wiser if ITN's Sir Alastair Burnet read the news without wearing any trousers. Hence this:

> A trouserless newsman went spare
> When his fans saw his knees on the air
> He looked such a sight
> As he yelped out 'Good night...
> Al Burnet, Nude at Ten, almost bare!'

I finally got my own taste of (local) fame in 1975 when I was appointed Southern Television's on-screen Kent reporter – and became something of a minor celebrity myself. I say this purely because in order to write about celebrities it is probably quite handy to have had a taste of it oneself. It was not a role I had particularly coveted, but I happened to be in the right place at the right time and in the right frame of mind. Having already worked for Southern Television in the late 60s as a bulletin sub-editor, I had decamped to Anglia TV for a while as chief bulletin editor.

At Southern I had worked alongside Brent Sadler at one stage. (I also worked opposite Tony Gubba, whose calm, dulcet tones would one day make him an excellent football commentator for BBC TV). Long before I started my on-screen career, Sadler was hungry to get on screen himself and, as a bulletin editor, he seized every chance. It was customary then for us to ape *News at Ten* by having a 'second voice' for some of the more important stories. The second voice would normally appear on screen at the beginning of any item, giving whoever it was some valuable moments of exposure. What we normally did, while writing the script early in the day when it was not certain who might turn out to be available for the 'second voice' slot, was to write something like this:

NEWSCASTER: There's been a big fire in Southampton Docks today. Scores of firefighters were called to the docks soon after 7am.

SECOND VOICE: The fire started when...

What Sadler managed to do, as the person who might have written that script, was to add his name to it as that 'second voice' later in the day, so that by the time the programme went on air, it was established that he was already in the slot. And so on screen he went, almost every time he was bulletin editor.

The programme editor, Terry Johnson – a rather fearsome but very able journalist – didn't like this practice and, much to Sadler's chagrin, banned it. As a result, Sadler, a likeable but ambitious young journalist, defected to neighbouring Westward Television where his on-screen ambitions were given full rein. He went on to fame and doubtless fortune as CNN's Middle-East correspondent.

Another presenter I got to know eventually – a little later in his career – was Peter Sissons, the long-serving BBC news reader. Sissons was a 'proper' newsreader in that he had served time as a news reporter, unlike some news readers who were simply former actors. I had an unexpected remote encounter with Sissons very early in his career. Working one night in 1968 at Southern Television, we got a message to say a young ITV foreign correspondent had been shot in both legs in the Nigerian civil war, and had had to be taken to the nearest field hospital in a pram, losing two pints of blood on the journey. He had just been flown back to Britain. Could I, as the newsroom man on duty, organise an ambulance to get him to hospital in Southampton?

Sissons was of course less mobile after that. 'You've got to be able to sprint occasionally in a hotspot,' he said, so he became ITN's industrial correspondent instead. And since this was the time of chaotic industrial relations in Britain, he was hardly ever off our screens.

My own TV career was never going to be one tenth as dramatic. After Southern and Anglia, there followed a spell at Independent Television News in London where I soon befriended the station's celebrated newscasters, led by the legendary Reggie Bosanquet, Andrew Gardner, Leonard Parkin, Gordon Honeycombe, Sandy Gall and Ivor Mills. Needless to say I was still flogging diary stories to the newspapers on the side, and my friendships with these screen idols (as well as Robert Dougall and Richard Baker at the rival BBC) were useful sources.

One story I picked up (rather later) was that when the Queen had opened the building, the 'early bulletin' director, Bob Verrall, hadn't quite known how to instruct his temporary PA to hit the button to open the show. In the end he settled happily for 'Cue, Ma'am!'

Once again my hybrid television-Fleet Street background helped me when I had the idea of monitoring newscasters' heartbeats for a *Sunday People* feature. Our guinea pigs were Andrew Gardner, and Leonard Parkin. How much, I wondered, did their hearts race when they were on the air on *News at Ten*, ITV's flagship main news, watched every night by millions? We wired them up to find out. Unseen by viewers, two electrodes and a tiny transmitter were taped to their chests, and technicians took readings from a cardiograph meter. Just 30 seconds before the programme started, Gardner's pulse rate was soaring, moving swiftly from a normal 73 beats a minute to 110. 'It's always worse at the start of the programme,' he explained. 'If I listen I can hear my heart pounding.' The tests showed that he worked himself up to peak moments of stress just before speaking. But once he started to talk, his heart rate went down. At the end of the commercial break, his rate surged again to 104, leaving the break resembling a deep valley in the cardiograph.

'A newscaster must look relaxed even when all hell is breaking loose,' said Gardner. 'There's no real let-up in stress. Often one is busier off screen than on, changing the running order. Part of the brain is concentrating on reading the news, another part is listening to the studio director to find out whether a late report will arrive in time, and yet another part is trying to work out what to do if it doesn't... That's when the heart really pumps.'

His chest was hairier than Parkin's, so Leonard needed less tape to stop the hairs getting in the way of the sensitive equipment. He sneezed as he was wired up, and the meter soared to a freak 250. But his results on air were less extreme that Gardner's. His pulse remained in the high 90s except for the occasional peak of 104. Some viewers thought he looked extra cool that night. 'Sometimes I feel completely worn out after a programme, but I try to hide it with a smile,' he said. (Parkin was occasionally accused of smiling too much during bulletins, when it was suggested he should look more serious).

When I asked their counterparts at the BBC for verbal feedback, the veteran newsreader Robert Dougall said: 'I still get sweaty palms.' And his equally urbane colleague Richard Baker admitted: 'Occasionally I think to myself: Oh God, I can't do it again! I have to control the panic and stop myself breaking into a cold sweat. The thing is, if you feel terrified, not to show it.'

The verdict of a doctor we approached was: 'This reaction is normal during emotional or physical stress. It's no more dangerous than rushing to catch a train and certainly will not shorten their lives. It's good exercise for the heart because even your arteries need exercise.' Gardner was only 66 when he died in flight en route to Madeira in 1999 – after suffering a heart attack.

Leonard Parkin, a delightful man, was very kind when I left ITN to freelance, and rang me on the very first day after I'd left to give me a story: a passionate fisherman, he had high hopes of improving his catch by fashioning some flies from his mother-in-law's coloured hat, and from some fur taken from an ITN PA's coat. Yes, it did get into print – in Londoner's Diary, 1970. (Whether the new flies helped him catch fish is not on record.)

Parkin continued to feed me nice little anecdotes about himself, almost always fishing yarns. One was about lending an ITN colleague his one and only sea fishing rod, only to leave it on the train when taking it home after his friend had returned it to him. A couple that weren't concerned with fish included a snippet about how he'd burnt his hair and eyebrows after using petrol to start a bonfire (luckily it wasn't obvious when he read the news) and how he used to sit down to be fitted for his suits to ensure they didn't get crumpled when he read the news. 'Normally when you go to a tailor you stand up to be fitted,' he explained. 'My tailor makes me sit down. Since I'm virtually always sitting down when I'm on television, it seems a good idea.' But what happens, I asked, when you stand up? 'Fortunately the wrinkling up process doesn't seem to happen in reverse,' he said cheerfully.

I made an immediate impact on Reggie Bosanquet – or rather he on me – largely because of circumstances rather than any desire by Reggie to be pals with a new boy who would be an extremely small cog in what was then Britain's most popular national news-gathering organisation. From time to time, ITN felt the need to close its Green Room hospitality area – whenever it felt the facility was being exploited by too much drinking. Reggie, of course, was commonly associated with drinking before and after going on air, although from personal experience I feel this was a reputation he didn't always deserve. Anyway, on my very first day in the newsroom at ITN – then in Wells Street, near Oxford Circus – Reggie came over to me and said (thrillingly, I felt, as here was one of my screen idols, face to face in the flesh): 'Ah, you're new here, aren't you?... I wonder if you could do me a favour.'

Wow. Just ask, Reggie, I thought.

'The buggers have shut down the Green Room again,' he said, 'and I could do with a drink. I wonder if you'd mind leaving the building by the back door, coming in the front door again, and telling the people on the front desk that you've been booked for an interview on *News at Ten*. Make up a name. Let's call you Doctor Fothergill. Tell them Reggie Bosanquet asked you to come in to talk about the rabies controversy.' (This was 1970 when there was a big scare about rabies outbreaks in the UK.)

'Here,' said Reggie. 'Take my briefcase. It'll make you look more genuine.' And so, just as if I were a new boy at boarding-school undertaking a chore for a prefect, I nipped out of the back, and duly re-appeared at the front desk (this was long before there were any anxieties about security), telling the charming ladies on duty that I'd come to be interviewed by Mr Bosanquet. They duly telephoned Reggie and within a few minutes he was bounding down the steps to greet me. 'Ah, Doctor Fothergill... Good of you to come. Before we go on air, would you like drink?' Then, triumphantly seizing the key to the Green Room, Reggie marched off in the direction of hospitality, closely followed by Leonard Parkin, his co-newscaster that night, and of course me. After *News at Ten* was over – with no appearance, it goes without saying, from Doctor Fothergill – he could be heard saying loudly: 'Doctor, I'm so sorry we didn't have room for your item. Would you like to come and have another drink?' Later, to maintain the masquerade, he even booked me a cab home in the name of Doctor Fothergill.

Of his celebrated screen partnership with Andrew Gardner, Bosanquet said: 'Andrew always exercised restraint upon my natural ebullience and I always had the capacity to make him laugh.' As for his drinking habits, he and I got to know each other much better a few years later when we worked together on a political programme called *Probe* (which we all nicknamed 'Grope') at Anglia TV in Norwich. Reggie was the presenter. I was the producer. We'd take the train to Norwich together, and Reggie might consume a gin and tonic or three. But he insisted that rumours of alcoholism were much overstated. 'It's true that I like a drink before I go on air,' he admitted. 'But it's definitely a mistake to have another. I honestly believe I perform better after one drink, but worse after two.' It might not have been a rule he was always able to live up to, but he was aware of his own failings and tried to control his drinking. At least he did when I knew him.

The format for *Probe* was that an invited panel of regional MPs would take the train to Norwich and discuss various topics of intense political concern to the folk of East Anglia. After the programme we would consume copious quantities of red wine. Early on, one of the MPs was Jeffrey Archer, who very quickly showed his true colours when he asked me what the first question was going to be, promising he wouldn't take advantage if I told him. He did, of course, and promptly rang Conservative Central Office for guidance just before the programme aired. For many years after that he knew me as 'Anglia' when I reminded him on the telephone, during the occasional interview, of the circumstances in which we met. Another of the visitors was Norman St John Stevas, the rather foppishly tailored future Arts Minister, anti-abortionist and TV personality (later Viscount St John of Fawsley). When I said I'd been a fan of his since before I was born, he came back– quick as a flash – with: 'which only goes to prove that there IS life in the womb!'

On one hilarious occasion Reggie was confronted with a technical problem that had nothing at all to do with whether he'd had a drink or two before the programme. At the end of *Probe* we would announce the names of the MPs we hoped would be in the studio for the following week's programme. This of course would be on autocue on one of the cameras. Just as Reggie was saying 'and next week our studio MPs will be...' the camera with the autocue he was reading from suddenly moved backwards away from him like a retreating Dalek, causing him to climb half out of his seat trying to read the rapidly retreating names.

Talking of Daleks, I was once invited to the mansion home of their creator, Terry Nation, near Sittingbourne. While his wife Kate played the grand piano in the rather splendid vestibule, he kept plying me and my then wife Veronica with huge tumblers of gin and tonic. After about three or four of these, I thought of saying: 'Perhaps we should wait for dinner before we have any more.' But something stopped me. And my instincts were correct. It suddenly dawned on me that dinner was not on the agenda. Thank goodness I didn't mention that we'd wrongly assumed we'd be fed. (How embarrassing that would have been – although, we had been invited for the rather dinnerish hour of 7pm.)

Even as a regional reporter I found my ten years on screen could have their drawbacks. Like the much more famous people I was interviewing in my spare time, I found even local notoriety could be tiresome. On my days off I developed a habit of not shaving, wearing my shabbiest clothes and looking down at the pavement in an attempt to avoid being recognised as I strolled around towns like Maidstone, Ashford and Canterbury. In a very small way, the poacher in me had become the gamekeeper. And I was quite happy to find myself in parts of the UK (anywhere north of London or west of Dorset) where I was no longer identifiable.

But for nationally known TV people like Reggie Bosanquet, there was no such escape. Thanks mainly to our journeys to and from Norwich, Reggie, the son of the cricketer Bernard Bosanquet, inventor of the 'googly', became a good friend, and also a useful contact.

One evening when I was doing a night shift at the *Daily Express* (having dashed up from my day job in Dover) Bosanquet phoned me to say he had a good story for me. It turned out that he had shinned up the outside of his ex-wife Felicity's London flat to discover the whereabouts of some previously shared furniture. 'You mustn't quote me personally,' said Reggie. 'But I guarantee the story is true.' I never did quite work out why he had done it, except perhaps to discover whether she had moved or sold the furniture without consulting him. But I duly bashed out the story and prepared to take on the *Daily Express* lawyers, who would doubtless want to know how I could confirm the story without an acknowledged source. Would Reggie sue if I had got it wrong? Would Felicity? I persuaded them the source was impeccable and the story 'copper-bottomed' and they ran it on Page One under the headline 'Bosanquet burgles ex-wife's flat'.

I'd worked for Southern Television twice previously, and as the weekend bulletin editor I would sometimes stay with Dickie Davies, of *World of Sport* fame, and his wife Liz – and what a hospitable couple they were… Here was I, a lowly sub-editor, being entertained by one of the most recognisable faces in sport. He also came up with some fun stories. On one occasion, not required in the studio that day, he'd gone to watch his beloved Chelsea in the 1970 FA Cup Final replay against Leeds United at Old Trafford. 'I shouted myself absolutely horse,' he whispered to me afterwards. 'My voice went completely, and now I'm trying to nurse it back in time for *World of Sport*… I do tend to get carried away when I watch live sport. I have so little opportunity because I'm always in a studio when it's all happening. It's just as well I'm not a football commentator. I'd have no voice left by half time.'

It made a story.

Another drama in Dickie's life came when he had to interview a boy on a roundabout at Battersea funfair in London for a programme called *Do Your Own London*. It should have been plain sailing – after all, Davies had spent ten years at sea as an entertainments officer on board the *Queen Mary* and the *Queen Elizabeth*. But viewers (with their then new-fangled colour sets) may have noticed that during the programme Davies looked a trifle green.

'I felt a bit foolish,' he told me later, 'but I have to admit that I am sick on practically everything that moves – from rowing boats to roundabouts. I thought the interview would last about a minute, but in fact it went on for almost four. I managed to stave off the inevitable, but as soon as it was over, I had to dash round the corner.' When he was at sea, Davies took pills to prevent sickness. 'But even after ten years, I never got used to rough seas – or any rough ride, come to that.'

When the job of Kent reporter at Southern Television came up, it seemed crazy not to audition for it. I was not the ideal candidate. In spite of having spent a few months learning radio technique at the newly launched BBC Radio Sheffield, I could hardly stand the sound of my own voice, was pretty nervous in front of microphones, and certainly scared of live TV. Nonetheless, like many other nervous reporters, I learnt as I went along, and gradually got used to standing in front of cameras in busy shopping arcades and other public places. While I still hated live television, and dreaded drying up, especially when people waved at the camera saying 'hello mum' and other gormless phrases, I gradually came to enjoy something of a love affair with the camera (as long as it was not live) and even started to enjoy showing off in front of crowds of people. This ability to make a fool of myself in public places lingers on to this day. Before I became an on-screen reporter I was petrified of public speaking. Now I almost enjoy the prospect.

My on-screen decade with Southern Television (and then TVS) turned out to be my longest period in regular employment. Working either from a small office in Maidstone or a remote studio in Dover, I was in some demand as a local 'personality' – but only really by default when local organisations found it was easier to book me than much bigger names from Southern Television in far-away Southampton. When women's institutes, parish councils and other local bodies wanted someone to open a fete, crown a beauty queen or make a speech, they would usually approach the station's press office in the hope of getting one of their big stars like Fred Dinenage, Dickie Davies, Barry Westwood or Trevor 'The Weather' Baker. As often as not they would end up with little old me, the best they could get – but at least I never charged a fee. To my great pride I even opened Margate Working Men's Club. I wonder if the plaque on the wall recording this historic event is still there. I imagine it was taken down long ago when people started asking – 'Arnie Wilson? Who the hell was he anyway?'

There were many memorable incidents when I carried out my duties as a local 'celeb'. I bumped into Norman St John-Stevas again in rather embarrassing circumstances in Maidstone, after I'd been asked to officially open an Oxfam Shop near Southern's office just off Week Street. As a gesture, I thought I'd better purchase something from the shop, and paid the not inconsiderable sum (then) of £10 for a pin-striped suit. As a dare, I told the film crew I routinely worked with that come what may, I would wear my Oxfam suit for work the following day. Who should be my next interviewee but Norman St John Stevas, elegantly attired as ever. So I was interviewing the Arts Minister while wearing a suit from Oxfam…

One of the more memorable moments came when I was asked to be the chief judge at a beauty contest in the village of Hothfield, just outside Ashford. The event had been organised as a way of launching the new village hall. The village had a large gypsy population back then, and this element would play a significant part in how the contest progressed. As the lead judge, I was seated at top table with the other judges. My companions were, as far as I can remember, the village post-mistress, the proprietor of the main store (who had donated the most generous tombola prizes) and the village headmistress. In the eyes of the local gypsies, dominated then by a single family, we were obviously seen as a posh and snooty lot. As the contestants lined up, I naively started to question them as if I were a genuine TV personality rather than just a district reporter, but soon gave up on that idea after an early encounter with one of the gypsy daughters.

'So what's your name?' I asked one of the first contestants.

'Ricanda!' she squawked loudly.

'That's a nice name,' I ventured, nervously. 'How did you get it?'

'Me gran gave it me,' she said. Further questioning of Ricanda, and indeed the next two or three contestants, turned out to be so uninformative that I pretty much gave up, and we proceeded with the selection process as simply and quickly as possible, pausing just to log their names. No further questions. We selected the prettiest girl, who was duly crowned and decorated with a purple sash. There was only one problem. We had chosen a non-gypsy. All hell was about to break out. Out of the corner of my eye I saw the matriarch of the family advancing towards our table. 'Was that you wot chose that girl as the beauty queen?' she demanded threateningly, focusing on me. 'Well yes,' I answered, 'I did – with my fellow judges.'

'Well' she screamed, 'you must have had fucking shit in your eye!' A brilliantly descriptive phrase I thought. I learnt too late that the mother had something of a violent reputation, and had even once attacked her own husband with an axe. Had she succeeded, and been arrested, it was pointed out to me, the village would have been conveniently rid of a couple of its more difficult residents.

We waited for the fireworks to begin. We didn't have to wait long. The mother was back in a trice, and poured a mug of beer over two of my fellow judges and this signalled the outbreak of a punch-up involving several bottles of beer. The unfortunate beauty queen took fright, handed over her sash and crown, and the runner up – a member of the gypsy family – was acclaimed the new 'queen'.

A week later I received a letter. It said: 'Dear Mr Wilson, we gather you was very upset by what happened at the beauty queen event and you won't ever come to Hothfield again. We wanted to apologise for what happened.'

I immediately wrote back saying: 'Far from being upset, I found the whole thing very entertaining. In fact it very nearly inspired me to try to turn the events of the evening into a script for the BBC's *Wednesday Play*...'

The only man who ever sent me a major gift for 'services rendered' (I hesitate to use the word bribe) was the great gambler and private zoo owner John Aspinall. Because both his zoos, or wildlife parks as he preferred to call them, were in Kent, I saw a good deal of him, and because his animals – particularly the tigers and gorillas – were very photogenic, we often featured him romping with them on our magazine programme *Day by Day*. When tragedy struck, as it did, sadly, all too often – over the years he lost five keepers, three killed by tigers, two by elephants – he would always allow me in with my regular film crew (George, Vic and Warwick), sometimes leaving the Fleet Street 'pack' baying outside the gates. It was during moments like these that my 'split-personality' as a TV journalist during the week and a Fleet Street reporter at weekends was at its most marked. It wasn't always necessarily a good idea to be given special treatment as a TV reporter when being watched by Fleet Street reporters I might well meet the following weekend when I changed hats.

But Aspinall obviously thought I gave him sufficient good publicity to include me one year in his Christmas gift list with a crate of champagne.

He, of course, may well have taken the secret of what happened to his great friend and fellow-gambler Lord Lucan to the grave with him. After hearing a story (one of many widely different rumours about his fate) that Lucan was hiding high in the ramparts of Saltwood Castle, the home of the celebrated Tory MP, diarist, and historian Alan Clark, I rang Clark's wife Jane and put it to her.

'Well, I don't think so,' she said gamely. 'At least, no-one has sent down for any food!'

Saltwood Castle was the location for one of the other embarrassing moments in my television career. I was interviewing Clark on the said ramparts, and we were both sitting in canvas chairs. During the interview – but mercifully not while George Pellett's camera was rolling, or it would have been a classic 'out take' more than worthy of *It'll be alright on the night* – my chair collapsed. I'm quite a heavy chap, and I'd split the canvas. A foot closer and I'd have fallen straight into the moat.

I did get very wet, though, when I interviewed the comedian Charlie Drake who was appearing in a show in my area. Instead of concentrating on his humour, the idea was to ask him about his black belt at karate – quite an achievement for someone so vertically challenged. At 5ft 1ins he was a full inch and a half shorter than Dudley Moore. By pre-arrangement, Drake and I did the interview on the edge of a swimming pool, and I pretty much knew what was coming. The idea was that I would 'come at him' with a knife. He would disarm me, and guess what. Splash. In fact I was easy meat. He was surprisingly strong, and I was in the pool – minus said knife – before I knew it. 'Aaa-Harghhhh!' as Charlie himself might have said – and often did.

On another occasion I was sent to interview Gary Glitter. This was long before his true colours as a paedophile had been revealed. He was still a big star. Somehow or other I got hold of one his jackets – the ones with the flashing lights – and started my report with a piece to camera actually wearing it. My daughters were disappointed that they didn't get to meet him, so I managed to track Glitter down in the phone so that at least Melissa could have a chat with him. She was thrilled. If only she'd known... If only I'd known...

Putting celebrities on the phone to my daughters became a regular habit. I remember when Melissa had watched one too many *Dracula* movies, which had caused her to feel really scared; I rang Christopher Lee (a fairly regular contact) and asked him to explain to her that he wasn't really a vampire and she had nothing to be scared of.

I lasted as Southern Television's Kent reporter for about seven years until it lost its franchise, and I clung on for another two or three years working for the new incumbents, TVS, but by now Kent had its own major studios in Maidstone. I was no longer the company's Kent reporter but simply one of many working in the county.

Later, tiring of TVS (and they of me) my (by now freelance) broadcasting career took me to Thames TV and LWT News. I was also doing some radio, principally for radio 4's *Breakaway* travel programme for which I covered skiing. Among the show's presenters were Bill Oddie, and the amiable Scot, Ken Bruce. We were already friendly after I had written numerous bits and pieces about him (after some excellent lunches together) in Peter Tory's diary page in the *Star*. This was the first time we had really worked together. He remains a good friend to this day, and we still see each other for very agreeable lunches.

One of the celebrities I interviewed wearing my radio hat was Barrie Humphries, dressed in his full Dame Edna regalia. I met him at a press conference to announce 'her' latest series for London Weekend Television. I was the only broadcast journalist there.

'LWT and I are getting together to interview not altogether willing celebrities,' he started. 'I should say it's been a lot easier trawling for celebs this time because they've been coming out of the woodwork, particularly in LA where one of your number actually spotted me in one of the luxury hotels. (It was the Hilton. But don't mention it possums, because I didn't get a discount...)

'He said What are you doing here? and I said I'm TRAWLING for celebrities. I can say now that Barry Manilow is going to be one of my guests, Liza Minelli, Tom Jones, to name but a few, and little Lord Linley, even if he just talks about his furniture. They're thrilled to be appearing. And as more people sign on the dotted, you will be kept posted with press releases faxes and telexes, possums.'

When Humphries/Dame Edna spotted my professional Sony tape-recorder – and in the absence of any TV crews – he used me as a kind of crazy lightning conductor for his humour, working the room through me and my tape recorder. 'It's question time,' he said, looking straight at me. 'I'm going to mingle now.'

The thing I remember most was that he was flirting with me, and fluttering those Dame Edna eyelashes at me.

'Suffice it to say,' he said, gazing mischievously into my eyes, 'that I've been to London Weekend and I don't want to sit in the yucky old studio this time. I want to be in something comfortable. I want to do this programme from my own home. Which home, they said. Malibu, Mustique, Montreux, or Melbourne? I said Mayfair will do because I'm into Ms in a big way. So that's how it's going to be.'

What was extraordinary was that although I knew full well that underneath all that get-up was a guy called Barrie Humphries, when he fixed me with direct eye contact and started the flirting process it was very easy to forget that I wasn't actually looking into the eyes of a woman.

'We're getting a rare glimpse of how I live in the megastar community,' he said... 'a bit of hoovering... something of the sort.' And then he started rhapsodising about this 'pretty pink suit of mine designed incidentally by my talented son Kevin.'

I was once told by a London cabbie that Humphries had dashed into his cab en route to a performance, and had changed into 'her' clothing on the way. The driver said that as he changed into 'her' clothes and assumed 'her' personality, so his character changed. And he wasn't even on stage yet. 'When Mr Humphries got in the cab he was quiet and introvert,' said the driver. 'Gradually, as he put on all that Dame Edna finery, he became loquacious, and very soon he'd become Dame Edna!'

Chapter 9
Wogan on Wogan

Said Terry 'I know what to do
Now I've eased up on Radio 2
My next major mission?
My lifelong ambition?
To be cast as the next Doctor Who!'

I crossed Sir Terry Wogan's path a few times (and even played cricket with him once). And long, long ago there was one moving story I worked on when a little blind girl of four insisted he was the first person she wanted to see when she opened her eyes after corrective surgery. And of course, kind-hearted Terry was happy to oblige.

Linda Johnson thought Wogan would be the most wonderful sight in the world. She'd been born blind, but after the operation she travelled from her home in Margate with her mother and brother to meet him, taking with her a photograph of herself holding a picture of him. And said: 'He's lovely. Even lovelier than I thought he would be.' In return, Wogan gave her a toy, pictures, and records as souvenirs of her visit. She also had the opportunity to say 'hello' to millions of Radio 2 listeners. Her mother said: 'When Terry was on holiday for three weeks, we had tears every morning because he wasn't on the air.' Wogan said: 'She's a lovely little girl. I'm only glad that I could help make her day'.

My one major interview with Wogan was granted to help publicise the BBC's *Children In Need* telethon, which Wogan traditionally presents. It was a far-ranging interview, much of which never saw the light of day. This was a shame because Wogan – at the time doing his thrice-weekly TV chat show – was generous with his time, and did not baulk at any questions I threw at him. Listening to the tape again for the first time in decades, I was struck with the good-natured way Wogan dealt with my endless questions and the candour of many of the answers. It took me a good day to transcribe the tape and I was quite humbled by the results. They make fascinating reading and even after so many years reveal much about the man that might not be suspected by his many devoted viewers and listeners.

ME: I'd like to try to get under the skin of Terry Wogan.

WOGAN: Sure. Fire away and see what you get.

ME: I feel there's a lot more to you than…

WOGAN: …than you see on television? Well it's always nice when people think you're more intelligent than you actually are. A good friend of mine is Ned Sherrin, a man I admire enormously. Ned is always defending me. He tells people 'Terry's not that lightweight – it's just the way he's doing the programme.' Patronising swine!... Of course he didn't mean to be. It's the idea that some newspapers have – and a lot of people have as well – that if you do light-hearted programmes, you are, by association – to put it mildly, a non intellectual, who never even picks up a book. I've never wanted to be Robin Day. Robin Day wants to be me, but I've never wanted to be Robin Day. I started on news and documentaries and while I find them fascinating and interesting, it wasn't my bent, as it were. I'm not really a serious-minded person, although I'm serious about some things like religion (always trying to fill in the gaps to give myself reason to believe) and philosophy. But I'm afraid good humour keeps breaking through; I don't see that you necessarily have to do serious things in order to be taken seriously. I enjoy doing light entertainment. Always have. It suits my temperament better than long-winded intellectual discussion, although I don't mind that over a dinner party. But in the end, someone's going to tell a joke – we hope. At least one of the functions of television is entertainment as well as information, and I think it's probably the most important function – certainly as far as the sanity of the population is concerned. You've got to have light entertainment, and television has been an enormous boon to parents and children and old people, and to people coming in from work wanting to switch on. Hitherto they'd either switch on the radio or go to the cinema. Now they have it at home. It's been a great invention, in my opinion, apart from great breakthroughs in medicine. Obviously it's not as important as medicine, but it's still very important for the well-being of the nation. Maybe it's a panacea. They said the first American television generation in the 50s would have square eyes. They said they would come out impaired – just as people these days will say 'I won't let my child watch television because it'll give them square eyes and atrophy their brain'. Yet that generation in America was the generation that protested against Vietnam. That was the most aware political generation that America ever produced – and so there's no question that television is valuable. I don't think it puts people to sleep – in the process of entertaining people you can inform people as well, and that's the ideal thing, which is what we've been trying to do on *Children in Need* of course. We've been trying to inform them, entertain them, and take money out of their pockets for that reason.'

ME: Do you think the *Wogan* from Radio 2 works on the TV chat show formula?

WOGAN: As a friend of mine said the other night, they were used to you on radio. In fact they were beginning to anticipate everything I was saying, and they understood my sense of humour. Then I suddenly appear on television doing a new thing, and naturally I'm apprehensive – and they're apprehensive for me. And therefore it takes them a little while to get used to it, because it's a new 'me' in a sense. Because you can't do the same kind of things on television that you do on radio. You just can't. You can't communicate as intimately, you can't create fantasy – because your imagination is limited by the size of the box. But at the same time, the main thing about me is me. So all I can be is myself. I think my upbringing and education, and my nature, militates against my becoming big headed. I'm the product of a bourgeois Irish upbringing and education, and a Jesuit training not to project yourself and to try to overcome any disability. So if you're shy you do amateur dramatics – or do what I'm doing on the radio or television. It's almost as if you're making yourself do things against your character. Having said that, what I've learnt over the years is to be myself and be in character. I'm not a pusher. I'm not a person who knocks on doors. I've always in a sense let the world come to me. I've found that every time I act out of character and try to push myself, it never felt or sounded right. I've been so lucky – everything has happened for me at the right time.

ME: So which is the real Wogan? The radio one or the TV one? [Back then he said the TV one, but then he'd have to, as that was his number one role. So one could say – 'he would say that, wouldn't he?' He was hardly going to say the radio one. And yet later in the interview he did, in a way, contradict himself by saying 'I love doing radio. I'll always love doing radio. Radio is my first love'. I think many or most of his fans would agree – for reasons he himself had advanced: you can't communicate so intimately on television. And after all, intimate communication is his strongest suit.]

WOGAN: I'd like to see if I can achieve the same kind of rapport between myself and the viewer that I was able to do on the radio. That's really what the dream is. It's not about money, and it's not about wanting to be on the television all the time. It's trying to establish a communication which hasn't been achieved yet by anyone else in this country. And who knows whether it can be done or not? There was a transition period – they heard me on the radio, they liked me on radio. They liked me on *Blankety Blank*. And then I made a transition into a new thing which I don't do as well, at least initially. It's a new thing for me as well, and what perhaps is forgotten is that it took me about four or five years to establish the radio programme. People didn't like me at first on that, either. I knew it would take me two years. I was either aiming at being the person most likely to be thought of as the most popular TV personality – or I might be the least popular TV personality. And there's no point in being in the game if you're not going to try to be the best or the most popular or the most familiar. I think if people look at me on a Monday and Wednesday then they've seen me, and if they want to watch something else on Friday you can't blame them for that. I've always said that the most you can hope for is that maybe most of the population will see me once a week for about ten minutes. I think a considerable number of people who watch me are my listeners – I hope a considerable number are. The reason I think *Blankety Blank* succeeded was that for the very first time I was able to do the kind of thing I was doing on the radio on the television. And I was able to walk around. But television, as we know from looking at old television programmes, moves on apace all the time. Television hasn't got any better. It's just got quicker. People's attention span is less. I find even the *Generation Game*, for which I have always admired Bruce Forsythe, was enormously slow when you look at it now. Terrifically slow. Very slow pace.

ME: Does criticism hurt you?

WOGAN: A newspaper recently asked this question about me: 'Is this man the biggest bore on television?' I am a target, I know. My name sells newspapers – especially if you can attach any scandal to it – or a question like that. Did it hurt me? Not really. No, hurt isn't the right word. It aggravated me. The only thing which hurts me is anything personal, anything directed at my family. The rest I can take. The other I regard as an unwarranted intrusion. I'll take gratuitous insults. I'll take sycophantic. I'll take anything because that's part and parcel of what I'm doing. I won't necessarily take it and not bite back, because I don't think it's part of the function of people like me to just sit there and take abuse.

ME: What about the opposite – being liked or even loved too much?

WOGAN: Unfortunately I work in an artificial world. Something that people find very hard to believe is when you say 'I love doing this'... but the aspects of it that I don't like are the aspects that you might expect someone like me to like – and that is fame, attention and notoriety. That's the aspect of the game I don't like. That's the biggest price for me to pay

ME: Does anything ever embarrass you?

WOGAN: My threshold of embarrassment is terribly low.

ME: What kind of things?

WOGAN: Nearly everything. I've been embarrassed lots of times. I'm always embarrassed when people shout across the street to me. That's why I like going to America – because no-one knows me there.

ME: Andrew Gardner once told me he'd gone to San Francisco and at first he was relieved that no-one knew he was a famous newscaster. After a while though, he started to miss being recognised. So he was quite pleased when a British ex-pat came up to him and said: 'I recognise you!' But he wasn't so happy when the man said: 'Welcome to San Francisco, Mr Honeycombe!' [Referring to a fellow ITN news reader who was also tall and balding.]

WOGAN: The person that really drives me crazy is the person who says: 'You don't remember me, do you?' And then you know they're going to be offended because you don't. You have to be honest with them. But if it's someone you should remember that is embarrassing. I was at the theatre once with my wife Helen and my daughter, and during the interval there was a party of schoolchildren at the back. And they came trooping down in a crocodile line. Most of the audience had gone out for a drink at the bar. And they came and asked me, one at a time, for my autograph on their theatre programmes. Now I couldn't refuse to do that – you would never refuse. Being rude to the public is the ultimate rudeness, because they are accepting you into their homes. I know that sounds sanctimonious but it's true. You can't be rude to the public, and you mustn't be. But at the same time you can be embarrassed if the schoolteacher hadn't had enough sense to realise that now everyone in the theatre had started looking at me. And you have to rely on the schoolteacher to say to the girls: 'No, you can't just go down there and ask for his autograph – there's 30 of you! I'll go with the programme and ask him to sign one.' It's hard to specify what actually embarrasses me, but the threshold is low. And that's why I'll never be a comedian or a stage actor, because I would be embarrassed if people didn't accept me. That's why I don't watch myself on television. I think I might embarrass myself. I always think of Alan Bennett, who's a marvellous playwright. And he watches all his plays from behind the settee – he ducks down behind it. And that's the way I watch myself. If I'm on the television and I walk in, say, to the breakfast room and find they're watching me on the television, I'll walk out again, because I find it hard to look at myself . I get embarrassed looking at myself. The great thing about doing a live show is that I don't have to look at it. I never worry about the show after it's over. And I don't think about the show on days when there isn't one.

ME: But you must often be pleased with your work.

WOGAN: Well yes, that's why you do it. You do it for the enormous satisfaction that you get when the programme works. It's the same doing five days a week on the radio. If I've had two or three days that really work, that a couple of things I tried worked, sounded right, came out correctly. But I always expect that in every programme – at least once or twice - I'd say something that would come out slightly wrong. And you have to accept that if you do something live it can't work out absolutely pitch perfect every time. And with a chat show three days a week – it's dependent on you, it's dependent on the mood of the audience, the quality of the guests, how relevant the items are that you can get in; a whole load of things that will work or not work. And you can't get too distressed if they don't. But there's enormous satisfaction when you get something that works. I'm a hard self critic, so for me maybe one in three shows works. In an ideal world – and I'm not saying it's an ideal world for anybody except me – doing the TV show five days a week would give me the kind of link with the public that the daily radio show had. I wouldn't lose the public for two day gaps. I could run on, and do continual links, which is the basis on which American chat shows work. So you can spill over, and say: 'Well, tomorrow night we'll continue this conversation.' You can't ideally do that when the programme's over on a Monday night, and we continue on Wednesday. Tuesday has intervened, and the moment is lost. The flow is lost.

ME: What's your formula for getting the best out of a studio guest?

WOGAN: You can't please everybody, obviously and once you accept that, you try to do your best with guests. You're trying to please yourself really. If we were taping the show, marvellous, because we could have 20 minutes of them and cut it to 10 really marvellous minutes of 'spontaneous' fun. Some people are marvellous performers, but you shouldn't have them in a live context, because the secret of their fun and the secret of their genius is their unpredictability – which can sometimes stray into unacceptability. And you need to have the scissors ready for people like that. You can't take risks with a live show at seven o'clock in the evening. Apart from that, people are in and out at seven o'clock. They're not sitting down watching television with their mouths open. But if the show were to go out at eleven o'clock in the evening, those who wish to, who are still up, will watch and you can take more liberties. I'll watch anything that's on television. If something which I'm really interested in comes up, I'll stay up all night to watch it. But I think there's an awful lot of sanctimonious nonsense talked about 'worthwhile' television. The classic case is *Points of View*. I've never ever heard a letter criticising a wildlife programme. Or a ballet programme. Or an orchestral concert. Or a programme on art. Because people think you're not supposed to criticise things like that. Intrinsically, it's worthwhile, and therefore if you say you like things like that, you are in some way superior to people who like *Coronation Street* and *Eastenders*.

ME: Have you ever been in awe of any guest?

WOGAN: No.

ME: Who would you most like to interview? The Queen perhaps?

WOGAN: Obviously I'd like to talk to the Queen but without going to the Palace to do it. That's the problem you see – you'd have to take her out of her context so that she felt less restricted. It might sound predictable, but I'd like to ask her what it feels like to be Queen. Does she think of herself as an ordinary person? How does she see her role? Has her role taken her over as a person or does she feel she has any identity as herself. Those kinds of questions. But this would be in the best of all possible worlds, and it's unlikely to happen.

ME: Wouldn't you perhaps be in awe of the Queen if it ever did happen?

WOGAN: No I don't think I'd be in awe of the Queen. I don't think so. I've been lucky enough to meet her, so I'd start with the advantage of having met her a couple of times. During one of my visits to the Palace, I shook hands with her, and while we were chatting about the programme, I noticed my wife going off to get a drink. So having shaken hands with the Queen, I started heading off to get a drink and I heard a voice say: 'Don't forget about us!' And it was Prince Charles and the Queen Mother. I'd walked right past them. And had to walk back to meet them of course. And I thought 'there goes my knighthood!' Anyway, if the Queen were a guest on the show, I'd know she was a perfectly nice and intelligent articulate woman. So I wouldn't be afraid of what she was going to say, or afraid of beads of sweat or fear, and that kind of thing. But that's one of the things you control within yourself – the fear, the awe you're trying to suppress so that you can do a programme in which you are in control. You must look in control. If you don't look in control, you embarrass the viewer. And that viewer will switch off. That's the cardinal sin.

ME: So what sort of things do you fear?

WOGAN: Nothing much scares me. I've always taken risks. I'm not great on spiders – and not too keen on snakes. If I found a big spider in the house I'd kill it. But I'm not an aggressive person. I've always been able to control my anger because I could never see that anger served any purpose. And if I ever lost my temper when I was younger, and hit someone, I used to feel guilty. I could hit people harder than most people could hit me. But the fights I was in were always arranged by bigger boys because I happened to be big and strong for my age. I used to play a lot of rugby, but I was never an aggressive player. Because I was big and strong, I could lean and I could push. I occasionally lost my temper with the children, but you always regretted it. There's nothing to be gained by showing either irritation or by being bad tempered with anybody. That way you get the most out of people. I can't work in an atmosphere of attrition, and never have. I can only work in an atmosphere of cooperation. I've had two bites at the cherry. I had success in Irish television before I came over here. I was very young, and in my formative years, and made the mistakes I had to make. Probably leaving Ireland and seeing if I could make it over here was the biggest risk I've ever taken. But even if I'd never made it in radio or television, I would have been quite happy to stay on at the bank. I was never bored working in the bank. I quite enjoyed it.

ME: I guess you'd have been a bank manager by now.

WOGAN: Oh yes. I had my bank exams and all the rest of it.

ME: Would you have made a good bank manager?

WOGAN: Yeh. I'd be all right. I wouldn't fret about it. If I made a good living and had a family and I was happy, it wouldn't worry me. I'm a conventional person. I was totally conventional at school. If my father had been an accountant I'd have been an accountant. If he'd been a doctor I'd be a doctor now. Luckily for me he didn't have a particular profession for me to go into. He was in the wine business, and he didn't particularly want me to go into that.

ME: How important is your family to you? Daft question, I know.

WOGAN: I don't know what kind of creature I'd be if I hadn't got my family. Probably a very lonely creature.

Chapter 10
Milligan madness

Spike Milligan taught me an important lesson about how to deal with celebrities: don't fawn over them. My first conversation with the complex ex-Goon happened when I was still in bed at my home in Old Wives Lees, Chilham, just a few miles outside Canterbury. I remember being stunned by the unexpected call and, quite frankly, I gushed. It's not that Spike reacted badly to my obsequiousness, but I could tell he felt a touch uncomfortable at being revered down the phone, and our conversation remained rather stilted and formal.

Of course by this time I should have been used to talking to famous people, but for some reason major icons like Spike sometimes did overawe me. I came to realise that all famous people tend to be fawned over by the general public, and henceforth I was determined to stop sounding like the general public. I realised the key to a rewarding relationship with major celebrities, especially someone a bit dotty like Spike, was not to fawn but to be chatty and even matey. Not too matey though, because there was always a danger of being too familiar – like an over-friendly waiter – which could tip the balance in the opposite direction.

The formula then was to be friendly, a little jokey, perhaps, and to try to make them feel relaxed with you in a not-too-familiar way, showing respect but a certain chumminess at the same time. It was good advice, even though it was my own advice, to me! And it was advice that came in very useful during the years to come when I realised that making an interviewee relax was a key component of successful television and radio interviewing – even when I was trying to hide my own broadcasting nerves.

Anyway, after this slightly stilted conversation with Spike, things between us got steadily more frisky as our friendship developed. Richard Webb, who eventually published my first ski book as a partner in Webb and Bower, but was then running the publisher Michael Joseph's PR department, made sure I received copies of Spike's war memoirs as each one was published. The first volume was, memorably, called *Adolf Hitler: My Part in his Downfall*. When that was published, a man from Finchley threatened to 'expose' Michael Joseph for contravening the Trade Descriptions Act because the publishers were claiming (thanks to Spike) that the book was written on edible paper, enabling anyone who didn't enjoy it to eat it. The man, a Mr A J Tew, claimed he tried a couple of mouthfuls and found it 'anything but edible', and would sue unless he received an autographed copy. Spike retaliated by saying: 'This man is a forgery. The original A J Tew is buried up a tree in Kiev.' However he later relented and did in fact sign a copy for him.

Thanks to Richard Webb, and my family's friendship with Spike's wife Paddy, I usually got a ringside seat at any publishing party to launch his books. At these, Spike was as unpredictable as ever. At a small get-together in the office of Edmund Fisher, Michael Joseph's MD, to mark the publication of volume two, *Rommel? Gunner who?* Spike did something typically goonish. While signing copies, including mine, he suddenly strode up to a painting on the wall by the celebrated artist Michael Ayrton and signed that in felt tip too. There was a sudden silence. We didn't know whether to laugh or look shocked. Fisher's jaw dropped. He was not a happy man. But Spike... was Spike. The painting, which had been left to Fisher by his father, had to be professionally cleaned. Eventually Fisher saw the 'funny' side, saying: 'I think we'll get it out. If it doesn't come out, I shall have stern words with Mr Milligan!' I can't remember whether he ever picked up the bill, but it was a classic bit of Milligan madness.

Spike, who was already working on volume three of his war memoirs – *Monty: His Part in my Victory* – said after the party that meeting seven old army comrades who had assembled to celebrate the publication of *Rommel? Gunner who?* had given him masses of new material for his memoirs. 'They have reminded me of some marvellous stories I'd forgotten,' he said. 'I've got so much material that I'm planning to write 108 volumes in all. Then we're going to start a Third World War so that I can write some more.'

When I asked Spike whether he was pleased with *Rommel*, as it had taken him so long to write, he said: 'I deny all knowledge of the book. I am a soldier on leave from the Palestine Liberation Army suffering from acute amnesia in an advanced stage, receiving medical treatment from the BMA at £3.50 a minute.' (Reading that some 35 years later, £3.50 a minute doesn't sound too steep.) As for my signed copy, I have it in front of me now. It says 'To Arnold. A Quvayker. From Spike Milligan.'

The Quvayker reference was the result of a funny story I'd told Spike that had rather tickled him. I'd been interviewing Warren Mitchell, who famously played Alf Garnett in the long-running TV series *Till Death do us Part*, and at one stage the conversation had turned to religion. 'What about you, Arnold?' Mitchell had asked, turning the interview round to me. 'What are your religious beliefs?' I told him my father was a non-practising Jew of Russian descent and mother was a Quaker; I'd been to a Quaker school and my ex-wife Veronica and I had married at the Friends' (Quaker) meeting house in Colchester, Essex. Quick as a flash, Mitchell responded with: 'Ah, so you're a Quvayker!' It was pronounced Ker Vayker and I was never quite sure how it should be spelt. It was Spike who decided on the Quvayker spelling, and from then on, every time he signed one of his books for me, he included the joke name. He also signed a copy of *Badjelly The Witch* for my daughter Melissa.

After spending time with Spike, you sometimes felt your own brain had become infected with his crazy sense of humour. I remember an occasion when he was anxious to promote a Beauty Without Cruelty concert at London's Mermaid Theatre which his wife Paddy was singing in. I suggested he might walk up and down London's Oxford Street with a sandwich board on which he could write 'Wife, four children and concert to support'. It appealed to him. He did it. Job done. I was rather proud of that – celebrity journalism for once put to good use.

His photograph appeared in two or three morning papers. In fact while writing this book I asked a friend, a layout artist on the sports desk of the *Sunday Mirror*, if he could possibly track down the photographs. With a little help from the *Mirror* photo archives in Watford, he did just that. They are very funny – especially pictures of Spike with a real sandwich board man, each checking the other out like a horse checking out a pantomime version.

David Whiting, whose mother Lady Dowding had started Beauty Without Cruelty, remembers it well. 'After the event I met Peter Sellers back stage,' he recalls. 'The rapport between Spike and Peter was like lightning as they bounced jokes off each other.'

One night I was invited to stay with Spike and Paddy at their home in North Finchley. I was having an early breakfast in the kitchen when their housekeeper mentioned with a giggle that although Spike was a vegetarian, there was some venison in the fridge. It went though my mind that this was quite a story, but immediately thought better of writing it. I felt it would have been a major betrayal. Instead I made the fatal mistake of mentioning it to a fellow diarist. I should have known better. My loyalty to Spike was not his.

'You can't use this,' I said, but told him the story. The next day I was mortified to find the story was in print. 'I couldn't resist using it,' said my colleague. 'But of course we'll pay you for it.' As if that was the point. I felt like Judas. Spike either never read it or just didn't bother to react. But it had taught me another lesson.

One day I found myself in Spike's Mini, being driven very slowly along the Thames Embankment. I say slowly because it's relevant. He was actually driving at 12 mph while he twiddled the knobs on his radio to try to find out where there might be traffic hold-ups. 'I hate traffic jams,' he said as the car crept forward. Driving and listening at the same time didn't come easily to Spike. He was not one of life's multi-taskers. But sometimes he would be so intent on tuning in to traffic news that he would virtually come to a standstill – inadvertently causing the traffic to back up behind him. 'If I kept listening long enough, I would find myself listening to my own traffic jams on the air,' he admitted.

One night during one of my regular *Daily Mirror* shifts I was asked to get some celebrity feedback about a TV programme called *Threads*, which imagined the destruction of Sheffield by a nuclear bomb. The problem was that the programme wasn't due to air until 10pm which was too late to whip up any reaction in time to catch early editions of the newspaper. So would I try to get reaction before the programme was screened, asked the news desk. Just as some MPs are useful 'rent-a-quote' sources, one's special VIP friends were often used to providing quotes in such circumstances, so I rang Spike and explained the problem. I expected a distraught reply, but got – not for the first time with Spike – something completely unexpected. 'I can't wait for the holocaust,' he said. Was I hearing things? No, said Spike. I'd obviously caught him in one of his legendary state-of-despair moods. 'It would teach us a marvellous lesson. I can't wait for the bomb to drop – and I'm perfectly serious. Mankind is utterly appalling. The human race is slowly massacring the earth – and they've got it coming. I'm prepared to sacrifice my wife, my children and myself. It's better they should die than their children's children end up in Ethiopian-style starvation camps. Four fifths of the world is starving. People are being raped and murdered everywhere, and kids go around sniffing glue.'

Spike's then wife Sheilagh and his four children were less eager to die. His only son, Sean, said: 'I think Dad's being a bit excessive.' But there was no holding Spike. 'The bomb would be like a massive dose of castor oil. It would do the world a power of good.'

Before I gave the story to the news desk, I did what I always did when Spike had given me controversial quotes – and nothing could be much more controversial than these. I asked him if he was sure he wanted his remarks published – hoping against hope, of course, that he did.

He never once, in any story throughout our long relationship, changed his mind about allowing me to use any of his quotes until the final story I wrote about him when for some reason he denied – retrospectively, when it was too late, and the story was already in print – some quotes he had given me about appearing in pantomime at the Chichester Festival Theatre. And that was the end of a friendship that had lasted more than a decade. Strangely, having allowed me to write so many controversial things about him, it was a comparatively innocent story that did the damage.

He was playing the 'good' robber in a production of *Babes in the Wood*. 'Some of my lines were corny when I cracked them the first time round, during the war,' he jested, when I rang him in his dressing room at the theatre. 'And I was scraping the barrel then! In fact some of the jokes are older than God. Let me give you an example: "Have you no scruples? – No, I've been inoculated against it." See what I mean? I wouldn't give that line to a comedian who was deaf and blind.'

He went on: 'Some of the material is dreadful. Why not come and see for yourself?' So I did – as his guest. 'Bill Pertwee [the 'bad' robber] and I have to rescue our material,' Spike told me. 'Once we've clowned around with the words it's almost good material. But if we can make terrible lines sound funny, imagine what we could do with good material... And another thing – why didn't they realise I'd be good at panto 20 years ago when I was longing to do it instead of waiting till I'm 67?'

It all sounded pretty innocent, knockabout stuff and it never occurred to me that it would cause problems when it appeared in print – certainly nothing like as controversial as other Milligan material I'd got into various dairies. So I was shocked when he wrote a deeply unpleasant letter to the *Daily Mirror* claiming I'd misquoted him, and demanding damages. To add insult to injury he even complained that I was 'digging for dirt'. I protested to the *Mirror* that I'd known Spike for years and he'd painted a thoroughly unkind picture of me and my motives. I suspect what happened was that he had been given a rollicking by the theatre management and his only way out was to say I'd made the whole thing up. He persisted with his complaint, however, and although the *Daily Mirror* accepted my account of events they paid him a considerable amount – running into thousands – as an out-of-court settlement.

After such a good relationship spanning some 15 years, I felt betrayed by Spike. Maybe he felt betrayed by me, but I can't imagine why. I did actually speak to him again, but he wasn't aware it was me. I was working on Peter Tory's *Star* diary one day and we needed to speak to him to clarify something. I plucked up the courage to call him, but simply said I was working for Peter. As far as I know, he didn't recognise my voice. It was a brief but poignant conversation. I miss him now he's gone.

Over the years I met and interviewed all the Goons, including Michael Bentine, although he featured in 'only' the first 38 of the classic ground-breaking shows that ran for almost the whole of the 1950s and comprised more than 225 programmes. Bentine was probably the only one to rival Milligan for goonishness, but an altogether gentler soul. In many ways he was my favourite. Harry Secombe, who I got to know quite well, along with his family, was a delight – but essentially the straight man of the outfit. Peter Sellers was much more complicated, and I found him quite arrogant on the only occasion I interviewed him. Throughout our interview he continually sprayed his mouth with some medication. Maybe he thought I was catching. Or possibly he was just going down with a cold, he never explained. I rarely asked celebrities for autographs, but on this occasion I did. Instead of signing his name, he drew the symbol of OM, the so called 'sound of the universe' – and the most important and significant word of mantra tradition. God knows what has happened to that little scrap of paper, but even if I still had it, and was considering selling it, who could guarantee it was actually Sellers' handiwork – unless he had signed it? But then he would have given me his autograph which he plainly didn't want to do. That was the catch, I suppose. A sort of Catch 22.

Years later, after Sellers' death, I interviewed his widow Lynne Frederick (30 years his junior), who went on to marry David Frost (and that lasted just 17 months before she married husband number three). To my astonishment she said she had been able to contact Sellers at a séance. It made the front page of the *Daily Mirror* that night. Not your average story, I guess.

Working nights at the *Mirror* was fun, and you never knew, of course, what was round the corner. Sometimes it was just a question of detective work – making phone call after phone call till, with any luck, you tracked down your prey. I remember being asked to try to find the wildly comic Freddie Starr after he had fled England for Jamaica to get away from it all when he was going through a particularly stressful time in his life. And to track down the celebrated England cricket captain Colin Cowdrey when he was staying in a remote part of Australia in between test matches. I found them both eventually. But God knows what the *Daily Mirror* phone bill was.

I remember spending my entire eight hour shift on the *Daily Express* one night ringing as many people called Smith (crazy, I know) as I had time for in the very vain hope that I might find the one Mr Smith we believed had a bird's eye view of the so-called Spaghetti House siege in Knightsbridge in 1975. The restaurant had been raided by three gunmen. The managers of the chain had assembled to pay in the week's takings of approximately £13,000. When the armed robbery did not go to plan, nine Italian staff members were taken hostage, and moved into the basement. Another staff member escaped and raised the alarm, leading to a siege of six days. My efforts were unrewarded, but the policy is always to try and try again – just in case. Talk about needles and haystacks.

[The best needle in a haystack quote I ever heard was while driving through Vermont recently and listening to the *Prairie Home Companion* live radio variety show created and hosted by Garrison Keillor: 'Serendipity is looking in a haystack for a needle and discovering a farmer's daughter.' Spike would have loved that.]

Chapter 11
Lean, Lawrence and Lara

Late one afternoon in 1990 at my home in West London, the phone rang. 'It's David Lean here. I gather you wanted to speak to me.' I was quite startled because I had heard that Lean was not newspaper friendly. I learnt later from his widow that in fact he enjoyed company and would like to have been more gregarious but was actually quite shy. 'People felt rather reluctant to contact him,' she said.

I had never met him; I had asked to speak to him for a feature I was writing for the *Observer* – but had pretty much given up hope.

'That's wonderful, Sir David,' I said. 'This won't take more than a few minutes.'

'Look,' he said, 'why don't you come round to my house and have dinner. There'll be just me and my housekeeper.'

'Well that would be really kind,' I said, 'but I only need a few sentences.'

'Come on over' he insisted. I could hardly refuse, and certainly didn't want to.

It was true that I needed only a few lines from him to complete my 'Experts' Expert' feature for the *Observer Magazine* – a regular series in which ten leading figures in a specialist field explained who they thought was the greatest of them all. I had already produced features on ten chief constables and ten explorers, and by now I had interviewed a galaxy of film directors, including Ken Russell, John Schlesinger, Alan Parker, Hugh Hudson and even Michael Winner.

I had decided to do without Lean (much as I would have relished speaking to him) and to find a lesser-known director to make up my ten contributors. But who knew what other tales I might pick up for other newspapers if I had dinner with Lean now?

I jumped into my car and made for the posher part of London's recently renovated docklands, with instructions from Lean on how to find the right door into his stunning riverside home in Limehouse. It was one of the more magical evenings I spent in almost 40 years of interviewing the glitterati – in the days when they actually glittered.

Lean's loft-conversion home was magnificent – though I would never see it in daylight. And to me, having been brought up in Canterbury, the floodlit grounds – the greenery lit by a subtle golden hue, with the Thames lapping idly by – resembled the cloisters of the city's cathedral (minus the river of course). I had no shorthand skills (I had given up trying to learn shorthand as a cub reporter in Maidstone when, the only boy in a class of girls, I had turned out to have no aptitude for it: rather like physics and chemistry at school). So I had brought two tape recorders with me – one as back-up (a precaution I had hit upon after one I had been using during dinner with the explorer Sir Ranulph Fiennes had embarrassingly packed up in mid interview). Luckily I had plenty of tape cassettes – the standard recording devices back then. The tapes moved slowly and silently and we talked after a candle-lit dinner. And talked. And talked. It was astonishing really. By then I was used to celebrities opening their hearts to me. It was my job, after all. But here was Britain's premier film director, who had conjured up some of the finest films of the age, from *Lawrence of Arabia* and *Dr Zhivago* to *Bridge on the River Kwai* virtually telling me, a total stranger, his life story. He told me *Zhivago* had made him more money than all the other films he'd made put together – it had already grossed almost £130 million by 1990, and had been 'a wild success'.

And yet initially, after the New York premiere, the signs had been ominous. 'We were having dinner up on the roof of the St Regis Hotel in New York City,' said Lean, 'and around midnight there was a dreadful hush and a terrible rustling of papers and I was thinking what on earth was going on? And the newspapers had just come in. And everybody read these terrible reviews. They were absolutely ghastly, I cannot tell you. Every critic was dreadful to it –

and in America they take more notice of critics that they do here in the UK. And all my friends and various other people were coming up to me and saying 'Well, David – I liked it…' Well, I don't think that was a bad film. I'm not ashamed of it.'

There were many more stories I'd never heard before, including the details of how Lean had painstakingly searched the globe for 'missing' sections of the original *Lawrence* movie after the producer Sam Spiegel had secretly cut it by almost an hour because, according to Lean, he was worried audiences would find it over-long at four hours. There were also commercial considerations – an over-long film could not be shown to as many audiences each day.

In 1962 when the film first opened, it was 222 minutes long, but it was subsequently cut to 187 minutes, and partially restored to 217 minutes in 1989.

'I only found out recently that he'd cut all this material out of the film,' said Sir David. 'When I discovered what had happened, I felt sick at heart. When you think that the man you were working with had, without saying a word to you, taken more than half an hour out of a film… I never knew while he was still alive.'

[Much later, when I was talking to Lean's widow, she described a bitter-sweet moment that occurred soon after his death. 'This will make you laugh,' she said. 'The other day we were sitting at the table, and it had been quite a lovely morning. And we were all very sad. And suddenly from nowhere there was an almighty clap of thunder. And I said: David's up there in the most utter anger. He must have met Sam Spiegel for the first time up there! Yes… I can imagine that.']

'*Lawrence* was shown at its full length when it first came out,' Lean continued. 'It stayed the right length for about two weeks and then, unbeknown to me, they started cutting it. All these years went by and I didn't realise what had happened. Nobody told me.

'To find out, you'd have to go to the cinema and watch your own work every night and I don't do that. Anyway, I was all over the world by then, making *Dr Zhivago*.'

It was no easy task, said Lean, after 27 years, to re-assemble the original version. The missing footage had to be tracked down in various places. 'They had one surviving sound track, the "marrying" track – dialogue, music and effects all on one track. So it was very difficult to cut and put back without making any jumps in the sound, but they did it. When the MGM labs put the negative on the printer, it started ripping immediately, so they re-stuck every join very lovingly, and did a wonderful job. Not one critic complained about the length. In fact the funny thing is that people who have seen the long version and the short version think the long version looks shorter, because it all makes so much more sense and is cut better and has a better flow. It's also a better, sharper print than the original. The focus is much better because it's been printed on the latest stock with far less grain than they had 27 years ago. So it looks just wonderful. I'm very excited about it. So are Peter and Omar. They're really quite stunned by how it looks.'

As the night wore on, there were stories about Peter O'Toole (as *Lawrence*), Omar Sharif (*Zhivago*) and three of the key actors in *Kwai*: Jack Hawkins, Alec Guinness and Sessue Hayakawa (Colonel Saito, the Japanese camp commander). This was fascinating – I had already become friends with Hawkins and interviewed him for BBC Radio in New York shortly before his death in 1973 (the same year that Hayakawa died) and Alec Guinness often generously picked up the phone to me for a relaxed chat, although I never actually met him. As a result of this captivating evening with David Lean, I would also – briefly and surreally – meet Peter O'Toole and Omar Sharif. And even end up with a pair of O'Toole's socks, as I mentioned earlier.

There was one story about Sessue Hayakawa that I liked: Lean told me that many actors, Hayakawa included, used to underscore their lines with a red pen and not bother to look at other dialogue – or indeed any scenes in which they didn't themselves appear. So when Hayakawa came to rehearsals, Lean talked him through the script, as he did with all the cast, and said something like: 'And that's when you die, Sessue.' And Hayakawa looked startled. 'I die?' he said. 'He had no idea that he gets killed at the end of the movie,' said Lean. 'It was quite comical watching his face when he discovered this.'

As a parting gesture, David Lean gave me a delightful memento. I had told him that one of my then teenaged twin daughters had been christened Lara, after the character played so poignantly by Julie Christie in *Zhivago*. He smiled, and wrote on a card for her: 'Lara, you were always my favourite.' My daughter treasures it to this day. That night, as I drove home from Docklands in the small hours, I contemplated my extreme good fortune to be in a career that brought me – completely undeservedly – into almost daily contact with so many talented people.

After such an exhilarating evening, I had to remember to include Lean in my Experts' Expert feature for the *Observer Magazine*. After all, this was the only reason I'd got the interview in the first place. So what did he say?

'It's awfully hard to talk about your fellow directors. As soon as I'd chosen one, I'd say, Oh God, I've forgotten so-and-so. I'd put Fellini up front, but in a specialised style. Nobody, however could touch Billy Wilder – you know, *Some Like it Hot* and *The Apartment*. I like him very much indeed. There are a lot of very good young chaps, but they're still learning like mad. I thought *Chariots of Fire*, directed by Hugh Hudson, was an excellent film. But I think it takes a lot to beat the old films. You can't forget John Huston or Orson Welles just because they're dead. They are two of the best directors of the whole lot.'

For the record, the overall Experts' Expert voted for by the 11 directors I finally interviewed was in fact Billy Wilder.

I never saw Lean again. I was invited to his sixth wedding, and flattered as I was to be asked, I couldn't go because I was skiing (by now my main occupation). Four months later he was dead, at 83 – from throat cancer, just like Jack Hawkins almost 20 years earlier. The evening we'd spent together now seemed even more poignant and magical.

Lean's sixth wife, Sandra Cooke, was an art dealer and designer who had met Lean by chance when they both visited the food hall at Harrods in 1985 (when he was 76) – she to buy vegetables, he to buy grapes. She told him how much she enjoyed his films. 'David was ageless to me because I thought he was going to be immortal, somehow,' she said later. 'Rather like you never expect your parents to die. It was a strange feeling. I never thought he'd go because he had the constitution of an ox. I was with him when he died. I sat on the bed, held his hand, and stroked his hair. He had lovely hair. And he said: "The battle's over. I'm going." But he's eternal. He always will be – to me anyway.'

Recalling the moment they first met, Lady Lean said: 'When I approached him in Harrods and told him I admired his films, I thought I'd get a peculiar, stuffy answer. But he said: Thank you very much. He was extremely friendly. And in fact he did most of the talking, despite being a shy man. But you have to remember that he did like the ladies – till his dying day. I loved that about him.'

Soon afterwards, Sandra had been chatting to an acquaintance about her recent visit to a clairvoyant who told her she would have a 'wonderful few years' with a man whose name started 'DA'. Jokingly, she mentioned her encounter with Lean. Amazed, the friend told her that only last night he had had dinner with a pensive Lean, who eventually admitted he'd met a 'girl' in Harrods and couldn't get her face out of his head. 'It really was fate,' Lady Lean says.

'David was never alone,' Lady Lean told me. 'He'd never lived alone. But I was never jealous of his past. I'm not a jealous person at all. And he never grieved over his past relationships. He was an enormously intelligent man although he didn't think so. He had a brilliant mind. A lot of people were in awe of him, but they shouldn't have been. He wasn't that sort of person at all. But he was totally unique and in his way a sort of god. There'll never be another like him in the cinema. There's never going to be another David Lean. Every movie was like a new love affair with a woman. And that, in itself, had kept him alive.'

Somehow Sandra provided Lean with the emotional security that previous wives seem to have been unable to offer. I asked whether she thought their marriage would have survived if she'd been his first wife rather than his sixth. 'That's very difficult to answer,' she said. 'Yes, I think it would, although I've no idea what he was like of course when he was a young man, and I myself was far less worldly and street wise. Who can tell? Put it this way – if we'd met years earlier but were more as we were now, I'm sure it would have lasted.'

Having missed the wedding I then found myself invited to Lean's memorial service at St Paul's Cathedral. Lady Lean startled me with a wonderful story. Peter O'Toole, she said, was going to re-enact the famous 'well scene' from *Lawrence* at the service in St Paul's. Wow! I went to town on this in Peter Tory's column in the *Sunday Express*. The well scene depicts the death of Lawrence's nomadic Bedouin guide Tafas after drawing water from a well in the Jordanian desert.

The dialogue proceeds like this:

> Sherif: He is dead.
> Lawrence: Yes. WHY?
> Sherif: This is my well.
> Lawrence: I have drunk from it.
> Sherif: *You* are welcome.
> Lawrence: He was my friend.
> Sherif: That?
> Lawrence: Yes. That.
> Sherif: You are angry, English. He was nothing. The well is everything. The Hasimi may not drink at our wells. He knew that. Sa'lam.
> Lawrence: Sherif Ali, so long as the Arabs fight tribe against tribe, so long will they be a little people, a silly people, greedy, barbarous, and cruel, as you are.'

The long section of footage that precedes the death of Tafas – Omar Sharif and camel, just a tiny speck on the shimmering horizon shuffling almost endlessly towards the camera, growing gradually bigger and bigger until they reach the well, was one of the crucial sequences cut back by Spiegel. Lean had deliberately shot it long for maximum effect, reasoning, correctly, that the audience would be spellbound rather than bored by the long build up. He told me that bringing the sequence back to its full length was one of the most satisfying moments he had in the reconstruction of the movie.

However it's generally agreed that the scene never happened in real life and is not taken from Lawrence's classic book *Seven Pillars of Wisdom*.

Unfortunately it didn't happen at St Paul's either. Although O'Toole gave Lady Lean 'one enormous hug' before the service, he plainly didn't like the idea of revisiting the controversial scene. After the service, I found myself asking O'Toole and Sharif why not.

O'Toole plainly thought the idea was daft, and became irritated when I asked him. Sharif, much milder, said: 'I would have done it if Peter had.' We argued about it as we left St Paul's, heading for the post memorial service wake where numerous fellow thespians including Terence Stamp, Sir Alec Guinness, James Fox, Sir John Mills and Rita Tushingham were gathering, and I suddenly found myself thinking: 'Ye gods, here I am on the steps of St Paul's having a heated discussion with two of my greatest screen idols. How surreal was this?'

Such is the life of a humble diarist.

Chapter 12
Actors galore

As a small boy, I adored listening to the classic radio series *Journey Into Space*. So did half the country. So meeting Jet Morgan– aka Andrew Faulds, then Labour MP for Smethwick – was almost as exciting as meeting Buzz Aldrin would be, a few years later.

That voice! In the early 1950s, only a few of the cult programme's huge audience had a TV to distract them from their wireless sets. Spooky music by Van Phillips and sound effects – plus a little imagination – were enough to send millions to their beds on Sunday nights with a delicious frisson of fear after Jet's latest adventures. Many deliberately listened with the lights turned off.

When Faulds and the rest of the cast discovered that the BBC had wiped the original series, they were horrified. 'We went bananas,' he said. 'Whoever took the decisions about what to save and what to put down must have a brain the size of a walnut.'

Luckily they managed to re-record it

'The lads within the BBC produced some very exciting sounds – with the help of Battersea power station,' Faulds told me. 'We were allowed to weave recordings of some of its sounds into the noises of the space-ship, like opening and closing airlocks.'

Unlike many actors who later resent being identified with the character that made them famous, Faulds has always been grateful to the space hero. Not that he would ever have wanted to 'be' him. 'I'm not interested in space in the slightest,' he said, rather disappointingly. It was like Dan Dare saying he'd rather be an accountant. 'I certainly wouldn't want to be a spaceman in real life. But Jet was an enormous boost to my career. I've always had a bit of a thrill when people come up to me and say they remember me as Jet Morgan. It's a golden oldie. I'm just glad I was in it.'

Over the years, inevitably, I've met and interviewed a good many actors, but few have moved me so much as Jack Hawkins. Back in

April 1973 I'd been pestering another celebrated actor, Stanley Baker, for a story he'd promised me. I had no idea what that story was (and still don't), but he'd kept saying to me: 'I've got a good story but I can't give it to you yet.' So of course every few weeks I'd phone him, and he kept saying 'Be patient'. Then suddenly one day he suggested I meet him at Heathrow airport, with my passport and some overnight things. I couldn't imagine what this was about, and assumed he'd organised some sort of joy ride to make up for the fact that he'd kept me waiting so long for the mysterious 'story'. I turned up at Heathrow and had one of the biggest surprises of my life. For some reason I never did fathom, he'd booked me on one of two British Caledonian inaugural flights to New York. I wasn't going to argue, especially when I discovered who some of the other passengers were. They included Lord Mountbatten, the racing driver Jackie Stewart (who once told me his eyesight was so superb he could identify faces in the crowd while he was racing), the actress Shelley Winters – and Jack Hawkins, then probably the most famous screen star in Britain. I remember having four drinks on my tray at the same time during the flight: red wine, white wine, brandy and Drambuie…

Once we'd arrived in New York, and made ourselves comfortable at the Plaza hotel, I got friendly with Hawkins who, it turned out, had another, far more serious, agenda. He had cancer of the throat, and was going to seek medical advice about the possibility of being fitted with an artificial voice box.

A three-pack-a-day smoker, Hawkins began experiencing voice problems in the late 1950s. In 1959 he'd undergone cobalt treatment for what was then described as a secondary condition of the larynx. In private, he used a mechanical larynx to aid his speech. In December 1965, he'd been diagnosed with throat cancer, and his entire larynx had been removed. From then on, his film performances were dubbed by other actors.

By the time I met him, his vocal chords were in such a bad way that he croaked more than spoke, which prompted the receptionist at the hotel to yell brutally at him: 'write it down – I can't hear you'. It must have been humiliating for him, but he took it magnanimously. She obviously had no idea he was Britain's 'most indubitable of matinee idols'. I felt embarrassed for him.

I was doing some radio back then, and – though I felt rather foolish asking, as he had such a croaky voice – suggested a radio interview. We went up to his room, where he towered over me in his white dressing gown while I asked inane questions. After a while I felt guilty about straining his voice and said: 'I think we should stop it there – you must be getting tired.' He replied in his growly, gravelly voice: 'No, carry on. I'm really rather enjoying it.' He said later that he was quite shocked to hear how bad his voice sounded, and that recording was one of the reasons he finally decided to have the voice-box operation back in London. He died very soon afterwards, in July. The BBC used an extract from my recorded interview on *The World at One*, and then promptly mislaid it. I have never seen or heard it since, which upset me as I was planning to give it to his widow, Doreen.

The last time I saw Hawkins was in New York. I had cunningly booked myself on the return half of another British Caledonian inaugural flight – from Los Angeles back to London. This gave me a wonderful opportunity to get my first serious look at America. By train. The journey, trundling on Amtrak through a dozen states, via Chicago, took two and a half days. People thought I was crazy – why didn't I fly? But for me, when it comes to trains or planes (with the possible exception of Concorde, which of course is no longer an option) trains win hands down. How many of those 12 states would I have seen in such detail – or indeed seen at all – if I'd gone straight from JFK to LAX?

I had the good fortune to meet the impossibly versatile actor, writer and film maker Peter Ustinov – he of *Hercule Poirot* fame - three or four times. On the second occasion he was with his Swiss wife Helene for an interview I was doing for the short-lived *Sunday Correspondent* newspaper about two novellas he'd just written. One of Ustinov's many talents was the ability to answer questions so fully that you scarcely need a second question.

Earlier that day, my explorer chum John Blashford-Snell had suggested over lunch that I should ask Ustinov whether it was he who – when filling in the visa form for a USA visit which asked whether 'any part of the purpose of his visit' was to 'subjugate the government of the United States' – wrote, 'sole purpose of visit'. It turned out to have been Evelyn Waugh, but it did prompt a Ustinov story.

'I got into trouble for completely different reasons,' he said. 'I was much younger and more naive at the time, and they asked you about your colour. And I put 'pink'. And I was told very sternly that I was white. And I said: 'No, I feel perfectly well.'

Here's another. 'At the White House there was a reception in honour of Prince Charles and Lady Di, and we were invited. Suddenly there was a tinkling of glasses and President Reagan wanted to propose a toast. And he said: "I just wanna raise my glass in this White House of ours to welcome the wonderful Prince of Wales and his lovely Lady David", and my dinner partner, a ballerina, gripped my arm, and asked: What did he say? and I said not to worry, he was only thinking of the week ahead at Camp Diana.'

We ended our meeting with Ustinov's account of how he failed to enter the world of espionage. 'I was once interviewed in order to see whether I would make a good spy,' he said. 'And I was supposed to go to Sloane Square underground station where there'd be a man reading the *News Chronicle*. Well there wasn't. There was a man holding the *News Chronicle*, but he was looking over the top of it, which I thought was a very bad performance. And I was supposed to go up to him with a password, and then he was supposed to answer, and we were to go for a walk. Well I went through the password, which I can't remember now, but it was something like The weather has improved recently – something really idiotic – and he was supposed to say: Yes, we've had several bright patches, and we went for a walk. Well, all that worked very well, and on the walk he said to me *Parlez-vous français*? and I said *Oui* and he said *Sprechen sie Deutsche*? and I said *Ja*, and he said Good man! And we went on talking about nothing in particular, and then he said he'd let me know. And I was turned down, which depressed me as a potential spy, but gave me enormous confidence as an actor, because the verdict was that I was refused because I didn't have the kind of face which could disappear easily into a crowd.'

Strangely enough, at the time I was seeing quite a bit of Peter Ustinov, I bumped into the 'other' Poirot, David Suchet, completely by accident. He was filming an episode of the TV series one night almost outside my then home in Twickenham. Well of course, I couldn't resist a quick chat during a break. He was utterly charming. Talk about the mountain coming to Mohammed – I suppose I should have asked him in for tea.

One of the nicest and most unassuming film stars I met was George Chakiris, a heartthrob who'd become famous for his role as the lean and dangerous Bernardo, leader of the Sharks, in the classic 1961 movie *West Side Story*. He still had the black leather wristband he wore in the film. I met him not in Los Angeles but in Richmond, south west London, when he was touring Britain as René Gallimard, the French diplomat in David Henry Hwang's *M. Butterfly*. It was exactly 30 years since Chakiris, by then 59 and as good looking as ever, had won his Oscar for his role in *West Side Story*. Incredibly, he said he didn't watch the film after its release until 1990, when he went to Paris to receive an arts award. After the screening, he said: 'I loved it. I cried.' And the fact that fans still remember him as Bernardo 'keeps me from feeling like this forgotten thing.'

He told me he and other members of the *West Side Story* cast still met from time to time. 'We all shared this wonderful experience and we all like each other too. None of us is temperamental and we all enjoy each other very much.'

Chakiris looked so good that I asked him whether he had interfered with his face surgically. 'No!' he chuckled. 'You know what, I have to tell you when you live in Los Angeles, it's such a different atmosphere, such a different world. I think that's why work-wise I've always preferred working and being in other places. I love – I have always loved – England, and working here, because people aren't looking at every line in your face. In Los Angeles there is such a preoccupation with one's appearance that it goes beyond what makes any sense. They are so obsessed with looking perfect, and beautiful bodies and all that sort of thing and you really get a bit fed up with it, you know. And you also feel in Los Angeles that virtually the whole city is in show business. It really does feel that way. The reason your question made me laugh is that when you're in Los Angeles you look in the mirror and you say: Let's see now, maybe I should do this... maybe I should do that. It's peer pressure, and it comes into casting directors' minds I think. When you walk into an office the first thing they decide is – well I suppose the first thing that hits anybody I suppose, when you walk into a room, is what you look like. But people hopefully will go beyond that. You feel this pressure to always try to look your best and it gets a little bit... it's a nuisance a lot of the time.'

In spite of his good looks, Chakiris has never married. 'The only time I thought about it,' he told me, 'and I'm not saying the girl in question thought about it... but I did think about marrying an actress I worked with in a film back in 1966. And we're still very good friends. She lives in France. That's one of the difficult things, I think, about our business – that we're all travelling all the time and so it's hard, by and large, to sustain a relationship sometimes.'

Peter Cushing was a neighbour when I lived in Whitstable, Kent. His private image could hardly have been more different from his film persona which, whether he was playing a goodie or a baddie, was nearly always involved in a sinister plot. We often bumped into each other, sometimes by appointment, and he was for ever, rather touchingly, leaving me little cards with his name embossed in red, which usually ended 'God be with you always.'

Apart from being religious, he loved animals. Picture the scene as I described it in the *London Evening News* John London column:

> Before six o'clock each morning a man whose business is horror walks stealthily along the mist-shrouded foreshore of a Kent resort, to keep a silent appointment – but the only victims are tennis balls.
>
> A glimpse of the grim face, lit by moonlight breaking through the sea mist, reveals Peter Cushing and... Thudder, a neighbour's

dog. Says Cushing – (star of assorted *Dracula* and *Frankenstein* movies, *The Mummy* and of course a few *Sherlock Holmes* epics, plus, later a couple of outings as *Doctor Who*) – 'Taking Thudder for a walk is part of my daily routine. It started when he chased after me during one of my regular early morning walks after my swim. I kicked a stone along the beach for him. He chased it and sometimes brought it back. When he didn't, he expected me to find another one to kick. Gradually he got into the habit of waiting for me. But now, instead of kicking stones, I use old tennis balls. It gets a bit expensive because he loses quite a few and I have to keep buying them – but they're easier on the feet.'

Cushing was pole-axed when his wife Helen died, and told me he had tried to kill himself by getting soaked to the skin and lying in the garden all night in the hope of getting pneumonia. Whenever I asked him how he was, he would simply answer 'thank you'. I began to wonder whether he was going deaf, and eventually had the nerve to ask him. 'No,' he replied, 'I'm not going deaf. It's just that since my beloved Helen's death, I know I will never be able to answer "I'm all right thank you" because I never will be all right again. So "thank you" is the only appropriate answer.'

Cushing told me once that when he received his contract for the then latest Frankenstein film, *Frankenstein Must Be Destroyed*, he carefully wrote, in brackets: 'Over my dead body!'

I did one major interview with him, realising that if, sadly, he did succeed in doing himself in, it would be a poignant feature. I kept a written copy of the interview in my loft for years, glad that he was still alive. When he finally did pop off, I was in Australia – about as far from my carefully stored feature as was possible. And in those pre-computer days, I didn't have it with me. Serves me right…

I got quite matey with Oliver Reed in the late 70s, and as a visiting journalist played cricket and football with him (and many others) at Broome Hall, his stately home near Dorking, Surrey. He once said: 'There is, of course, a world of difference between cricket and the movie business… I suppose doing a love scene with Raquel Welch roughly corresponds to scoring a century before lunch.'

He admitted to me that his cricketing statistics contained an untruth. 'When I was at school, I got a wicket by cheating,' he said. 'My cap blew off as I was chasing a ball. I picked it up with the ball, and then threw them both at the wicket. The ball missed, but the cap hit the stumps, and the batsman was given out.' Reed's career figures? 'Something like 50 overs, 0 wickets for 500 runs,' he grinned. 'One of the reasons I get knocked about a bit by batsmen is that I'm usually anaesthetised by alcohol.' But to be fair he did have one other excuse. After getting measles as a child, Reed developed a 'terrible squint'. Fortunately for his acting career, it was corrected, but left him with a vision defect. 'I have problems playing cricket, squash and tennis because the balls are too small for me to see properly,' he told me. 'Rugby's fine because the ball is big.'

My ex wife, Ronni, was quite excited about my friendship with Reed as she had always thought he was rather dishy, and indeed even said I reminded her of him a little. Seen together, any resemblance was pretty sketchy. He was quite a bit taller, bulkier and stronger. So when we played football, he found it fairly easy to bounce me off the ball.

Ronni's interest in Reed rather fizzled out when I triumphantly introduced them – only for Reed to clumsily spill a large glass of red wine all over her jeans. I half expected her never to wash them again, as it were, but the magic spell was broken, I fear. Reed eventually died of a heart attack in a bar after (reportedly) downing three bottles of Captain Morgan's Jamaica rum, eight bottles of German beer, numerous doubles of Famous Grouse whiskey and Hennessy cognac, and after beating five much younger Royal Navy sailors at arm-wrestling. His bar bill for that final lunch time totalled 270 Maltese lira, almost £450.

One amusing problem I had with Reed was that he and his brother David, who was his business manager, sounded identical on the phone. Luckily Simon, their half-brother – now a prominent sports broadcaster – didn't sound like them, which was handy when I was trying to work out who exactly I was speaking to on the phone.

I had an unexpectedly bizarre experience when I met Charles Hawtrey – famous for his *Carry On* film roles – when I was in the attractive Austrian resort town of Seefeld for a 'Miss Cinema' competition in the early 70s. I hadn't realised that Hawtrey, a fellow panellist with the utterly delightful fellow thespian Billy Whitelaw and others was hardly the kind of chap to take much of an interest in beauty queens. (In her autobiography, Barbara Windsor wrote about Hawtrey's alcoholism, and his outrageous flirting with the footballer George Best.)

Born in 1914 as George Frederick Joffre Hartree, he took his stage name from the theatrical knight Sir Charles Hawtrey, and encouraged the suggestion that he was his son. However, his father was actually a London car mechanic.

One night when the Miss Cinema judges were enjoying a few drinks in our hotel, Hawtrey became quite tired and emotional, and asked me whether I'd see him to his room. Being a relatively callow youth, I didn't realise what was coming. When we got to his room he asked me to lock the door. I asked him how this would be possible without his key and it gradually dawned in me – to my horror – that he meant lock it from the inside. Of course I made my excuses and left. But it wasn't over. Hawtrey shortly re-emerged at the bar. In floods of tears because I had abandoned him.

Years later, on his deathbed, the poor soul supposedly threw a vase at his nurse who asked for a final autograph. It was the last thing he did. His ashes were scattered in Mortlake Crematorium, at Chiswick. I was told no friends or family attended. Sad that.

Chapter 13
The royals

At the time of writing, the Prince of Wales is still without a proper job. This once led me to write a limerick about what he might do to get one while he was waiting to be King.

> Prince Philip saw Charles and said 'Heck!
> What's that collar you've got round your neck?'
> Said Charles with a sob
> 'One's been given a job –
> I'm the Rev at All Souls, Tooting Bec!'

I'm not going to pretend I have spent much time talking to royalty, though I have bumped into the Prince of Wales twice, his dad once, watched Princess Diana skiing in Lech, Austria, and of course there was that lunch in neighbouring Zürs with Princess Caroline. Oh yes, and I once found myself, with ex-King Constantine of Greece who was wearing a white dressing gown, sharing a lift in Villars, Switzerland, which, much to his exasperation, refused to take him to the correct floor for the spa (and yes, we did chat, briefly).

My first meeting with Charles was at St Margaret's Bay coastguard station in Kent. He'd been up since 6am for a special briefing before he took the minesweeper HMS Bronington into the English Channel. Bronington (M1115) was a mahogany-hulled coastal minesweeper. She was the last of the 'wooden walled' naval vessels – being used to keep an eye on ships operating under flags of convenience that were defying the two-way traffic system in the channel, and attempting to avoid any responsibility for clearing up any spillage in the event of collisions with other vessels. As one nameless wit put it, it was his first day as 'Charlie the Channel Cop'. At the coastguard station he watched how radar was being used to track so-called 'rogue' shipping. The role of Bronington's crew of 32 was to chase these ships, warn them, and – like channel traffic wardens – make a note of their registration.

I asked Prince Charles if he'd enjoyed his briefing, and he said: 'As much as one enjoys any briefing.' When the subject of looking for 'rogues' came up, he looked at me and two colleagues and said: 'I think I've already found the first ones!'

Policing the Dover Straits was and still is a serious business – particularly back in 1976, not so long after the disastrous winter when two vessels went down within weeks of each other with the loss of 51 lives.

My only serious friendship with anyone royal was, as I have mentioned earlier, with Lady Brabourne, later Countess Mountbatten, a cousin of The Queen. Even then we rarely had a conversation that didn't at some stage or another include her regular 'Now you won't quote me, Mr Wilson, will you?' And I never did, except when she lost her cat and I was able to run a little story in the *Daily Mirror* diary that led to her pet being recovered. But over the years (after establishing that Lord Mountbatten was indeed her father) I found her a great help on occasions when there was a royal story on the go. She was always immensely discreet and her integrity was without question. While she never gave me any information – and I wouldn't have expected her to – she was a kind and useful sounding board for my own stories about the royal family. Then, when certain red-top publications started making up 'royal sources' I pretty much gave up pestering the countess. What was the point of having a genuine royal contact, albeit an extremely discreet one, when some newspapers just made up royal contacts who, by definition, had much more to say for themselves, since they didn't actually exist?

I recall an excellent lunch with Lord 'Bill' Deedes, however (we used to dine together at least once a year) which turned out to be focused on the rift between Prince Charles and Princess Diana. Deedes had been my MP in the Ashford area of Kent, and we often met in varied circumstances.

Deedes, who was of course Denis Thatcher's golf partner, was also an unlikely chum of the Princess. He had travelled with her on her missions to remove land mines from some of the world's trouble spots: specifically Angola and Bosnia.

He was a wonderful lunchtime companion. We normally met at his favourite London restaurant, Paradiso E Inferno, in the Strand, where we once sang an impromptu duet while discussing his travels with the princess. Our tongues loosened by a bottle of wine or two, I asked him what his take was on her relationship with Prince Charles. 'Well, Arnie,' he said, with that famous Deedes twinkle in his eye, and that equally famous slushy 'esh' lisp, 'it's a little like the words of the song…I get along without you very well…' – at which point we both tried to sing through the remainder of the poetry made famous by Hoagy Carmichael. But neither of us could remember the words. We both tried to sing it together, thinking perhaps that where one of us had a mental block, the other might come to the rescue. Indeed the entire restaurant became hushed at the sight of these two ageing crooners struggling to sing such a famous song. It was something of a Bateman moment – fellow diners halted with forkfuls of food in mid-air, wondering what to make of such a tuneless duet. We both managed 'I get along without you very well, of course I do' but the next few lines – *Except when soft rains fall, and drip from leaves, then I recall the thrill of being sheltered in your arms* were left hanging in the breeze.

When I got home, the image of Bill Deedes singing for his lunch intrigued me, so I thought I would try to find a home for the story in Richard Kay's diary in the *Daily Mail*. Richard had taken over from the notoriously temperamental Nigel Dempster (I'd got used to offering stories to Dempster's much more considerate deputy Adam Helliker) and, fond though I was of Nigel, Richard – himself a genuine friend of Princess Diana – was also a far more relaxed and calming person to deal with. But the first thing I felt I had to do was call Deedes and see whether he had any objection to my selling the story. 'My dear boy,' he said. 'Feel as free as the air to offer it to whoever you please.' Only a former diarist such as he would have been so understanding, I suspect. My next task was to try to establish the words of the song. This was before the Internet had taken over our lives, so I figured the quickest way to do this was to ring a very good friend, Tony Coe, a jazz saxophonist and clarinettist whose instrumental skills had been put to good use on the sound tracks of some of the *Pink Panther* movies and *Superman II*. Tony himself wasn't certain of all the words, and he in turn gave me a phone number of a singer he felt was certain to know them. Thus it was that a complete stranger sang the song down the phone to me while I scribbled down the words.

Well, it paid for lunch – almost.

Once, I managed to lure Deedes to my favourite restaurant for a change – in London's Farringdon Road – and we dined at sub-pavement level, Bill's weathered face bathed in candlelight as he regaled me with fascinating titbits. It was he, he revealed, as Minister Without Portfolio in the Macmillan government, who had quite innocently typed out on his portable typewriter John Profumo's famous speech to the House of Commons in which the former War Minister had lied to the house about not sleeping with the call-girl Christine Keeler. There was also a funny story about how the Thatchers couldn't understand how it could take very long for mere mortals to get from Dulwich (then their home) to Downing Street. 'What Denis failed to mention,' recalled Bill, 'was that when they made the journey they usually had a police escort.'

One of the more curious royal stories I was involved with (through a mutual friend) concerned the mother-in-law of one of Prince Andrew's flying chums, when the prince was still flying helicopters. It occurred in the officers' mess at Portland naval base. The woman had been invited to await her son-in-law, a naval lieutenant, who was flying with Andrew on a sortie in their Lynx helicopter.

As she sat watching TV in a cosy armchair, she began to feel drowsy. Having a fairly ample figure, she undid a button on the waist of her pale blue pleated suit and fell into a gentle slumber – only to be rudely awakened by this: 'Mother-in-law, I'd like you to meet Prince Andrew – Prince Andrew, meet mother-in-law.'

Uncomfortably aroused from her sleep, she scrambled to her feet. Her skirt, unfastened, fell away and stayed in the chair. With a hand half-outstretched towards the now ashen-faced royal pilot, mother-in-law stood there in her white surgical stockings, 'hoping' as Peter Tory put it in his *Star* diary, 'that merciful death would swiftly claim her'. Andrew was speechless. Some few days later, however, he was telling the other chaps in the mess that he had 'told the story to the Queen'. Her Majesty, by all accounts, had 'practically fallen off her perch with merriment'.

Chapter 14
Stateside

The highlight of my diary days was a wonderfully self-indulgent but productive two week tour of the USA – mainly California – in which Peter Tory and I, along with a photographer, Tony Fisher, were given virtual carte blanche by the *Star* newspaper to interview any celebrity we could persuade to talk to us. The choice of subjects was largely down to me. I provided the contacts (his contacts book was rather a shadow of mine) and we did the interviews together, with Peter providing the main writing skills and final flourishes.

It worked like this. I flew alone to Los Angeles to prepare the ground, staying with two of my oldest friends in America – Robert Mintz, a former film producer, and his Australian wife June. I'd met Robert during an early foray to the Cannes Film Festival, where in the early 70s I'd been a guest on a yacht being used as a base by the production company associated with the British actor David Hemmings (famous for his roles in *Blow-Up* and *The Charge of the Light Brigade*). Hemmings and Mintz had directed and produced a film being shown at Cannes called *The 14* (aka *The Wild Little Bunch*), a true story about a family of British children causing havoc by going on the rampage after being orphaned. So it was appropriate that Hemmings was one of the names on our hit list.

I spent the week hunched over my phone numbers, calling just about every celebrity I knew in America. In the UK in those days it was simply a matter of calling celebrities direct – assuming you had their contact numbers. Luckily I had a few useful numbers in the States too. But of course there were myriad stars in America. And although I was doing all this in the Los Feliz hills, just a hoot and a holler away from Hollywood, trying to lure some famous names into our net whose phone numbers I didn't have, proved quite tricky. So while I did manage to get through to various household names (like *Star Trek*'s William Shatner, and Telly '*Kojak*' Savalas) or their agents (and I almost succeeded in hooking Jimmy Stewart) we were still struggling a little. At this stage Bo Derek hadn't committed, and we ended up with the following short list: William Shatner, David Hemmings, and Dudley Moore (whose phone numbers I did have). I also managed to get to an astronaut at NASA's Houston HQ – Robert 'Hoot' Gibson. By the time Tory and Fisher flew out to join me I had established a basic timetable. First out of the hat would be Shatner – aka Captain James T Kirk, commander of the USS Starship *Enterprise*.

We found the Canadian-born actor riding a horse at the Los Angeles Equestrian Center. Shatner loves horses and once bred them. He was passionate about the saddle-bred variety – 'the peacocks of the horse show world'. He also told us he had a pilot's licence and loved flying microlights, difficult though it was to picture the captain of the *Enterprise* bobbing about in the sky at sub-warp speed on such a flimsy craft…

He might have been good at understanding Klingon, (and might conceivably have managed *Nuqneh-Nooknehh*, for example – as in 'Greeting, what do you want? State your business') but he was less skilled at determining our accents. 'Are you guys from Australia?' was his opening gambit. I quite liked him, but Tory, a more cynical, world-weary writer than me, was not quite so impressed, although he did allow himself to write: 'We found him to be an engaging and enthusiastic man – the occasional faint suggestion of self-esteem seemed to be entirely reasonable under the circumstances.'

However Tory told *Star* readers that the current joke on the *Star Trek* flight deck was that in the next epic (written, directed by and starring Shatner) our hero would arrange for the *Enterprise* to blow up in the first few frames, killing all the personnel but himself, leaving him to play all the parts. 'This,' wrote Tory triumphantly, 'would involve Mr Shatner beaming himself up – a task that would be daunting to even the most experienced astronauts.'

Although Shatner seemed very much at ease with us, he did say he wasn't keen on interviews. 'That's probably why we hardly ever read about you in the British papers,' said Tory. 'I think British readers would like to know a bit more about you.'

The first thing we were surprised to learn was that although he'd started acting as a child, Shatner studied economics at university in Montreal, his home town, although admittedly he was 'doing amateur and professional theatre all the time I was there'.

He told us: 'I was supposed to be adept at handling books and business, and things like that. The truth of the matter is that I was terrible. I had a smattering of English literature, and I had some performance classes and musical classes, and some psychology which stayed with me, but the rest of that information just went over my head. So the irony is that although I got my first job in a professional theatre as assistant manager on the basis of my new degree, I proceeded to destroy the theatre's books and accounting by my ineptness. I was fired – for total, utter incompetence, but I was kept on as the juvenile [actor]. That happened twice, in two different theatres.'

The *Star Trek* phenomenon started when Gene Roddenberry, the series creator, who'd been asked to recast the pilot after the network failed to buy the original, had 'seen Shatner in something or other' and called him in New York, where he was working and said: 'Please come to Los Angeles and see this pilot I've made.'

Said Shatner: 'And so I went to see it – it was a two-hour movie for television. He asked me to play the lead part. And I said I would if there were certain corrections made. Basically I think everyone took themselves too seriously.'

'Needed slight tongue-in-cheek?' suggested Tory. 'Well,' joked Shatner, 'I think the tongue-in-cheek is for the viewer. The actor has to not stick his tongue in his cheek otherwise it makes a lump and it's hard to talk! The tongue-in-cheek is in the eyes of the beholder. I think the character can take himself seriously, but the actor can't – if you follow.'

'Beam me up Scottie!' – which Kirk never actually ever said – was a good example of tongue-in-cheek material, and 'had a certain grating quality', admitted Shatner. He also mentioned the 'Christmas reel of out-takes which were put together by our editors for our amusement at Christmas parties, and they were supposed to go on the junk pile when the series was over. Well, that's become very popular. The thing which is irritating about that is that it's often played on television and the actors never get compensated for it.'

Did they have a lot of fun on the set? 'Not really,' said Shatner. 'It would be more like a school reunion. You don't really have much in common. All you have in common is some nostalgia and reminiscences. It's a pleasure to see them on the set, but I've never seen anyone off the set except Leonard Nimmoy. He's a friend of mine.'

It's worth remembering that although the 79 episodes of the original TV series were often repeated after NBC cancelled it ('it was only middlingly popular,' said Shatner), and were eventually followed by the big-screen versions, there was more than a decade between making the TV series and the movies. So while for *Star Trek* fans there didn't seem to have been much of a gap, Shatner, and the rest of the cast, were busy doing many other things during the 12 years in between, and not giving the Starship *Enterprise* much thought. So for quite a long time in his life he forgot about being Captain Kirk, while for the viewing public – watching repeats – Kirk never really went away.

'Did you ever want to become an astronaut?' I asked.

'No – I'm quite happy being an actor,' he laughed. 'And being a pretend astronaut. Although I'd like to go up!'

Shatner revealed that he used to hunt big game with a bow and arrow. This now filled him with shame and horror, he said. 'I've stopped hunting,' he told us, 'for philosophical reasons. I breed Dobermans and horses. In effect I bring living things into the world. I'm terribly moved by the birth of a horse. Tears come to my eyes every time I see it happen. And the birth, even of a puppy, is an enormous, magnificent event – like the birth of a baby.

'I've looked animals in the eye and shot them with an arrow. I've had to cut the throats of wounded creatures. I look my horse in the eye – and it is actually looking back at me. There comes a point when it is quite impossible – a monstrous act – to kill a living creature.'

To end on a more light-hearted note – Shatner confirmed what most people have already guessed. Those sliding doors on the bridge through which Kirk comes and goes are actually opened by two men hidden behind the set. *Pssshhhhh*. That's the noise they make, but although Shatner did a funny impression of the sound, we forgot to ask him how the sound effect was produced. Presumably it was done in post-production. Ah well. Kirk out.

Then we were off to meet Dudley Moore, who was easily short enough to be an astronaut, at least back in the cramped Mercury spacecraft days when there were limits to how tall you could be to fit inside one. We found him with his delightful wife-to-be Brogan Lane. I'd been hounding Moore on the phone in recent months and he'd reluctantly agreed to give us a 'few minutes' in LA. 'Normally I'd have asked you to talk to my agent,' he said. 'But there was something in your voice.' And if that wasn't a compliment, what followed next certainly was. I was rewarded with the sound of one of Britain's funniest (and later most tragic) comedians laughing uproariously at one of my quips.

Tory remarked – and later mentioned in his column – that a height difference of only 5½ inches was something of an achievement for this 'actor, musician and comic genie', since most of his previous partners had been virtual Amazons. 'His nose almost travels through life on the same level as hers, and he needs only to stand on tip-toe in order to place an affectionate peck on her brunette fringe.'

Moore said: 'Every time I went through Heathrow airport, the newspapers would describe my arrival as Sex Thimble Dudley Moore, en route to wherever, with towering blonde. You'd think they might have found a variation occasionally.'

'How about towering inferno?' I suggested, referring to the film of the same name. There was a slight pause, and then Dudley simply exploded most gratifyingly with cackling mirth. 'Towering inferno!' he repeated. 'That's good!' I still have that moment on tape. It may not sound so funny in the cold light of day, but it was just one of those throw-away remarks that happened to hit the spot at the time.

'Most people tower over me actually,' he said. 'That's the way it is when you're 5ft 2½ – I always have to mention the half because every little counts!'

We'd found Moore on the brink of returning to film work after a two year break. 'I just wanted to stop for a while,' he said. 'I thought amazingly interesting, important things would occur to me to do – but they didn't. I didn't really do anything madly creative. So I'm just basically going back to work again.'

At this point the delightful Miss Lane entered the room, offering us a drink. She called him Dud. Wine was one suggestion. 'What do we have?' asked Moore. 'Do we have anything worth drinking?'

Of the many thoughts and tales he shared with us, perhaps the most poignant – bearing in mind that Moore himself eventually died in tragic circumstances – was one in which he was convinced he'd deeply offended Rock Hudson, the handsome screen star who shocked his female admirers when he later died of AIDS.

'Rock and Liza Minnelli were at a do,' he told us, 'an Oscars ceremony. And I knew Liza of course, from doing the film *Arthur* with her, but it was really the first time I'd met Rock Hudson. He was looking terrific – maybe a little drawn, a little gaunt. I didn't think anything of it. Apart from that he looked as handsome as ever.

'I'd always worshipped his good looks. As a kid, I'd thought I'd give anything to be able to do my hair like Rock Hudson. He was so glamorous to me. And Liza said to me: You're looking terrific! And I said: So are you, but it's Rock I'm worried about. And he looked at me as if to say: What have you heard?

'Obviously he took it the wrong way. What I meant was: Look at you with your looks; you've got nothing to worry about. It was an attempt at total flattery, but he misunderstood. I couldn't work out his reaction until I heard later that he'd died of AIDS. I felt a chill when I heard. I mean, Christ, when you're dying of AIDS, that's the last thing you want to hear from anybody!'

After our interview, Moore offered to drive us to his restaurant, 72 Market Street, just ten minutes down the road. He rang to make sure there was a table. 'Can you accommodate three friends of mine in about 15 minutes or so?' he asked. 'Name of Tory. T as in Tom, O as in ovula, R as in arsehole, Y as in Why me? Thank you so much. I will bring them there and drop them off.'

He was as good as his word, driving us there in his Bentley, sitting on a pile of cushions to enable him to see over the steering wheel.

Moore died in 2002 after suffering a terminal degenerative brain disorder. Years after our meeting in California, I had met him again in the Colorado ski resort town of Telluride where he was already behaving very strangely. He was completely unable to remember our day-long visit to his former home in Los Angeles, and looked very puzzled when I told him about it. At the time I simply put this down to the fact that he must meet many people in his life and couldn't possibly remember them all. Later, of course, it all made sense.

Tory and I moved on to New Orleans, where we started writing up our various notes beside the hotel swimming pool. This turned out to be a mistake – not because of the strong sunlight, but because it started raining bars of soap. As *Press Gazette* (the journalists' magazine) reported at the time, under the headline 'Arnie's soap opera': 'Apparently Wilson, anxious to maintain his bronzed Rambo appeal, opted to type out his exclusive tales by the poolside of the grand hotel where they were staying in New Orleans. The clickety clack, however, was not entirely appreciated by the bathing beauties and residents enjoying the peace and quiet in the rooms above, so they took it upon themselves to silence him by throwing bars of soap out of the window. The soap storm started turning nasty when great blocks of the stuff were being tossed at a height of around 100 feet and exploding like pistol bullets as they hit the ground. The subtle innuendo was immediately picked up by sensitive Wilson, who was forced to continue tapping out his gems in the shade.'

For some reason this makes no mention of Tory, who was subjected to the same soap storm. Indeed, he says today: 'I was nearly killed by a bar of soap dropped from altitude by a kid and then I walked into plate glass which indented a half-moon scar from the centre of the sunglasses above my nose. I looked like a cult member for weeks.'

Tory and I were about to split up and do separate interviews – me with David Hemmings, whom I already knew, while Peter was due to fly to Miami to spend a day in an under-cover van with the Miami Vice police. And then we got a phone call that sent us both winging our way back to Los Angeles. Bo Derek, who had co-starred with Dudley Moore in the movie *10*, had agreed to see us.

Back at LAX, we drove up the scenic route via Santa Barbara to the Santa Ynez mountains (named after St Agnes), where Bo and John Derek, her film-director husband of ten years, hung out in a spectacular ranch with horses and dogs galore. Derek was recovering from a heart attack. At the time, she was 30, he 60. She'd been 19 when they had married. 'I've spent all my adult life with him,' she said. 'We don't ignore the age difference,' added Bo, looking her usual glamorous self on very little make-up, and later cantering around the ranch on a handsome steed, looking suspiciously bra-less. 'He talks about it all the time until I get sick of it. So we're very realistic that way. But we both ignore the real thing. We talk about when he won't be here or if he should have a heart attack. But I'm an ostrich. I stick my head in the sand. I'm not ignoring it but why bother to think about it? There's too much to do. There are so many people who say: Oh I would die if this person weren't there – but they seem to go on. All your logic tells you that you couldn't go on, you've spent too much time with this person, it's too much part of your life, but people do go on. He wants to think I'll go on without him. But, erm... who knows?'

John Derek had quite a reputation for temper tantrums, and shouting. (Even when he was having his heart attack, she said, he was 'angry – not scared'.) How did Bo cope with his anger? 'I don't like it,' she said. 'Especially when it's directed at you! But overall, that's part of who he is. He was always the tough guy. He's very strong. And very hot-tempered. He does intimidate people. And that's something he doesn't always understand at first. Yet in many ways he has more compassion than I do. But he's totally intolerant of premeditated laziness, or someone who knows they are doing you wrong but they are still doing it. We have people like that in our lives. It's not that I don't forgive them, but they don't need us in their lives, and they're really screwing up our lives.'

At this point John Derek came outside into the California sunshine to join us. 'You'd better come and hear some of this,' I told him, hoping he'd take it the right way. Nervous laughter all round. How did she cope with cinema audience's perception that she (in many of her films at least) appeared to be something of a dumb blonde when it quickly became evident to us that she was far from dumb. We couldn't help feeling that sometimes her arguably poor choice of movie selection would be likely to provoke scorn even before the critics had seen it. 'It's not really that necessary for people to know who I really am,' she said. 'We'll make a picture for the people first and foremost – but the critics can get in the way. They may not be able to kill a movie but they can certainly put a dampener on it.'

I had the temerity to ask Bo whether she had ambitions to become a 'serious' actress. She took no offence. 'I don't actually like acting that much,' she said. 'I like making pictures, yes. But not acting. It's too embarrassing.'

Tory pounced on this statement. 'I used to be an actor,' he said. 'And the reason I got out was that I too found it embarrassing. That's the first time I've heard that said... by someone else.' Bo laughed loudly at this.

'I don't enjoy acting myself that much, I guess,' she continued. 'It's not me. I think it should be left to the people who have studied hard and worked for it.' As if to emphasise this point, Bo has the dubious honour of winning three Golden Raspberry Worst Actress Awards, and was nominated in 2000 as the Worst Actress of the Century.

I asked Bo whether her husband gently reassured her, to try to minimise her embarrassment, and said things like, 'come on honey, that's wonderful, that scene'. Bo paused for a second and then said: 'He talks a little differently than that!' More laughter. 'No, but he's great, because I can get lazy. I fall asleep. And it's very easy to get embarrassed and walk through a scene, and just say your words and do your little tricks that you know how to do.'

'What are your tricks?' we ask.

'Just different things. And if I were just a normal actress, I would be such a pain to the director, I know. I need a kick sometimes.'

'Do you shout back at him?'

'Not when I'm wrong. When I'm right, yes! John says the older I get the more I talk back. I think that's because I was with someone so strong when I was young. When it comes to being on stage, you have to really love it because you give up your life. Say somebody offered me something and the money was tremendous. OK, I'd go back to New York, and rehearse for this many weeks and we do it for so many months, but I have to give up my love, my marriage, my life, my everything. And that's not worth anything.'

Bo told us that she was only in *10* – the 1979 film that made her and Dudley Moore stars – for about ten minutes. 'Well, it may have been 15 or 20 minutes,' she added. She described Moore as a 'complex, very brilliant, very funny man – but also very serious and in a way tragic'.

The conversation switched to films the Dereks were about to start work on. The most intriguing seemed to be one that John Derek had written many years earlier with the actress Rita Tushingham originally in mind. It was due to be titled *Ice Box*, set at the North Pole, and to be filmed in Norway. 'I play a skinny girl in a whorehouse who can't get laid,' Bo said, to disbelief from us. The plot already sounded unlikely. 'It's about these huge, gigantic men who do contract work for 18 months, and when they come in from the cold, they want big, voluptuous women to keep them warm. But beauty is in the eye of the beholder, and beauty has a different meaning there. My kind of figure would appear to be a little scrawny for them, so she gets rejected. It's fun because it's making fun of yourself, which is good. We've always meant to make comedies. This one will be hard to take seriously. My character is that of a runaway – who has never been able to run away from this man – and finally she runs to the one place where he'll never find her. My character is a bit of a misfit. She's led a very sheltered life. When these men first see her they decide they'd rather just wait for one of the other girls who they know they can release all their frustrations with and have a good time with, so they're not too sure about me. She doesn't understand her role and pretty soon the word gets out that she's not very good.'

As far as I know, the film was never made. A mixed blessing perhaps. John Derek died ten years after our meeting, in 1998. And yes, Bo did survive without him.

Next stop was David Hemmings – me on my own this time, while Tory did his thing in Miami. 'Stepping over what could well be the tail of a slumbering alligator,' Tory's column would relate later, 'I extend my hand to the white-haired Englishman who is swatting mosquitoes from the side of his neck in the humid heat of the Deep South sunshine.' (Well, it was Tory's column and it had to look as if he was the one doing the interview, not me.) 'David Hemmings, I presume,' wrote Tory.

With Tory actually 715 miles away, here's how that conversation really went: 'Hello mate,' said Hemmings. 'Nice to see you.'

Then 45, he was making the pilot for a TV series called *Three On A Match*, about a chain gang trapped in swampland, a sweaty 50-mile journey from the romantic jazz capital of New Orleans. Even I was surprised by the white hair. He'd aged noticeably since we'd last met, spoofing for champagne at Pinewood Studios in Teddington. 'Yeh, we'll you've got to face it mate,' he said. 'I am not Joan Collins. Of course I've changed. But the same old willing spirit is there. And, thank God, the flesh isn't yet weak.'

Hemmings was playing an English con man. 'He's a bit of a bullshitter – a chameleon-like figure,' he said. 'Yup, the part, I have to admit, is based very much on aspects of my own personality. But there you go.' Our conversation was interrupted. 'You are wanted in this scene, David,' said one of the crew. It was certainly an action-packed scene, with one actor playing a state trooper cracking a bullwhip a lot of the time.

It was a slightly moving situation – Hemmings in a rough, tough movie but, whenever they broke from the set, wanting to talk mainly about the prospect of being reunited with his eldest daughter, Deborah (from his first marriage), whom he had last seen when she was only four. One day, he said, without warning, he'd

121

received a letter from her. 'It was wonderful. I was absolutely thrilled to bits. I was very young when I got married for the first time. Seventeen. We divorced three years later. I was banished from the family home – probably rightly. I never kept in contact at all. I didn't even send birthday or Christmas cards. I didn't want to be a Sunday-afternoon-at-the-zoo father. Now it's so nice to be able to start to tie up all the loose ends; to clear up some of the slagheaps of your life that you have left around.'

(I have no idea whether they eventually met but I hope they did, and I hope it made them both much happier. I last spoke to him years later, back in the UK, and rather stupidly forgot to ask. He died in 2003.)

For Tory and me it was time to return to reality after our fun-packed fortnight. The reality of an office in Fleet Street, and the rather more mundane but very pleasant routine of trying to fill a daily column without any Hollywood celebrities in the flesh to help us.

Chapter 15
Playing politics

I've been lucky enough to meet a few former British prime ministers, including Harold Macmillan (on the receiving end of the Profumo scandal), and even to spend a little time with former president Jimmy Carter in Crested Butte, Colorado, where he turned up (with wife Rosalynn and skis) for the local ski-film festival for which I was one of the panel of judges. I even grabbed the opportunity to give him one of my ski books.

In terms of PMs, finally getting to meet Harold Wilson was hugely exciting. He'd been something of hero of mine since I emerged from my teenage years, and I remember being upset about a very difficult reception he'd received from booing protesters in Sheffield in January 1968, soon after I'd started work there as a very green broadcaster with the local BBC radio station.

He'd come to the city to help celebrate 40 years of Labour rule. But all police leave was cancelled as 1,500 demonstrators yelled for the PM's blood outside City Hall. As Wilson slipped in through a back door, anti-Vietnam war protestors burned an American flag in a nearby garden. Students battled with police, and cries of 'fascists' rent the night air. There had been numerous arrests.

I was so upset that I naively (even for a very young journalist) wrote a supportive letter to Number 10. I received a friendly letter in reply, not from Wilson himself, of course, but from Gerald Kaufman, then his parliamentary press liaison officer, who thanked me for writing, and effectively told me not to worry – the PM had taken it in his stride.

'The Prime Minister was not in fact at all disturbed by the demonstrations in Sheffield,' he wrote. 'This kind of thing does happen from time to time, especially with university students gathered from miles around. Nevertheless the Prime Minister took away from Sheffield the memory of the very kind and favourable reception he received inside the City Hall. He realises that there may be misgivings about some of the government's policies, and respects those who hold those misgivings sincerely.' (Well, he would say that wouldn't he? – I can see that, now that I have acquired a little world-weary wisdom. This was spin before the political implications of the word had been invented. *Plus ça change…*)

Mr Wilson, in the more peaceful surrounds of BBC Radio Sheffield, was asked – by Michael Green, the future controller of Radio 4, but then a humble but rather good presenter – to request a record. He chose *Thank U very Much* by The Scaffold, which includes the lines:

> *Thank you very much for the Sunday joint*
> *and our cultural heritage, national beverage,*
> *being fat, Union jack,*
> *nursery rhyme, Sunday Times,*
> *napalm bomb, everyone!*
> *Thank you very much.*

Years later, when I grabbed the chance to interview Wilson, who was by this time 69, it became clear, that something was wrong. Alzheimer's had begun its unforgiving grip, but of course no one knew this at the time. His celebrated mind was beginning to let him down. 'It's a terrible nuisance because I never know from one day to the next whether or not I can rely on it,' he said. 'It's most unfortunate because I think it's fair to say that during my time as Prime Minister my memory was widely regarded as being one of the sharpest in the House.'

Wilson freely admitted there were some days when he got his dates muddled. Even as we talked, he had problems remembering during which period of his life it was that he had gone to Moscow. Was it on a secret fact-finding mission for Churchill? He wasn't sure. 'I do know that Churchill had asked me to try to find out whether the Russian factories were producing domestic goods or war materials,' he said. 'I took a photograph of a little girl with a fairy cycle and I was promptly arrested. It turned out the Lubyanka was situated just behind the girl and the authorities thought I was taking pictures of that.'

At that stage, Wilson became confused about the timing of various Moscow visits. He remembered Moscow, but it was as if all his Russian memories had merged in to one. Was it during the war, he wondered out loud, was it when he was Prime Minister, President of the Board of Trade under Attlee, or just an opposition MP? He couldn't really say. 'Yet there are some things I can always seem to remember. I could quote you the national coal production figures for November 1945 quite easily,' he said, and promptly did so. Wilson had his critics, and there were all those conspiracy theories about him too, but at the end of the day I felt saddened, having finally got to meet him, that it was the beginning of the end for him.

I enjoyed making the occasional phone call to Harold Macmillan (later Lord Stockton) whose number in Chelwood Gate, West Sussex, was in the phone book. Occasionally he would pretend to be someone else when he answered the phone (like the butler, for example), but when I called him to discuss Mandy ('I was certainly game – but I wasn't on it') Rice-Davies, with Christine Keeler, in the infamous Profumo Affair, he made no attempt to do this. The conversation, however, did not last long. I had just interviewed Miss Rice-Davies for Peter Tory's *Star* diary, and felt like having a bit of fun. It seemed Mandy was to be formally introduced to Princess Anne at the Royal Premiere of *Absolute Beginners* in Leicester Square.

'Lord Stockton?' I asked when that familiar 'you've never had it so good' voice answered.

'Yes?'

'Ah, Lord Stockton, I've just been interviewing Mandy Rice-Davies. It seems she is to meet Princess Anne. I wondered...'

'Who?' the grand old man interrupted.

'Mandy Rice-Davies, sir.'

'Who's she?

'Well, I rather believe she was part of the Profumo scandal which almost brought your government down...'

'Never heard of her,' said Macmillan. 'Goodbye.' And slammed the phone down.

I got back to Rice-Davies and asked whether she was put out by Macmillan's loss of memory. 'Certainly not,' she said. 'Good for him. He's a wonderful old man.'

There was even a limerick in *Time* magazine, not one of mine this time, but by an unknown author:

> What have you done, cried Christine
> You've wrecked the whole party machine
> To lie in the nude
> Is not at all rude
> But to lie in the House is obscene

Although my instincts – and upbringing – are socialist, my political allegiances have never been terribly specific, and I have always tended to vote for the man rather than the party. And that meant, in my formative years, voting for Bill Deedes who I admired and respected enormously.

I knew him as my local MP, travelling companion on many commutes to London, dining companion, and most of all, mentor. As a young reporter on the *Kent Messenger* in Ashford – Bill's constituency for very nearly a quarter of a century – I enjoyed a fairly typical journalist-MP relationship with him. Like my colleagues, I found him approachable, fair, witty, amusing and modest.

It was only when I befriended his son Julius – also employed by the *Kent Messenger* – that I got closer to Bill. Julius suffered from a rare medical disorder that meant that he had to have his blood 'topped up' by regular transfusions at the children's hospital at Great Ormond Street. He was always very brave about this. He would disappear, on his own, to London, have the transfusion, and on the way home take in the odd football or cricket match. One story that sticks in my mind is that one day when Julius got back to the family home in Aldington, after one such medical ordeal, his mother Hilary asked: 'Was it dreadful, darling?' to which Julius replied: 'Yes mother. They lost 2-0.' He was speaking of his favourite team, Arsenal. (They used to lose occasionally in those days.)

Julius died in 1970, aged only 23. Although it was a terrible blow to the Deedes family (Bill and Hilary had three daughters and another son, Jeremy, who also rose to great heights at the *Telegraph*), it had been expected. Indeed, Julius had survived longer than expected. By now I was working at ITN and, working mainly on *News at Ten*, often found myself sharing a late-morning railway carriage with Bill as he trekked up to London to his desk at the *Daily Telegraph* Peterborough Column. (I would shamelessly barge in to his first class compartment where, as a Home Office minister and book reviewer, he would be devouring vast tomes on law and order, drugs, Northern Ireland and other issues of the day, and engage him in conversation. No doubt he was irritated by my serial invasions, but he never showed it). With a patient sigh he would put down any books he was studying and we'd chat away happily till we reached Charing Cross. If I happened to be Fleet Street bound rather than going to ITN, we'd often walk down the Strand together, continuing our conversation.

When Julius died, I asked if might write his obituary for both the *Kent Messenger* and Southern Television, two of my previous employers. This is when I first encountered the more intimate warmth of Deedes' friendship. For the best part of a week I was invited to share the daily comings and goings in the Deedes household, and was made to feel almost one of the family – an experience I have never forgotten.

Over the years, sometimes with long gaps, Bill and I kept in touch by letter and occasionally lunch or dinner. Because, like Bill, I had always enjoyed writing 'diary' stories, I treasure one letter which informed me: 'You accuse me sometimes of being bad about personal items of news. Well, here is a surprising morsel. Yesterday, in a field of 40 at Littlestone Golf Course, I won the Denge Medal, played for annually – I believe since 1889 – for the best medal round. Score was gross 76, less 10 handicap, 66. I think it is 40 years since I played a competitive medal round and won – on the old Hythe golf course. If you want a quote: After two days in Northern Ireland I took a day off to watch the pros at Wentworth. After watching Arnie Palmer putt I changed my own system – and surprisingly, it worked!'

One of my proudest moments was interviewing him for the *Evening Standard* to mark the completion of his 70 years in journalism. I started my piece by saying that after the death of former Prime Minister Sir Alec Douglas-Home (who once told me he polished his black shoes with brown shoe polish) people said he was the last of the gentleman politicians. 'Shum mishtake, surely,' I wrote, echoing Bill's trademark lisp. They had forgotten Bill Deedes, reporter, soldier, minister, editor and legend, more or less in that order. *Eminence grise* to Princess Diana, inspiration for *Private Eye*'s Dear Bill feature, and, much earlier, following his coverage of the war in Abyssinia, for some of the material in Evelyn Waugh's *Scoop*.

Things got much more serious when World War Two came along. Deedes fought instead of reporting the war this time. And won a Military Cross. 'I did eight years in journalism before the war,' he told me, 'and then I did five years of the war. On the whole I was more confident as a soldier than a journalist. I hadn't done too badly as an officer, so when they said "would you possibly like to command something and attack Japan?" this struck me as quite a good idea. It didn't materialise because they dropped the bomb on Hiroshima. A bit of luck for me but not, of course, for Hiroshima.'

Deedes received a lifetime achievement award from Tony Blair. 'It said something about me being a Fleet Street legend,' he told me, relaxing on a sofa at the *Daily Telegraph*, his employer for virtually the whole of his distinguished career, and gazing wistfully out across Canary Wharf. 'I would describe it as a survivor's medal. To tell you the truth, I haven't dared look at it. It should be taken calmly, as it were, bearing in mind – whether you're a legend or not – you're no better than the last piece you've written. I do a Monday column, so presumably that was the last piece I wrote.'

And was last Monday's column any good, I asked him? 'It's always good,' he answered. He went on to describe his role as

Minister Without Portfolio in the Macmillan government ('Minister of Information in disguise') between 1962 and 1964 as being 'mainly bomb disposal'. The concept of spin had scarcely been considered. 'The more I look at what Alastair Campbell has been doing, the more incompetent I realise we were in those days. I'm probably a stronger supporter of Alastair Campbell than most people in journalism because I've seen enough of the interplay between Labour governments and the press.

'And although I don't necessarily approve of it, I think Blair was dead right when he came into office to say: This time we are not going to allow the newspapers to get our knickers in a twist – we're going to twist their knickers. I mean, I can remember the Labour Party in the time of Michael Foot and the time of Kinnock – I can even remember the Labour Party at the time of Ramsay MacDonald. The fact is they are justified in feeling that newspapers are not altogether on their side. Of course there are tabloid newspapers that support Labour, but secretly – and it's a secret that you will now reveal – I think Blair had a good reason for trying to make certain that Labour took the initiative with the press rather than having the initiative taken against them. So I'm a hidden supporter of Alastair Campbell. You can make what you like of that.'

For a quarter of a century – no time at all, really, on the Deedes scale of things – the charming doyen-to-be of Fleet Street combined distinguished and concurrent careers as politician and journalist, until giving up the night job in 1974 to concentrate, finally, on the road to legendhood. This entailed editing the *Daily Telegraph* as a 'stop-gap' editor. The gap turned out to be 12 years. He stepped down in 1986 – a still very sprightly 73 – and was ennobled with a life peerage. Some, including his wife Hilary, thought he would then finally start taking life a little more easily. Not a bit of it.

'When my wife realised I wasn't going to leave the *Telegraph*, she went to live near our daughter Lucy in Scotland, waiting for me to retire,' he said. 'It's very difficult for me to commute from Berwick on Tweed to the office, and so that's a real handicap. I see her as often as the railway allows. You have to be enormously loyal to your wife to take that line very often, but we do see each other quite a bit. The journey is every bit as difficult as getting to East Timor.'

Forced to make a choice, he said he would always chose journalism above politics. 'You're front row, you're in the stalls, you travel, you see things.'

Of his award, he said: 'It was a very nice gesture. But I'm not good at being a legend at all. If you want to go on being a reporter, you can't be a legend at the same time. And I want to go on being a reporter.

'After a minor stroke during the Indian earthquake, some people thought that's it... that's it. That's the end, yes. I was dead lucky. I tend to be touching wood quite a lot these days. You have to go abroad from time to time, so I do a bit of that, and I tend to be dead lucky with travel. I have been in aeroplanes which have run out of petrol, and had all kinds of adventures. I'm a survivor. I have discovered that I have made, in the last four years, 30 foreign trips. All, I may say, at the expense of the *Daily Telegraph*.'

Bill Deedes' writing seemed to become better as he got older. He was still writing brilliantly in his 90s, by which time he had acquired the wisdom and experience of more than 70 years in journalism. He was, of course, irreplaceable.

'I shall keep travelling,' he said. 'Partly to get away from Canary Wharf, and partly to escape the wet and cold winters here. I don't mind my life being shortened by adventure, but to have it shortened by the weather would be ridiculous. I've never imagined myself dying in my own bed. If I die at all, I'll die in my boots. But it'll be a while yet...'

After Bill's death in 2007, the family home at Aldington was put on the market. This provided the opportunity to resurrect a delightful story about him exploring the extensive grounds of this fine Victorian building just after he'd purchased it in 1946. He returned to Hilary after his initial walk-about and, scythe in hand, reported triumphantly: 'Darling, I've jusht dishcovered a tennish court!'

I met both Margaret and Denis Thatcher briefly – and Mark too. (By sheer chance I'd even been on duty at the *Daily Mirror* news room on the night in late March, 1982 when Argentine scrap-metal dealers had made their second unauthorised landing on South Georgia, a fortnight before the start of the Falklands War. The Argentinean flag had been raised and shots fired, and somehow we in the newsroom had heard about it before the British government. I rang the people at Number 10 to check the story and they claimed it was the first they'd heard of it. Fancy that – did I really know about the incident leading directly to war in the Falklands before the PM?)

It was Carol – who doesn't have much time for her twin brother – I really got to know. We shared a mildly affectionate knockabout friendship because for many years she was a ski writer like me. And was thus subjected, I'm afraid, to a diarist's constant scrutiny whenever we skied together. To her I must have seemed like a vulture waiting for pickings – rich or otherwise – or an irritating bluebottle buzzing about. But at least I always made a point of asking her whether she would mind if I wrote about her. 'If you must,' was usually her slightly vexed but not unkind reply.

So when poor Carol became the victim of a practical joke in Austria, I couldn't' resist offering it to Peter Tory, whose column on the *Star* I worked for each summer (between skiing trips). What happened was this: while we were relaxing with a few glasses of schnapps in a mountain restaurant after skiing, an Austrian asked Carol if she would blow into the sails of a little wooden model windmill to see if she could get the sails to go round. It was a set-up, of course. She puffed into the contraption as requested and was immediately half blinded by soot. Game girl that she was, Carol said: 'I didn't really mind, although the soot got into my contact lenses and all over my dress.'

Some time later in the Italian resort of Courmayeur, when our party was preparing for an off-piste ski excursion, she asked whether I'd mind carrying her rucksack, which had our packed lunches (and her notebook) in it. Then announced to the team: 'Everybody – if Arnie falls down a crevasse, please rescue notes.'

Another anecdote that ended up in Tory's column was less well received. While skiing together in another Austrian resort, St

Anton, Carol and I shared a glancing blow when I was drifting to the right and she to the left. She came off slightly worse than me, losing her skis and tumbling into the snow. As she scrambled back to her feet, shaking snow off her ski suit, she said loudly: 'Gosh Arnie – it's a good job I'm not a fragile blonde!' Peter Tory happily used the story, but Carol had a slight problem pronouncing her Rs, and Tory's mischievous headline was Cwash Bang Cawol. I felt that as she'd been so cheerfully philosophical about being knocked flying off her skis, this was literally adding insult to injury.

Maybe it was my carelessness too that sent the former Foreign Secretary Lord Carrington home nursing a bump on his forehead during a spontaneous interview outside a Kentucky Fried Chicken restaurant where he was throwing a farewell party for his chums before leaving the UK to take up his post as secretary general of Nato in Brussels. The amiable Lord reeled backwards clutching his forehead and said: 'Oh my God,' after he and I looked up at the same moment and bumped heads. I apologised profusely, naturally, and we shook hands to show there were no hard feelings. Just a hard blow to his Lordship's forehead. Fortunately this appeared to have no long-term effect on his health or indeed on the running of Nato.

I bumped into Lord Carrington again, so to speak, at a private viewing of portraits of prominent figures of the time, including Admiral Sir John Forster 'Sandy' Woodward of Falklands fame and Sir Peter Hall, the celebrated theatre and film director. Carrington, who said he had forgiven me for the clash of heads, informed me that he had developed a passion for gardening. 'He spends every weekend pulling out weeds,' confirmed his wife Iona. 'That's all I'm allowed to do,' said Carrington. 'I'm not allowed to do any of the really good stuff – I'm just the handyman. I certainly don't do any digging – not if I can help it. We do have a gardener – and machinery. I'm not allowed near the machinery either. And my wife always uses the Latin name for plants so I never really know what she's talking about. And she never seems to come down to my level.' It was left to Lady Carrington to explain: 'Latin names seem to come to me and they stick rather better than one's friends' names.'

Sometimes being (unavoidably or carelessly) late on a story can be quite serendipitous. I remember the Fleet Street 'pack' descending on a London address when the Conservative Party chairman Cecil Parkinson was embroiled with the saga of being revealed as the father of his former secretary Sara Keays' yet-to-be-born daughter Flora. I arrived to find the Press had all cleared off without realising that Parkinson was actually having dinner with friends in a different part of the building. I hung around, got an interview and – the pièce de résistance – he even gave me a pair of brand new trainers later which I asked him to autograph. I was jogging every day then, and Parkinson had been sent a huge box containing several pairs. He would never have managed to wear them all out no matter how often he himself jogged or fled from Her Majesty's Press.

Chapter 16
Explorers

To the natives in the fearsome forests and vast swamps of Panama and Colombia, he will always be 'El Quebracha' – 'the Axe-breaker'. To many of his friends, he's known simply as 'Blashers'…

Thus, in 1977, I started my script for a five-minute TV film about one of the last of Britain's great explorers.

Over the years, I have bumped into quite a few explorers, but only two on a regular basis, and of those two, one has been such a regular part of my diary-writing world that he has become a close friend. His name is John Blashford-Snell – feared by lions, tigers, crocs and sharks the world over. John, president of the Scientific Exploration Society ('a group of other nutty explorers', as he puts it) is perhaps the last of a breed. Pith helmet. Hacking through the jungle with a machete. Wrestling with boa constrictors. That kind of thing. The stuff of *Boys' Own* annuals. Straight out of Hollywood (or Pinewood) casting. Except that he's real.

My script (back in the 70s before he became a full colonel and an OBE) – continued thus:

> 'Lieutenant Colonel Blashford-Snell, MBE – 14 stone of hard muscle – is a veteran of many expeditions to some of the most hostile jungles and deserts in the world. Still ringing wet from a cliff exercise, he takes stock of his new surroundings…'

The Colonel should have been knighted (and actually has been, in error, on the Internet, but hates my even mentioning this as he feels it sounds like self-promotion) but so far has escaped the royal dubbing. I think that of all my diary contacts, John has been the most prolific. What I mean by that is that of all the hundreds of celebrities I have written about, I have written more stories about him than any of the others. I think John would agree that the scores of mentions I have served up about him have not done his career as an explorer any harm. It hasn't done my bank balance any harm either. But this isn't the point. Out of that serendipitous early relationship has sprung, as I say, real friendship

I first encountered this good natured and very funny army officer way back in the mid 1970s, when he was appointed CO of the Junior Leaders Regiment of the Royal Engineers at Dover – the Kent port where I worked for Southern Television at its local studio. We conducted an interview in an inflatable craft somewhere off Dover Harbour. It was a little choppy out there.

'This is all a far cry from the mosquitoes and swamps of the Darien Gap,' I reported. 'Or the rapids of the Blue Nile. This exercise would normally be done at night. It's happening in daylight for our benefit. German soldiers are defending the White Cliffs against a surprise attack by British soldiers. That's not quite how it happened in the war, but in this exercise the invading party – led by frogmen – have to win, so it has to be the wrong way round. The young soldiers are already tasting the kind of excitement that follows Blashers around wherever he goes.'

It all made for an action-packed report. We seemed to hit it off OK (Blashers hits it off with most people) but the next day I was ready for my next assignment. At that stage the good Colonel was yesterday's news and I thought 'that was fun – wonder if we'll meet again?' We did. Sooner than I could have guessed. He phoned me. 'John Blashford-Snell here. Thought you'd be amused to hear that we have just blown up a pond near Canterbury.'

A local farmer – Alf Leggatt, MBE – an ex naval reserve lieutenant, former trawler skipper and hero of a million catches – had complained that his goldfish were all being eaten up by a monster perch. He'd already tried to kill it with rod, net and even rifle. So Blashford-Snell had 'taken some lads from the regiment, with a scout car, and blown it up,' he said. 'Seem to have got rid of the perch!'

'Why on earth didn't you tell me you were going to do this?' (This was relatively early in his career and for some reason he didn't understand what a cracking photo opportunity it would have been. But he was quick to remedy the situation.)

'I could always do it again!'

I didn't need to be told twice. The film crew and I headed for Ickham – a small East Kent village where nothing much had happened for years – and this might well have remained the case if it had not been for Blashers. And 'Mini-Jaws'. The perch had helped itself to about 2,000 of Alf's goldfish before he'd called in the Army to deal with the creature.

According to one local historian: 'The golden plenty among which it lived disinclined the perch to vary its diet with barbed bait. So the Army was called in and tried to blow up the voracious perch. The attempt failed. Mini-Jaws champed on.

'A second attempt was made by none other than the resourceful explorer and big-game hunter Lt-Col Blashford-Snell,' the official records continue. 'He set about the problem with characteristic directness, eventually increasing the amount of explosive and confidently asserting that …that must have done the trick.'

That night my report about Blashers' heroic triumph was featured on *News at Ten*. There was even a Giles cartoon in the next day's *Daily Express*.

For the next 30 odd years he sent me postcards from assorted expeditions around the world, knowing full well that any anecdotes he included were liable to end up in a diary page somewhere. He can still be found in rain-soaked jungles, snake-infested swamps and scorching deserts, paddling, hacking and trekking his way to the ever-diminishing remote areas of the world. And our relationship survives to this day. In 1990 I even joined one of his expeditions and spent a month sleeping under the stars in sleeping bags (no tents) in the Kalahari Desert and other regions of Botswana.

John is interested in concrete jungles as well as tropical ones, and a few years back he invited me, on behalf of the *Financial Times*, to join him in the heartland of Brixton, a part of London that has not always enjoyed the best of reputations.

A sea of dark faces watches the great white explorer as he enters their village,' I wrote. 'The sun beats down, but he wears no pith helmet to protect his head. The vegetation is dense but under control. There is no need for Colonel John Blashford-Snell, OBE, veteran of more than 70 expeditions to virtually every jungle in the world, to hack his way to this particular destination.

A man whose head is swathed in dreadlocks approaches, wearing a shirt of red, gold and green – the colours of the Ethiopian flag. He wears a hat bearing the Imperial Lion of the former emperor and God, Haile Selassie. The Colonel greets him in Amharic, the language of Ethiopia. '*Tenastalin*,' he says. ('Good Morning').

This one word, I learn later, is the equivalent of nine in English: 'May God answer my prayers and give you health!' The Rastafarian has no idea what he is talking about. He speaks only English.

For the 'village' the Colonel has arrived at is in London, not Africa. We are in Brixton's notorious Moorlands Estate, dubbed – by some of its long-suffering residents – the 'wild west' of this once deeply troubled neighbourhood. 'It really is just like entering an African village,' says Blashers. 'All eyes are on you, and you feel a little threatened, and then you realise it's simply curiosity. They don't mean you any harm.'

More than a decade earlier, just a few hundred yards away, I had experienced a night whose imagery I will never forget, when a colleague with whom I was covering the Brixton riots was attacked by a mob of looters and slashed twice across the face in front of me. Through a terrifying obstacle course of blazing cars, I had dragged him – half blinded by his own blood – to safety.

Now, the redoubtable Colonel had persuaded me to return – on a goodwill mission. As well as his much more widely publicised career as a pith-helmeted hero, Blashers has had a long association with underprivileged teenagers. He combined his two passions under a single banner by starting Operation Drake and its successor, Operation Raleigh. The Prince of Wales, who thought young people could benefit from 'some of the challenges of war in a peacetime situation', became its patron. Although he had now retired from the army and Operation Raleigh, Blashford-Snell was still battling the soul-deadening effects of inner city life.

'You walk a tightrope between the gangs, the police and, in this case, Lambeth Council,' he said. 'It requires diplomacy of the highest order. Decent, articulate young families trying to make the best of things are living here side by side with the Yardie culture. Alcohol, drugs and video pornography are gnawing away at the soul of the country like a cancer. A nation's most precious asset is its youth. And we are in danger of losing an entire generation. Our aim is to get kids off the streets – and stop them mugging old ladies or breaking in to cars. We are hoping to promote happier, healthier, better-informed and self-motivated young people.

'It's the ultimate challenge,' said JBS cheerfully. 'I enjoy challenges, but I wouldn't pretend it hasn't been an uphill battle.'

My other explorer chum is Sir Ranulph Twisleton-Wykeham Fiennes – known to most people simply as Ran. He and Blashers are friends, but they are very different characters. Fiennes likes it cold. Blashers prefers warmer climes. Fiennes likes to subject himself to hardship. Blashers would rather not. In fact the Colonel once told me that if he had to try to climb Everest (as Ran finally did in May 2009), he'd put scaffolding up. 'Why not make it easy for yourself?' he asked.

Blashford-Snell's attitude to mountains (compared with that of Fiennes) was rather neatly summed up by a chance remark he made when he was running Raleigh International (formerly Operation Raleigh), an organisation he'd started to galvanise young people into travelling abroad on gap-year expeditions and helping people in third-world countries by building bridges, improving water supplies and helping with myriad projects all over the world to improve standards of health and education.

'What we're doing,' Blashers had told me, 'is blending adventure with worthwhile tasks. We don't just do a task like climbing a mountain because it's there. But we would climb a mountain if it were necessary to get some people who lived up a mountain down to a clinic and back up again afterwards.'

By coincidence Blashers had given Fiennes a helping hand early in his career. 'I helped get Ran started,' he says, 'by being his rear-party link for his first expedition.'

I'd first 'met' Ran during a night shift on the *Daily Mirror* in 1984. Mikhail Gorbachev had been to London on an official visit just before starting his historic term as leader of the Soviet Union. At the time, Fiennes had just started working as the personal representative in Europe of Dr Armand Hammer, chairman of Occidental Oil. Hammer wanted to present Gorbachev with a portfolio of newspaper coverage of his visit. Fiennes rang the *Mirror* and by chance got me. I proceeded to cut all the references to Gorbachev's visit from the *Daily Mirror* files. Very naughty. But Ran was delighted and we also became friends.

Fiennes is one of the most courageous men I know – an almost absurdly pragmatic hero. In 2000, attempting to walk solo and unsupported to the North Pole, he sustained severe frostbite to the tips of all the fingers on his left hand, forcing him to abandon the attempt. On returning home, his surgeon insisted that he should retain the fingertips for several months to allow re-growth of the remaining healthy tissue before amputation. Impatient to remove the source of considerable pain, Fiennes tried to remove them himself in his garden shed with a fretsaw. When that didn't work he used a Black & Decker to cut them off just below where the permanent damage had been done.

Here's Fiennes on his fingers and toes and other appendages after returning from one of his epic expeditions in 1990:

'They heal so quickly, it's unbelievable. The body just heals so quickly. They really looked a mess and felt a mess only two weeks ago.'

– But you've lost one toe, haven't you?

'Yes but even they heal terribly quickly. They probably look like your toes now. I mean, look at that [holding up a recently frostbitten finger]. That's going to slough away and in a few days it won't be there. And that was really bad about two weeks ago. And that toe is less by about a third than it was. That bit there fell off one day into the sock, and I had a skin graft right down from there to there. But that's going to be all right. You have to take lots of penicillin – we learnt that in the early days – so the poison doesn't spread, gangrene doesn't spread.'

– You've got a sore spot on your chin as well, I said.

'Yes, that's from tearing off my face mask too quickly. The skin came right off there. But when it's cold you can't feel it. And I tore it off and didn't know till I saw all the blood, the skin and the hairs stuck to the ice on the inside of the face mask. We've got big scabs on the inside of our eyes – cold cutting into the skin – and on the nose, and everywhere else. Sight is quite important to one, but the specialist has already said I shouldn't go blind in the right eye. As for the left eye – they haven't come up with a conclusive report yet...'

Like all brave men, Fiennes has a couple of Achilles heels. Like the skier Franz Klammer, he's uneasy about being in the dark. 'If I happen to be somewhere rather remote I will be happier if I have some sort of deterrent close by,' he says. 'Not to use against animals, or ghoulies or ghosties, but other human beings.' He's also a serious back-seat driver. But he believes in God, which helps. 'Very sincerely, totally and utterly' he says.

'I don't believe in the concept of someone treading along beside you, or anything spiritualistic like that. I'm sort of standard Church of England, but I certainly believe that if things go well, it's because you've been treated kindly by The Creator. And if you say to yourself, at the simplest level, for thine is the kingdom, the power – ie, the ice, the wind, everything, was created by Him – and the glory, ie, if you should succeed in the expedition, there's no glory in it for you, because everything is God. You're just an ant – you're one of 800 million people or more, and you'll be dead anyway shortly, and before you there were hundreds and hundreds and hundreds of other humans who are all dead and after you for thousands of years there will be many more humans who'll be dead, so what you're doing means nothing in the general aspect of things. So why get excited if a ski breaks?'

'Follow that...!' I said. 'Do you pray?'

'Yes, but I must admit I pray more when I'm on the ice than when I'm back here. Here the telephone's always going. Out there, it's not.'

Like many people, I am surprised Fiennes is still alive. To this day I can't believe that in 2003 he ran seven marathons on seven consecutive days in seven continents. He did this after surviving a heart attack at Bristol airport, followed by heart bypass surgery. The man must be mad. He knows I think this.

His incredible back-to-back marathons were accomplished with the nutrition specialist Dr Mike Stroud. This was curious because during one of their polar treks together he and Stroud had allegedly fallen out. I was dying to ask him about this. Fiennes became angry when Stroud – who normally led – fell back one day when he was ill. Ran accused him of risking the expedition's success. The story goes that Fiennes later apologised and said Stroud was a 'brick' for carrying on. In his diary, Stroud later described Fiennes in less affectionate terms.

'There are rumours that you and Mike didn't always get on together' I said, pitching it gently.

'Yes there were' said Fiennes.

Had they made it up (in either sense)?

'Both of us sold thousands of books based on the newspapers saying that we hadn't been getting on,' agreed Fiennes. 'Which you might say is dishonest. But if the newspapers wish to do that they will do it. The big headlines – that our smiles when we got back were all a sham – were totally untrue. Of course people have words with each other on a trip like that. When you've got gangrene you get irritable.'

Was there even an element of truth in the story?

'Well, there is an element of truth if you say that people who are in business together sometimes have a dispute.'

I wondered how he and I would get on during a similar trip. Would we fight?

'We would be far worse, infinitely worse. Anybody other than Mike Stroud and me on that expedition would have fallen out in a very, very big way. But of course we made the most out of those words in the diary. There is, after all, so little to write about. You are writing about whiteness, you are writing about 160,000 words about crossing snow with no view, no history, no people, no animals, no birds. I mean even if you've got a thesaurus for the word white…

'So I borrowed Mike's diary and where I found him saying, Ran said to me this morning you're a real brick carrying on, he had added Ran Fiennes is a real prick. That formed the basis of what became a complete myth between us and of course we remained the best of friends because we never weren't the best of friends.'

Having got to know these two wonderful characters so well helped when I offered to interview ten explorers for the *Observer* Experts' Expert feature – the same series that had prompted Sir David Lean to contact me when I was writing about film directors.

The man who got the vote? Wilfred Thesiger. Sir Laurens van der Post described him to me thus:

> Armed with a shotgun and a couple of guides, he followed the course of the Awash river from the great high mountain plateau of Abyssinia into the Danakil basin, one of the hottest and most inhospitable places. People had tried to get across before, but were murdered. Wilfred got though... and made his way back to civilisation, having cleared up one of the last land mysteries of Africa. I think that comes the nearest to exploration in the old sense of the world.

I was also lucky enough to get an interview with Lord Hunt – who'd led the first successful Everest expedition, timed perfectly to welcome Princess Elizabeth to the British throne in 1953 – through his actress daughter Sally Nesbitt, who was at the time doing PR for the Portes du Soleil ski area. (Sir Ranulph Fiennes says of the Everest triumph: 'I was a nine-year-old schoolboy with wide eyes when he led this incredible expedition which put Hillary and Tenzing on Everest.')

At the time I interviewed Hunt, there had been controversy over whether perhaps K2 might, in fact, be the highest mountain in the world after all. As it turned out, it wasn't. 'I don't think there's any question about it,' he said. 'I think there's a clear difference of about 800 feet.'

Would it have been devastating if it turned out that K2 was in fact higher?

'Well it was so long after the event. We'd climbed Everest – supposedly the highest mountain at the time. If it transpired 35 years later that the other mountain was higher... well, just too bad!'

– You wouldn't think your whole life had been wasted?

'Not at all.'

Shortly before I'd interviewed Lord Hunt, he and his wife had visited the Galapagos – where, at the age of 78, he'd had an encounter with a sea lion.

'I was charged by an enormous great bull,' he said. 'I may have got a bit close to one of his females. Luckily they can't propel themselves very far without collapsing. They get up on their flippers and they come at quite a big speed. It was making a hell of a noise too – a great roaring noise. In my mind as I ran was the possibility that I might fall over on my face. Normally the only time I run is to catch buses.'

I also met the youngest member of that triumphant 1953 British Everest Expedition, George Band. He was by now 78 – but still in great shape. Sprightly, even.

I met him in Zermatt, Switzerland, where the Alpine Club was celebrating its 150th anniversary; Band joined a group of them who celebrated by trudging up the relatively easy local Breithorn (at 13,661ft, less than half the altitude of Everest).

Band, whose book *Summit* chronicles the history of the Alpine Club, said he 'continues to enjoy modest climbing and escorting treks in the greater ranges' and had recently visited India, Nepal, Sikkim, China, Tibet and Bhutan.

Chapter 17
The final frontier

I am passionately interested in all things related to space travel, an inveterate reader of Dan Dare in the *Eagle* comics of the 1950s and 60s, who managed to persuade the *Financial Times* to run my 50th anniversary feature on 'The Pilot of the Future' in 2000. And, as previously mentioned, an obsessive listener to the great 1950s radio series *Journey Into Space*.

So I was glued to the TV when Apollo 11 touched down on the Sea of Tranquillity on July 20, 1969 (who now recalls that some of the early black and white pictures were transmitted upside down?). I was on the team during ITN's coverage of Apollo 13, when I was given the task of monitoring live Houston sound because there was so little interest in this mission that they gave it to the office junior. Until, of course, it became a major news story, when my elders and betters took over...

Glued to the TV again in 1980 for Professor Carl Sagan's brilliant and memorable programme *Cosmos* (which he, for some reason, pronounced Kas Moss) which also introduced me to the wonderfully evocative music of Evangelos Odysseas Papathanassiou – aka Vangelis.

Bearing all this in mind, you'll understand that the morning of July 11 1999 was the beginning of one of the most exciting days of my life. It wasn't quite dawn, and the thinnest of crescent moons was still visible. The man I was going to have breakfast with had actually been there. Indeed he was only the second man to set foot on the moon. Somehow I had managed to get an interview with Buzz Aldrin. It had taken months to set up, but now it was about to happen. It was for the *Financial Times* newspaper's 'Lunch With The FT' slot, but for the purposes of this chat, it was actually breakfast with the FT.

A champagne breakfast was definitely out. Aldrin is a recovering alcoholic, and had not had a drink for 20 years. 'After going to the Moon, it was a question of readjusting to a non-focused existence,' he said. 'And that was coupled, I think, with a genetic pre-disposition that exhibited its traits in my parents which moved me towards alcoholism which finally I was then able to identify. And then, in a very difficult struggle to re-adjust, I had to overcome that.'

As he strolled into the courtyard restaurant at the belle époque Halcyon Hotel in West London I saw not a veteran astronaut but a sprightly marketeer, better looking and taller than I had imagined, with eyes that twinkled like Venus and a rather fetching, if slightly flashy, hand-painted blue silk tie bedecked with stars and moons.

A gold ring depicting a star and moon adorned his finger, and an official gold pin – recognising his historic ride to Tranquillity Base with Neil Armstrong and his record breaking space walk (EVA) during the Mercury programme – was pinned to the lapel of his blazer. Buzz, whose mother was born Marion Moon, is almost a one-man lunar boutique. I wondered aloud if he ever looked up at the moon and said 'Wow – I was there!'

'Sure – it does cross my mind,' he said. People have long memories when it comes to the first men on the moon. 'I have a sense that people come up to me and say: You're still flying aren't you? – as if they're disappointed that I'm not still flying my own airplane,' he said. 'Well you either afford exotic toys because you've earned the wealth, the wherewithal to have a yacht in the Mediterranean or an airplane you can fly, and that's a symbol of your achievement… But I haven't achieved that financially, so I don't have the time to devote to playing airplanes or taking care of a yacht even if I had the money to support that. I'll fly your airplane if you have one, but not one of my own. It's expensive, it's very time consuming and so I don't have either of those two ingredients.

'I don't really miss it, and I don't feel compelled to do it just for the reaction that it may have on other people. I will dive, I will ski, I will go to the Titanic, I will do unusual travel events. But I don't have the need to be a macho guy who fits in with other macho guys. I don't need to do that any more.'

Sometimes Aldrin the skier would find himself up against interesting opposition. It was always a 'great challenge', at celebrity ski events, to be paired against William Shatner. 'The idea of a real-life astronaut skiing against a Hollywood version like William Shatner was intriguing,' he said.

'So who won?' I asked.

'Well, this guy, you know, he's over the hill, he doesn't look in as good shape as I am. But he's Canadian and he's been skiing all his life,' Buzz chuckled. 'And he usually won by a little bit. So I guess my perfect skiing day would have to include beating Bill Shatner.'

Although he co-wrote two science fiction novels, Aldrin likes to separate fact from fiction in space travel. When I asked him his views of the conspiracy theory that the Russian cosmonaut Yuri Gagarin, the first man in space, didn't actually leave the surface of the earth, he said: 'When reality makes news, then the non-reality people want to create something that will draw attention to them as revealers of the real world.' This doubtless includes the urban myth that the whole Apollo Programme was faked. I didn't dare ask for a comment on that. Even at the (then) age of 69, Aldrin could easily have made me see stars...

Aldrin expressed little desire to return to the Moon. 'Anyone who's flown in space would like to experience that again, but the system will not reach back into the early pioneering days again. Because they did it once, they certainly have no need ever to do that again. Just because they flew John Glenn again, they don't want to start a precedent where they want all the early people to say: Hey – how about me too?

'John Glenn's flight in the Shuttle was the rewarding of an American hero who flew in orbit first for us – a one time opportunity to refly somebody from the early days – we'll fly him again, they said. It's a symbol. And it was a symbol very well received by the American people because they recognised that if John can fly then why can't other people?'

146

The Aldrin I met preferred to talk about the future rather than the past – and getting tourists into space. So much so that as breakfast proceeded I could hardly get a word in edgeways. He wanted to be a pioneer in the space tourism industry. To stimulate the private sector and help design and build re-usable rockets to do the job. Rather than for ever being feted as the pilot who took mankind to the surface of the moon for the first time, or having a huge crater named after him, Aldrin, it seems, would rather be celebrated as 'Mr Tourism In Space' – a visionary who inspired the space tourism industry.

He agreed that in a sense when he set foot on the Moon, he was in a way a space tourist himself. 'I'd like to have spent more time looking around as a visitor,' he admitted, 'but with only two hours on the lunar surface, it was precious little time to even accomplish what you were supposed to be doing.'

One idea he had was to offer flights in a space shuttle as lottery prizes. 'The evolution of the re-usable rocket leads towards putting hotels in space,' said Aldrin. 'We'd make use of the big empty hydrogen tanks that go into orbit as the building blocks for the hotels. Kind of bizarre, people say; what are you talking about, space tourism? Well, it's no longer a giggle factor. It is becoming serious.'

So if Aldrin were ever to go back into space this would presumably prevent a repeat of the touching do-it-yourself religious service he carried out on the Moon. 'I was very conscious of the significance of the landing, and the responsibility of doing the appropriate thing,' he said. 'I asked people to pause for a moment and give thanks in their own way. I had brought with me, wrapped in appropriate plastic sealing, fire-proof and everything, a little silver chalice, and a little bit of white wine and a wafer. So I opened those things up and proceeded to serve myself communion.'

Was it Californian wine?

'I have no idea. But if I were to do it again, it would convey an erroneous signal to those other people that I shared my recovery with. And anyway I guess my spirituality has moved beyond identifying with the particular rituals that might be identified with one particular part of religious thinking more than others.

'The Muslims don't serve communion, and the Buddhists don't. What I feel about spirituality now is something which over-rides all of those, including Christianity. When I am asked questions about this, I say that by far the more important change in my life has been that I came back as a person who had been on the moon in the eyes of those who I meet. And now I have to live up to that. I have to deal with the anniversaries, the celebrations, the publicity, and that has a greater impact on the rest of your life, I think, than the actual experience.'

'What I'm doing now is pursuing flights for private citizens, opening up space tourism. People will assume that either I want to fly again and that's why I'm doing it – or if I don't fly then it's Buzz doesn't want to fly again.

Being a keen student of things lunar, I just happened to have my Rand McNally map of the moon with me. Indeed, I had spilt coffee on the Hercynian Mountains while I was waiting for Aldrin to join me. And I had noticed a major crater called Arnold. But where were Aldrin, Armstrong or Collins?

'There are three craters named after us,' said Aldrin, 'but they're so small they wouldn't show. They're in the vicinity of our landing site. But of course anything on the nearside of any appreciable size has already been named. So our craters are very small. There are quite a number on the other side but they're all named after Russians, because they were the first to send a satellite round the back of the moon with a camera. One of the most beautiful sights when you leave the moon – we were in a close orbit around the equator – is the Tsiolkovsky crater. As you leave, you can look back at the backside of the moon at this beautiful crater named after the Russian rocket scientist and pioneer Konstantin Tsiolkovsky. It's the most prominent crater on the far side of the moon.'

Rather proudly I showed Aldrin some newspaper cuttings recording his epic journey with Armstrong. I pointed out that in one of them there was no mention of 'Buzz'. He was referred to throughout as Edwin – his real name. 'Well sometimes it was

Edwin Buzz E Aldrin Junior, he said. (The second E stood for Eugene – his father had the same names. The nickname 'Buzz' originated in childhood: the younger of his two older sisters mispronounced 'brother' as 'buzzer', and this was shortened to Buzz.)

'Edwin Buzz E. Aldrin Junior is unwieldy and always has been. So I legally changed my name, and my drivers' licence and passport are all just Buzz.'

There was an amusing sequel to this interview. When we'd finished breakfast, Aldrin said his wife would like to meet me. She was still upstairs in bed, suffering from jet lag. Buzz and I made our way to the rickety old lift – and he searched for the appropriate button. His room, he thought, was number 50. But that didn't correspond with any obvious floor. We ended up on the wrong one, searching for the right room. It suddenly occurred to me that the lunar module pilot of Apollo 11 had been unable to pilot us to his accommodation. This struck me as hilarious. It wasn't his fault at all – the Halcyon lift system was not exactly NASA technology. I rang a chum on Londoner's Diary. A good friend, but a young one. I gleefully explained what had happened. There was a pause. He said: 'Sorry, Arnie – but who's Buzz Aldrin?' Ahem. Well I suggested he check with someone with a longer memory. He came back saying 'my editor would like the story'. I bet he would. And of course it was used that very day.

A decade or so before I breakfasted with Buzz I had met another astronaut – nowhere near as famous as Aldrin – indeed hardly famous at all outside the USA, but it was a fascinating experience nonetheless. I met Robert 'Hoot' Gibson at NASA's Lyndon B. Johnson Space Center, in Houston – a wonderful opportunity for Peter Tory and me to visit the celebrated Mission Control Center. Gibson had been due to be commander of the next Space Shuttle until the Challenger disaster of January 1986 aborted his own Orbiter mission.

Of the Challenger explosion, he said: 'I saw the puff, and thought, Well that is not good, but maybe it's just a main engine or something. For a while your eyes fill in what they want to see. But within two minutes of lift-off, I realised that was it. It was a terrific shock. We had the misfortune of watching seven of our friends go die.

'It was a tough day to live through, I can tell you. We could not have sunk any lower. That has been the worst tragedy I have ever bumped into. I have been a test pilot and I have lost friends before. You never get used to it. I have never lost so many friends at once. We were all one big family.'

When we asked him if he would ever like to fly a mission with his wife Rhey (a doctor and fellow astronaut) in the crew, he said: 'We've always said we'd love to fly together. But it would probably be unfair to our son. Anyway I think NASA would look at that, and say: Come on, that's just too cute! It would never work anyway because I might say, as commander, Go open the sunshields, and she'd say Go open them yourself!'

As one would expect, Gibson was of the Right Stuff. Peter and I would write:

> Physically fit to highly-tuned perfection, clear-eyed, straight-featured, and with a brain as sharp as a *Star Wars* laser, he is one of America's most treasured heroes. Spaceship commander.
>
> You can't do better than that in this most proud of countries.
>
> Curiously, astronauts are purely regarded in these parts as 'government employees'. They are not movie stars. And the salaries they receive are certainly not spectacular. A junior astronaut [remember this was 1987] makes $27,000; the more senior get $70,000.'
>
> Gibson told us: 'I want to help us recover from this [the Challenger disaster]. I don't want to see any of my friends go fly until I am convinced the Shuttle is safe and ready. [This was especially understandable as his wife did in fact fly two more missions after Challenger.] I am going to stand up and make a lot of noise if I don't think it's safe...
>
> What's the launch like, we asked. He replied with an energetic twitch of his aviator's moustache [Tory, once a keen and moustachioed aviator himself, must have loved writing that]: 'You get there on the pad, you light everything off, you say bang, fire

the bolts –and up you go. Eight minutes later, you're going 17,000 miles an hour. Wow!'

Sadly, of course, despite Gibson's great concerns and efforts, the Challenger disaster was followed 17 years later by the equally tragic Columbia Space Shuttle explosion in 2003.

Someone who I'm sure would have liked to be a spaceman was Peter Fairley, ITN's science editor, who covered some of the Apollo space missions, including the one I worked on myself, Apollo 13 – the one that almost didn't make it home in 1970.

Shortly before his death in 1998 he told me how he'd had to resort to fairly desperate measures when the spacecraft was crippled by an explosion.

'It happened just an hour before we were due on the air,' he said, 'and apart from a colour transparency we had absolutely nothing to illustrate the story with. I happened to have a model of the spacecraft, so I grabbed some scissors and gouged a jagged hole in it to show viewers where the service module had been damaged in the explosion. I remember being terribly embarrassed about letting anyone see me doing it, so I hid in the ITN loo.' Fairley's improvised broadcast worked so well it was repeated later on the main 10 o'clock news, by which time they had satellite pictures too.

Another intriguing Fairley story was that when it emerged that Apollo 13 was safe, and the whole world breathed again, Peter's eyes were manifestly moist on air. In fact he told me he shed a tear or two, although I don't recall this happening. He said ITN's editor Nigel Ryan had mildly rebuked him for 'crying on air'. I have no idea how true this story is, but it's what Fairley told me.

One of my favourite space titbits involves a momentous event on June 3, 1965, on the occasion of the first American space walk, when Ed White was climbing back into Gemini 4. As he was hauling him in, his fellow astronaut James McDivitt's glove came loose, and drifted off into space. What had become of this lonely accoutrement? With great excitement, I rang NASA to try to find out. 'Sir,' said a testy voice, 'there are 4,000 man-made objects orbiting the Earth. We do not track space junk.'

Not true these days, says Mark Frary, a former astro-physicist who once worked at CERN, the world's largest particle physics laboratory in Geneva, referring me to this:

> The NASA Orbital Debris Program Office, located at the Johnson Space Center, is the lead NASA center for orbital debris research. It is recognized world-wide for its initiative in addressing orbital debris issues. The NASA Orbital Debris Program Office has taken the international lead in conducting measurements of the environment and in developing the technical consensus for adopting mitigation measures to protect users of the orbital environment. Work at the Center continues with developing an improved understanding of the orbital debris environment and measures that can be taken to control debris growth.

Its website reveals images of huge clouds of debris in orbit round the Earth. 'One of those dots is presumably the missing glove,' speculates Frary... 'Unless it has now burned up.'

I still occasionally watch Sir Patrick Moore on the BBC programme *The Sky at Night*. At 87, he's a national treasure if ever there was one – and probably the only astronomer alive who can claim to have met Orville Wright, the first man to fly; Werner von Braun, the Saturn V rocket scientist who helped pioneer the Apollo moon missions; Yuri Gagarin, the first man into space; and Neil Armstrong, the first man on the moon. He also once played a duet with Albert Einstein.

Since the wonderful old stargazer's phone number is readily in the phone book, I do ring him occasionally, and recently paid a visit at his Selsey, Sussex home accompanied by his friend David Whiting, the stepson of Lord Dowding.

We found the veteran astronomer in great spirits, holding court, Buddha-like, in a huge red kaftan, and making a fuss of his two cats, Jeannie and Ptolemy. Both front and rear doors of his house have inner doors which carry notices saying, in *Space Odyssey* style prose: 'Cats' airlock. Please keep shut at all times!'

'Patrick was my house master at Holmewood House School, near where we lived in Tunbridge Wells in the late 40s,' Whiting had explained on the way. 'Dyslexia was not known in those days, so I used to receive several lashes with the bamboo cane from the headmaster for being lazy. The idea in those days was that a little bloodletting around the rear end stimulated the circulation to the brain. Well, it didn't work with me! I used to run away from school at the beginning of most terms – school was not the happiest time of my life. On returning home from her dancing classes, mother would find me hiding in the bushes. She would make a phone call to Patrick telling him she was putting me in a taxi and would he please keep an eye on me when I arrived. Patrick became a close family friend. He composed the music for the school plays, and played the xylophone faster that he could talk.'

Sadly, as we discovered on our arrival, his arthritic hands mean he can no longer play the xylophone – or enjoy his other passion: cricket. His celebrated Ford Prefect, with 900,000 miles on the clock, tends to languish in the garage, and Sir Patrick spends much of his time in a wheelchair.

As we left, he said: 'I have to accept that I am now a senior citizen [translation, 'old coot' – his words, not mine] and must now watch cricket rather than spin my leg-breaks. But I have lived through an interesting period, and met a great many interesting people.'

Chapter 18
Eric Morecambe

Their agent said 'Listen you guys -
'Eric's real name we'll have to disguise...
'This Bartholomew thing
'Doesn't have a good ring.
'Let's agree – you'll be Morecambe and Wise.'

Eric Morecambe told me he was 'petrified' of water – yet liked being on board the Q2. The comic genius behind the *Morecambe and Wise* shows was a complex man. Very likeable and matey, but underneath all that there was definitely quite a lot of insecurity as I discovered when, with two *Sunday People* colleagues, Peter Oakes and photographer David Graves, I paid him a lengthy visit at his home in Harpenden, Hertfordshire. It was 1976, and he'd just turned 50.

Morecambe told us, perhaps unexpectedly, that he didn't think of himself as a purveyor of happiness. 'People come up to me and say: You'd be surprised how much happiness you give to people – how much people enjoy meeting you. But I never see it that way. I never want to be remembered for giving people happiness. I would like to be remembered as one of the best English comedians. But that's an ambition that's maybe yet to be achieved. There's a lot of other great comedians as well. But I'd like to be in the top ten. What I'm saying here is that I get paid for making people happy, if you want to call it that. I don't call it making people happy. I make people laugh, for which I get paid, and I'm very professional about the whole thing. What I want to be remembered for is being a very, very good comedian – a great comedian.'

By 1976 he and Ernie Wise had dabbled in three films, but were never entirely happy with the results. 'I still feel there's a good film in Ernie and me,' he said, 'but it's a bit like how everyone thinks there's a good book them. It was as much our fault as anyone else's. We felt it was a great chance for us, but we were "guided" – we should have put our foot down. That's what we do on TV, good bad or indifferent. Ernie and I have got to say Yes, that's the way we're going to do it, and not rely on someone else. If we don't do it that way, then we don't do it. Ernie and I were in awe of being in films, or being big stars. It didn't work.

'It's all about timing. George Burns has a great definition of timing: You finish your joke. You get a laugh. You move on to the next joke. That's timing. I like Tommy Cooper. He's a very funny man. He could make you laugh if he said My father died yesterday.'

They went on to do one more film – *Night Train to Murder*. Morecambe died soon afterwards.

We moved on to Morecambe's trade-mark glasses. 'I've worn them since I was 13,' he told us. 'I have two pairs. One pair I've had 15 years. They hide the bags under my eyes. I've had big bags there for years.' But he told us that they'd caused a strange thing to happen while he'd been fishing recently in Derbyshire, when his surroundings started 'swimming' in front of his eyes.

'I was fishing on the banks of a very fast moving stretch of water,' he said. 'Really concentrating – trying to catch a big trout. A two-pounder. And I missed him. I got him on line, and lost him. I was at it for almost an hour, in very high, hilly country, with caverns all round me. It was quite frightening, like something from a modern horror movie, with these huge granite slabs rising up. And suddenly it felt like the whole area was moving. I think it had something to do with my glasses. Or my fear of water.

'I can't swim, and I never go in the water. That's why I won't buy those big waders which come up to here – I won't fish in water. Only on the bank. I'm petrified of water. As a kid in Morecambe baths, I nearly drowned. I went in with a school mate, and he held me under. It was a kids' game. A prank. He held me under for just a bit too long, and that was it – I said never again.

'There's a lot of lake fishing I could take advantage of, but I won't go because it's on a boat – a little rowing boat. I'd certainly never try shark fishing...'

What about taking a cruise? 'Oh yes, we've been on the QE2. That was marvellous. And if the QE2 goes down... well that's a 20-to-1 chance, isn't it?' (Someone said: 'I hope the odds are a bit better than that!')

'I'm fatter now, but when I was a young boy, you really could kick sand in my face. On holiday I never go in the sea. I'll wade – paddle – right on the edge. I have swimming trunks on just to get brown. My wife says go in, you'll enjoy it. People can't understand why some people don't enjoy it.

'I've got a pool here at home. I've never been in it – or on it. A heated pool. All my family swim. It's 8ft 6ins at the deep end. I only stood in it once, at the shallow end, just to have my picture taken, with a lifebelt, funnily enough. I wanted it around my waist. That made it into a funny picture.

'So water just frightens me to death. Flying doesn't particularly worry me though. Sometimes I get a bit worried on those motorways. Tyres worry me a bit. It's not you having a blow-out. It's the other fellow. I won't drive in fog at all on the motorway. I'll come off. I don't care if I'm late for appointments, although I'm usually a very punctual person. It just isn't worth it. It's the other berk – this is the part that always worries me. If his number's up, I don't want it to be my number as well.'

At this stage, my *Sunday People* colleagues were expressing similar fears. Morecambe gulped and looked over the top of his glasses. 'I'm in a room full of cowards!'

'In our business, you can get pissed on from a great height. We get our share of unpleasant letters. Of course there are cranks who don't sign their names. I send them on to Ernie, and he opens them.

'I thought when I was a young man that if I didn't make it by the time I was 40 that was it. By 40 you're an old man. But I was actually 40 when we really started to move. I see it this way. I say that in ten years time, how can Ernie and I walk out there and do gags like "you can't see the join" or "my little fat friend" and "short fat hairy legs"… and the slap on the cheeks – it'll have gone by then, even though it will be a new audience. But Ernie says, "Ah but we said that ten years ago".

'I'm a born pessimist. I say: That gag didn't go well so the whole show was no good. Ernie's the optimist. Ernie and I have worked together as a double act since 1941. So if Ernie feels it's time to pack up, fine – there's no argument either way. There's nothing signed. There's no contract. It's all based on… fear!'

'We're not a comic and a straight-man any more. Ernie's now become a character in his own right. This is good for his image. And this has helped us tremendously, the fact that Ernie has moved on. If you saw the early Dean Martin and Jerry Lewis films, the only reason Dean Martin was there was to play the handsome fellow, be the love interest, be a role model. Ernie used to be like that. Small and handsome. Tiny love interest! But he's developed over the years.'

We asked Morecambe whether he'd ever done anything he was ashamed of.

'I once stole a pear from a shop in Morecambe,' he said. 'From Mr Hoyle. My mother sent me to the shop for half a pound of sugar or something. I'd known Mr Hoyle all my life. I'd be about nine years old. Eight or nine. You know how they have the pears, apples and vegetables stacked up. While Mr Hoyle was out the back I took a pear and was about to put it in my pocket when he comes back – fortunately – otherwise it would have been so easy – and says: What are you doing, Eric? Are you going to buy that?

'No Mr Hoyle, I said, I haven't got any money. I was in tears. He never told my mother though, which was marvellous, and I've never done anything like that since. He did it in a nice way. He didn't slap me or anything like that. That helped set me on my way in life. If I'd taken it, I'd have tried for the apples eventually, then the bananas and then the money – you never know, do you?'

The subject moves on, somehow, to Lord Lucan, the missing earl who allegedly murdered his nanny thinking, in the darkness, it was his wife

'I've heard he's here,' says Morecambe.

'What? In Harpenden?' I suggest, to much mirth. 'Yes' said Morecambe. 'In this house. I am Lord Lucan.' We talked about how he might have disguised himself. 'Fake glasses and a limp always work better than a false moustache,' said Morecambe, giving us a quick demonstration. 'But I can't keep this up very long.'

As we were leaving, we spotted a hand-written verse entitled 'Ode to Eric'. Could this be from Ernie? No, it turned out to be from Morecambe's wife Joan, written to celebrate his 50th birthday. She was on hand to read it too.

> The time has come, you've had such fun, in all your work and play.
> But now you've reached, I think, your peak, so may I have my say?
> You cannot lie about your age, the ghastly truth is known.
> It's not the time to rant and rave, your wild seeds you have sown.
> So why not try the gentler pace in all the things you do?
> Remember life is not a race, so why get in a stew?
> I want to say now, Eric dear, in spite of all my warning,
> Throughout a darned good year, with your second innings dawning
> Please may I add you do look nifty to say you now have just reached fifty,
> So just refrain from getting frantic when all of us just love your antics.

Chapter 19
Music

You don't need to go to Los Angeles to find talent. It's amazing who turns up in your life even if you never leave your home county – in my case Kent (where my mother, a concert pianist, and my father, an unsuccessful composer, had moved to when I was eight). One day when I was living near Canterbury, I was told the Beach Boys had surfed in and were staying fairly anonymously just outside the village of Challock. And lo and behold, when I popped round to see then – there they were. Not ALL the Beach Boys, I must confess, but three of them. All I can remember now is that they were very relaxed, with no self-importance, and were extremely polite and friendly. And it made a piece for the following day's nationals.

One Saturday night when I was working at the *Sunday People*, we got a message saying Boy George was going to see Frank Sinatra at the Albert Hall – would we like an interview (with Boy George, not Sinatra)? Why not? I arranged to meet him outside the hall, where a large crowd was building up (for Sinatra, not Boy George).

The crowds were being held back by crash barriers, so as I had a little time, I approached the nearest police officer, explained the situation, and he assured me that I would have access to Boy George as he arrived. And why not, anyway?

Half an hour later, Boy George's car drew up. I made a move to meet him and found myself being flattened against the wall of the Albert Hall by the very same policeman I'd spoken to just a while earlier. He was about 6ft 2 in, and well built to boot. For some reason I have never worked out, he flung himself against me, his back against my front and made it impossible for me to move.

I was so furious that he'd not only reneged on his promise, but had also effectively assaulted me, that by the time the scrum was over and Sinatra was on stage, I was determined not to lose out. I found a back way in to the building, somehow slipped past security and managed to find Boy George's box, where I did a token interview. This left me free to watch Sinatra for the rest of the evening from the relative luxury of Boy George's box – something I would never have done if that police thug hadn't attacked me.

It was also at the Albert Hall – in rather more peaceful circumstances – that I met one of my favourite artists, Leonard Cohen, backstage. He was charming and polite. And OK, I admit it. I shamelessly asked for his autograph.

Another wonderful singer I spent time with was Dame Vera Lynn, who recently made such a spectacular comeback with her old recordings. Dame Vera is a near neighbour, but the last time I saw her turned out to be rather embarrassing and, coward that I am, I have never had the courage to ring her since. She wanted me to spend the day with her at the Dame Vera Lynn School for Parents to help support children with cerebral palsy, a specialist building in West Sussex. We had a very happy day there but the following day I discovered that while she was with me her home in the picturesque village of Ditchling had been burgled. I was so embarrassed I didn't dare contact her. Silly of me really. I'm sure she would have forgiven me, even though I was only indirectly the cause. But now I fear 'we'll never meet again'.

Tony Coe, who hails from Canterbury, is one of the finest jazz clarinettists and saxophonists ever to walk the earth, and I got to know him long before I had become a writer. Before I had left school even. He and I had been to the same grammar school in Canterbury, although he was just a few years ahead of me. It was because of a friendship between Coe's uncle and my father that Coe and I met, and I ended up learning the flute on an instrument purchased or borrowed from Tony. Much later, it was this very flute that I lent Spike and Paddy Milligan's daughter Jane when she wanted to learn to play. As I've known Tony for so long, there are many stories I could tell. He has several claims to fame. He was Humphrey Lyttelton's clarinettist for five years when 'Humph' was still trumpeting away as leader of his jazz band. Lyttelton paid him this compliment: 'Tony Coe is one of the most remarkable and brilliant musicians in the world. The sheer range of his musical activity is staggering and testifies to an awe-inspiring instrumental mastery.' Coe is also a doctor of music in Paris. He played with the John Dankworth Orchestra, Stan Tracey, Stan Getz and Dizzy Gillespie.

He might possibly be the only musician to have turned down a job with the great Count Basie because he simply refuses to fly. 'If God had wanted us to fly, he'd have given us airline tickets,' is one of his favourite sayings. I suspect he stole it from Ronnie Scott, whose club in London's Soho he often played in. Another of his favourites was Scott's joke about bouncers. 'We have them at Ronnie's, to throw people *in*,' he'd often say.

But even with his feet firmly on the ground, Coe is not the most organised of travellers. Caught short on his way back from Haywards Heath, where he'd been doing a bank holiday gig at Jeremy's, my favourite restaurant, Coe asked his colleague John Horler (formerly John and Cleo Dankworth's pianist) to pull up near a church so that he could take advantage of some nearby bushes. Climbing back into the car, Coe was puzzled to hear Horler playing loud Dixieland jazz. Or so he thought. 'You don't like Dixieland,' he berated his chum, settling comfortably into the passenger seat once more. 'Why are you playing it?'

'Who are you?' asked the driver – not John Horler at all, but a completely different motorist – a complete stranger – driving a very similar car.

'He was quite benign about it,' said a slightly embarrassed Coe, who has never bothered to learn to drive. 'It was dark, and I thought John had driven closer to make life easier. The cars looked identical in the darkness.'

My favourite story about Coe concerns his being told, quite recently, to leave a five-star London hotel after a row over an interval drink during a jazz brunch in which he was the star performer.

Coe says he was asked by a waiter at the Landmark Hotel's 'soaring atrium' where 'selected premier musicians take the stage of the Gazebo' to play for guests, what he and his accompanying guitarist Ed Renshaw would like to drink during the interval.

'I asked for a white wine, but I was told that was not possible,' said Coe. 'So I wandered downstairs to the bar and bought my own. I had hardly started to drink it when I was confronted by an officious member of the hotel staff saying "her" musicians were not allowed to drink alcohol during a performance. She seemed like an ambitious little woman in a smart suit wishing to impress.

'I pointed out to her that it was the interval – not during the performance. But she insisted that either I stopped drinking the wine or I would have to leave. She seemed to have a strong German accent [I discovered later she was Dutch] and I accused her of being a fascist. She objected to this, so I called her authoritarian. Either way I wanted to finish my drink. At this point she asked me to leave.

'I thought it would hard on the hotel guests for me to take Ed with me so I said he should stay and keep the music going alone – and walked out. Of course I could have made a speech to the guests saying they were going to be deprived of half their music because I'd had a glass of wine. I think the rules are crazy. I have played before at the Landmark and no-one ever mentioned this drinks ban then.'

When I checked with the hotel I was told: 'We have a rule that when musicians perform at the hotel they have to observe the same rules that apply to the regular staff, who are not allowed to drink on duty… It was quite right for him to be asked to leave. Rules are rules.'

Nonplussed, Tony told The Landmark Hotel to give his fee to charity.

The only time I met David Niven he was pretending to play the piano. It was all in aid of the Bond movie, *Casino Royale* (the spoof version). Again, there was a 'local' Kent angle. Coached by Edward Rubach, Niven had to mime playing the piano to recorded music in a scene being filmed at Mereworth Castle, just outside Maidstone.

'The only other time I've had to play the piano in a film,' Niven told me, 'there was a pianist crouching under the keyboard who actually fingered the keys.' Whatever – the director, John Huston, seemed pleased with Niven's performance.

That story reminds me of an extremely unlikely tale about the ground-breaking BBC TV series *Z-cars*. But for piano keys, read pedals…

Apparently when the four main characters were signed up for the series, which ran for 16 years, two of them – James Ellis and Jeremy Kemp – couldn't drive. We were told that a shortish stunt man was employed to lie on the floor of their Z-car and, by looking through specially drilled holes in the chassis, to operate the clutch, brakes and throttle. We actually ran the story in the *Sunday People*. No, I didn't believe it either, but no one ever complained or said it wasn't true, so who knows? I like to think it was.

Chapter 20
Back page stuff

I'm not a huge fan of sport except for soccer and skiing. I was quite a decent wing-half, as we used to call midfield players, and captained the school team. At the age of 13, I decided for various reasons (red shirts, Robin Hood, and a centre forward called Wilson) to support Nottingham Forest. I have followed them through thick and thin – mainly thin. I never met Brian Clough, but I did briefly work with the former Forest Scottish international Stuart Imlach's son Gary at TVam, and I did play in a few charity football matches (especially during my Anglia TV days) in which my opponents included Billy Wright, Ian St John and Jimmy Hill. I've met Jimmy Greaves a few times and have forgiven him for scoring all four goals against Forest in his last game for Chelsea in April 1961. One reason is that although I was there, I didn't remember Forest scoring at all, but when I looked up the record I discovered to my amazement that the score was actually 4-3 so, half a century on, that has cheered me up no end.

I've been a guest at Chelsea once a year for some time, hosted by the Austrian National Tourist Office for ski writers, and we have lunch in the Bobby Tambling suite before the match. Normally there are some old Chelsea hands there who entertain us with a question-and-answer session. Ron 'Chopper' Harris, the former Chelsea defender, is a regular, and he sometimes appears with 'Greavesy' when Jimmy is doing his very entertaining stand-up comedy routine tours with well-rehearsed jokes about football.

My favourite Mike Yarwood story happened in Great Yarmouth. I had arranged to see this very gifted impressionist and took an old school friend, Graeme Johnston, along for the ride – probably to impress him. But I ended up getting frozen out. Yarwood discovered my friend, a passionate Luton Town supporter, had an encyclopaedic knowledge of football. Yarwood, as it turned out, had too. Gradually all attempts at interviewing him faded as the two of them pitted their wits against one another, asking more and more obscure questions about teams from the distant past. I gave up. Eventually it was time to go. Yarwood was beaming all over his face. He turned to my friend and said: 'That's the most enjoyable evening I've had for months.' I soon forgave him. And of course it made Graeme's year – and possibly Yarwood's.

Then there was the time Erica Roe – she of the 40-inch bust – streaked at Twickenham in January 1982. I got to her first after the event – unfortunately not in the flesh, but on the phone. It was really all down to the enterprise of one Roger Insall, a colleague on the *Sunday People*. Roger went to every pub in the area leaving a note asking 'whoever it was who streaked at the rugby match' (we didn't know her name) to ring the *Sunday People* news desk where I was deputy night news editor. Well, it worked, and I got the first interview. In fact Erica talked so much that there wasn't room on the *People* front page for everything, so I sold the remaining titbits to the *Sun*. It was the only time I ever managed to get the front page lead story in that newspaper. It had been one of those classic weekend stories that was still buzzing on Monday. The angle the *Sun* went for was that on the Saturday of the streak Ms Roe was supposed to be working at a bookshop in Petersfield, Hampshire. She'd been 'off sick' that day. Then advertised the fact that she was very fit and healthy to millions of TV viewers.

Although I never met Erica in the flesh, I did spend a little time with another woman famous for her ample bosom – Samantha Fox. I went with her and her mother Carole, along with Shirley Anne Field and Ian Ogilvy to Cyprus on a press trip.

I may be one of the few men to have not only dangled grapes into Sam Fox's mouth (it was over dinner, nothing untoward) but also to have picked her up bodily and thrown her into a swimming pool. I have the photos to prove it. She took it very graciously. But it was explained to me that had it not been a friend who had grabbed her, it might have been a very different story. As I wrote at the time:

It's definitely look but don't touch where Samantha Fox is concerned. The Page 3 girl has built up a formidable armoury of unpleasant tricks to deter the dirtiest of old men.

'Putchyer hand on my knee and you'll see what I mean!' she said, as we dined together at a plush hotel in the Cypriot resort of Paphos. Grateful for the opportunity, I reached out gently and clutched her right knee.

Ouch! My little finger was bent back and felt as though it was almost being ripped off.

Yeow! A long finger-nail gouged its way into the nerve between my thumb and forefinger.

Bash! Her little fist whacked me right in the solar plexus. 'I'll spare you the knee in the groin,' she said generously.

But Sam hadn't finished yet. Her hands flew up to my face, and she dug a finger under each ear and pressed. Hard.

As I yelped, she brought her right foot down on my toes, and stamped hard.

'I'm getting pretty good at defending myself against anyone who tries anything funny' she said. As if I needed to be told. 'Just because I'm little (a matter of opinion, I thought) it doesn't mean I can't look after myself.' It was a good job, perhaps, that I'd only gone for her knee.

I was pretty poor at cricket, though I fancied myself as an agile slip fielder and once made double figures in a charity match for a side captained by Terry Wogan. I got to know Colin Cowdrey quite well (I used to live opposite the county ground in Canterbury when I was at the local grammar school) and I even walked up the Old Dover Road arm in arm with the great Rohan Kanhai and O'Neil Gordon 'Collie' Smith, after asking them both for their autographs.

Denis Compton, my biggest childhood cricketing hero, turned out to be a disappointment when I finally met him. But he provided a good tale. My mother's parents were great Middlesex supporters and took me to watch Compton play Surrey at the Oval. He scored a century. My mother, a stickler for what she believed was correct pronunciation, always called him CUMPTon. (She also called Coventry CUVentry.) I guess it was the fashion then. Anyway, when I bumped into Compton, I used the pronunciation my mother had taught me. Mr 'CUMPton', I started...' It's COMPton,' he said. Maybe I'd already displeased him because he then demanded money for the interview which surprised and disappointed me. I had never paid for an interview in my life, and wasn't about to start. I made my excuses, as they say, and left – marching to the nearest phone box to call my mother.

'Guess who I've just met... Denis COMPton.'

'It's CUMPton dear.'

'No it's not,' I said triumphantly. 'It's COMPton. I asked him. And he should know...'

'Well, it's still CUMPton darling.'

Kanhai and Smith were both contemporaries of another of the all-time greats, Sir Garfield St Aubrun Sobers. Golf is not among my skills – just ask Franz Klammer. (But I do have one of Sean Connery's cast-off drivers, a generous gift from Paul Chase-Gardner, a former ski tour operator who is rather good at golf and whose mother was once Ladies' Captain at Sunningdale. Very recently I offered to return it to Paul, as I'd not struck a ball with it for 15 years, but he was adamant. 'That's yours for keeps' he said. 'No going back'). But for one bizarre feature in the *Financial Times* I found myself in Barbados playing with Sobers, the first cricketer to hit six consecutive sixes in one over. It was a bit overwhelming because a) he's a great golfer b) it was drizzling and I had to hold the umbrella c) I had to keep the score, and d), worst of all, I had to try to hit the odd shot in a vaguely workmanlike manner while performing my other chores, including taking notes.

No matter what sport Sobers tries, it seems he always looks as though he's playing cricket. If he'd only been wearing his cricket whites during our knockabout, the illusion would have been complete. He even plays golf wearing two gloves, batsman-style. 'I just couldn't get used to the feeling of wearing only one,' he grinned, wielding his Number 4 iron with the expertise and panache of the world-class cricketer that of course he was.

Sobers is a golf addict. He took up the sport almost 50 years ago when some Australian test rivals invited him to play. A detached retina ended his first class cricket career, but 'I can see well enough to play golf for the rest of my life,' he said. And though he has arthritis, when I played that round with him at Sandy Lane, where, back in 1992, he had the freedom of the course, he said: 'I don't feel the pain. I don't even notice that I walk with a limp except when I see myself on TV.'

As a prolific all-round cricketer, he said he became fed up with having to produce match-saving feats to order. 'People always expected me to produce a brilliant innings or take a few wickets even when I was playing only once or twice a year.' So even friendly matches were discouraged. 'I don't enjoy the game any more.'

He says golf is good for your cricket, but not the other way round. 'If you don't keep your head down at cricket, you can sometimes get away with it. But if you do that playing golf, you normally hit a bad shot.

'Golf teaches you patience, which I need, because I'm no good at waiting for people in front of me – I get so cold and stiff that my golf suffers. Your golf stops being so fluid if you have to wait around.' When I told him that as long as I hit one good drive every game, I was happy, he said: 'Don't be so negative. Try for two or three – or four! When you start playing golf, the most important thing is to hit the ball as naturally as you can – it doesn't matter where it goes as long as you hit it. Then, when you know with reasonable certainty that you're going to hit it, you can start worrying about where you're going to hit it. That's the trouble with most beginners. People have been playing golf for years who still can't hit it straight. '

The bunker in front of the third green was full of rainwater. Plop. In went Sobers' ball, with an answering plop from mine. Scooping the balls out to the damp sand nearby, both our sand-wedge shots failed. 'We both made the same mistake then,' he said. 'We didn't follow through properly.'

When we were finished, and the sun was going down, the whistling frogs were beginning their dusk chorus. Sobers had a flight to catch. He was representing the Barbados Tourist Board in London, and then going on to play some more golf. Back then, he couldn't leave the game alone. 'Golf is the easiest game in the world – to get hooked on,' he said. 'I guarantee that if you play for a year – not every three weeks, but two or three times a week – you'll be hooked. That's the kind of game golf is.'

Among my cricketing souvenirs is an amusing gift from Bill Frindall, then the commentary team's jovial statistician. It was a letter from one K R Bhat in Mangalore, in south-west India, typed in purple. 'Dear Sir' it said. 'On August 10, 1974 will you please answer my questions on 15.20 PM (or 20.50 PM according to Indian Standard Time) which I have asked below. I have given the names of 17 Pakistani cricketers. You just read their date of birth, highest score in first-class cricket – where, when, against whom? Same about best bowling also. I'd prefer 10th August. Read their names in the same order as given below: Intikhab Alam, Asif Iqbal, Majid Khan, Imran Khan, Mushtaq Mohd, Sadiq Mohd, Wasim Bari, Zaheer Abbas, Aftab Baluch, Aftab Gul, Asif Masood, Sarfraz Nawaz, Wasim Raja, Mohd Nazir (Jr) Shafiq Ahmed, Naseer Malik & Maazullah Khan. Sir I am grateful if you furnish these information about Pakistani Cricketers who are playing so well in England. Thanking you again, Please note that on 15.20 PM on GMT on 10-8-1974. P.S. Please answer just after TEA on 10th Aug 1974 P.S. 10th August.'

My favourite cricket interview was with the great Brian Johnston, one-time grenadier guardsman. I had first met him during the lunch break in the commentary box at the Oval and, in mid-conversation, I felt a tap on my shoulder as John Arlott returned, wanting his chair back. And so to Johnston's home near Lord's cricket ground to finish the interview with the owner of that wonderfully recognisable voice, which blended so well with the sound of leather on willow... 'When I went recently to my cleaner in

St John's Wood,' he said, 'there was a new woman behind the counter. I said: Would you please clean these trousers for me? She said Certainly, Mr Johnston, and when I asked how she'd recognised me, she said, Oh, I recognised your voice before you even spoke!'

Johnston had been a bit of a cricketer himself, although he described his skills as 'hopeless'. That's why he felt so lucky, as an 'indifferent amateur', to count so many famous professional cricketers as friends, initially at least because of his work as a commentator.

'When I joined the BBC after the war,' he said, 'I played charity matches on Sundays – like the Lord's Taverners do now. And in those days there was no professional cricket on Sundays so we had all the test players and all the visiting teams available. I kept wicket to all the great bowlers like Laker, Lindwall, Truman and Bedser, which was great, and I had a marvellous time for about the first 15 years after the war, keeping wicket for all these people on a Sunday. They were quite tolerant of me, because I was pretty inefficient. I used to count the number of people I'd caught and stumped, but I was a very poor batsman, and I do remember that in my second year at Oxford, when I probably played more cricket that I've ever played in my life, I normally went in about Number 9, 10 or 11, but that year I made seventeen hundred and something runs. I used to make the odd tens and twenties, so that shows how many innings I had. But I did hit 75 against Tavistock for Bude, the north Cornwall team I used to play for.'

And what about this business of cricket commentary? 'Well we all sit in a little box that wouldn't pass the factory act – it's very small, it gets hot and Fred (Truman) smoked his pipe and cigars – all the sort of things to get people annoyed and angry, but I've never had a quarrel with anybody in the box, and I've never seen one. We're all extroverts. I think it's the innate love of cricket and the fact that all of us think it's fun. Which is the be-all and end-all of our broadcasting really – to make cricket fun. All right, we go over the top sometimes and we're schoolboyish, but we go to enjoy it just like any other people.' And what if things go wrong? 'Of course things go wrong, but when they do we normally corpse and get the giggles. I don't think anyone ever gets annoyed with anyone.'

What about John Arlott, I asked. Didn't he get a bit tetchy sometimes? (Johnston talked about him partly in the past tense only because Arlott was no longer, at the time of the interview, still in the commentary box). 'Well old John wouldn't basically – and he's an honest man – approve of my method of commentary. You see Arlott was a tremendous personality. I think he did more for cricket than anybody. He had this marvellous Hampshire burr, and all that, and he was a poet, who could paint pictures with words. He wouldn't go along a hundred per cent with the kind of schoolboyish things we do now.'

Were there raised eyebrows occasionally? 'Oh yes. When we were talking about chocolate cake and things like that. But on the other hand he had his bottle of claret, so who was he to complain? Originally, for anyone to be having a drink in the box would have been unheard of… Arlott used to arrive in the box with a brief-case, and I'd think, gosh, he's got a lot of *Wisdens* in there, and then he used to open it up and say [and here 'Johnners' does an impression of Arlott's 'burr'] "what about a bottle of Beaujolais?" I think he thinks that I make it too much of a personality cult, which is strange really, coming from him!'

Two things in particular stand out from the interview. One was the protective cricket box on Johnners' office wall. 'What's that doing there, Brian?' I asked. 'It's a present from my godson, Graham Cowdrey,' he said. 'He never wears it,' whispered his wife, Pauline. 'Why not?' I asked. 'It's too small – but don't quote me!' I'm afraid I couldn't resist doing so. What a cad! The other great revelation came when Johnston explained why the family dog was called Larwood, after the controversial and infamous bodyline bowler Harold Larwood.

'It's because his balls swing both ways' he said.

A final thought on cricket. The game is one of the astronomer Sir Patrick Moore's passions too, and David Whiting says today of Moore's playing days: 'His slow run up to the wicket was like a heavy bomber on takeoff. Then he'd launch one of his deceptive

171

spinners (often with success) on the amazed and bemused batsman. Umpiring the inter-school matches was another issue he took seriously, always accompanied by his pipe. On one occasion, when the game was becoming intense, Patrick put his lighted pipe in his pocket and stooped to watch the ball. Patrick as always was so engrossed in the game that he did not notice the smoke billowing from his pocket, and had to hastily discard his jacket, to much applause from the audience.'

Just as people who don't know much about skiing always seem to have heard of Franz Klammer, everyone knows vaguely who Sir Stirling Moss is, even though they never saw him race in any of the extraordinary 212 victories he achieved out of 529 races he entered (including 16 Formula 1 races). Even now, that mythical question posed by policemen pouncing on speeding motorists – 'And who do we think we are sir, Stirling Moss?' – has virtually passed into the English lexicon. He even claims it was once said to him, and he took great delight in answering: 'Yes, I do, actually!'

And while in my travels I have bumped into Damon Hill (and his much lamented father Graham) and even attempted to interview Felipe Massa (who at least smiled) and Kimi Raikonnen (deliberately monosyllabic, even though we were hosted by Ferrari at Silverstone), the only driver who really put himself out for me was the great Stirling, whom I visited two or three times at his home in Mayfair. He is often called 'the greatest driver never to win the World Championship'. We sometimes talked about how things have changed on the F1 circuit.

Moss would compete in as many as 62 races in a single year and drove 84 different marques of car over the course of his racing career, including Lotus, Vanwall, Maserati, Jaguar, Ferrari and Porsche. Like many drivers of the era, he competed in several formulas—very often on the same day. He was placed second in the Drivers' Championship four times in a row from 1955 to 1958. But rather like Brian Clough never won the FA Cup, Moss won everything but the championship.

'In my era drivers got along very well with each other,' he told me. 'Nowadays they're not very compatible. For my first wedding, all my ushers were racing drivers. I think today if a driver got married and he needed five or six ushers, none of them would be from racing. I wouldn't like to race today. I think there are very great corporate pressures on you, enormous sponsorship. If I were racing today I would be expecting to earn, I don't know, between three and five million pounds a year. I was the highest paid driver in '61, and my total gross income was £32,700. And that was good money. I first drove a car when I was about six, possibly earlier – sitting on my mother's lap – just up and down our front drive at Maidenhead. I think we had a Lancia. Then when I was six or seven I had my own car – an Austin 7 – on my father's farm. I hadn't decided to be a racing driver then; I was expecting to be a dentist like my father. But I wasn't bright enough to be a dentist, so I became a driver. I first raced at 17. If you're not bright enough to do anything else you have to be driver or an MP, and I didn't want to be an MP, so what else do you do?'

Although Moss was close to death in two major crashes, he claims it left him none the worse mentally. But to my mild surprise he said he believed in divine intervention – of a sort. 'Each time I had a crash, with the exception of my last crash when I don't know what happened – but in the other crashes... I had a wheel come off at 140mph at Spa, at the Belgian Grand Prix, and broke my back and my legs, and finished up in hospital, obviously, and although it concerned me, because you don't want to crash, at least I knew what the reason was! And it wasn't my own shortcomings. Yes, there were times when I thought I was going to be killed. I thought I was going to be killed at Monza, when I was doing 165mph and the steering sheared, and my car smashed into the barrier, and I closed my eyes and I thought I was going to die. But really nothing much happened except the car spun to a standstill in the dust. And I opened my eyes and thought this must be hell but it isn't that hot. It was a serious accident but it could have been extremely serious. I thanked God afterwards.'

'Do you believe in God?' I asked.

'Yes I do believe in God. Otherwise I don't think I'd be alive. I think He did look after me. Otherwise if He'd wanted me it would have been so easy for Him to say, All right, come in. Maybe He didn't want to mess the place up. God moves in mysterious ways and I don't know the answers. I don't know if there's life after death, but otherwise it's all such a waste of time. One builds up all these relationships, but where the hell we're all going to go I've no idea. I'd like to think there's motor racing wherever it is. I've had a fantastic life from it. But of course I don't know what the options are... I'm not religious. I'm a believer – but I'm not a religious person. And I'm not a solo person at all. I don't enjoy my own company.

'The first important success I had was when I was 20. A journalist friend offered me his Jaguar XK120 to race in the RAC Tourist Trophy which is a classic race, because he was driving something else. In 1950 it was held at the Dundrod Circuit, high in the hills above Belfast. Nobody else would lend me a car – I think they thought I was going to kill myself, and it was pouring with rain and I managed to win the race outright.'

He did the same the following year, and dominated the event for the next decade as it switched to Goodwood. It was at Goodwood, many years later, that Moss was badly injured in a crash while driving a Lotus in the Glover Trophy. The accident put him in a coma for six months and partially paralyzed the left side of his body. Although he recovered he decided to retire from racing the following year.

'Motor racing today is much safer – 'the way the cars are built,' he said. If cars had been built in the 50s as they are now, people like Jimmy Clark would still be with us; Peter Collins would be with us; Eugenio Castellotti too... Really and truly, the magnet of death today in a racing car – a good driver now and a good car – they may be more lethal in one way, but far safer in another. At Imola in 1989 Gerhard Berger crashed at 160 mph and the car burst into flames, but he was racing again a week or two later. The modern racing car is built very well, has on-board fire extinguishers and has a life-support system so that instead of breathing flames the driver has a tube going in to his helmet which gives him so many seconds

174

of fresh air. And all those things are obviously greatly beneficial to the safety of the car and driver.'

So what was it that Moss had that he would use to such spectacular effect throughout his career that would make him a household name? 'It's tenacity, the feeling of balance...' he started to explain... 'It isn't courage – it's being able to make the best possible use of the skills you've got. It's rather like the strongest man isn't necessarily the best boxer. Just because I can hit you harder than you can hit me doesn't mean to say I'm going to beat you. It takes a lot more – there's skill in it. In motor racing it isn't just a question of bravely putting your foot down. There's a lot more to driving, and driving particularly in the wet was beneficial to me – I happen to be good in the wet, I suppose because I have a feel for the car.'

At (then) 60, Moss, still dabbling on the race track in the Supersports Car series, was thoughtful about how the ageing process changes your attitude to driving. 'Youth gives certain benefits to a driver, because as you get older your threshold of fear gets closer – there's no two ways about it. Not demonstrably closer, but it is there. There are corners I go into, and I think I should be able to take that flat out, but I can't quite do it, and I think Gosh, and the next lap I try, and I can't. I haven't got the... I suppose one has to use the word courage. It's a bad word because courage and stupidity are very close together, because sometimes it's a stupid man who does something brave or it might be a courageous man. Stirling Moss in the 50s would have had the bravery or the courage or the stupidity – whichever it was – or a balance of them all, to have done it. You see, if you have sufficient confidence – it's confidence I'm lacking these days, I think – because I'm pretty sure that this particular corner should be flat out. When I was younger I would have had the confidence to know that if it isn't quite flat out, and I get into trouble, I reckon I've got the confidence to correct the problem. Nowadays, although I'm pretty convinced I'd have the confidence to correct the problem, I don't know that I would. I'm sure when we get older we reckon we're better lovers than when we were younger. I don't know whether I am or whether I'm not. But I would like to think that I have more expertise. More stamina.

Not, if you like, more virility, but more stamina. One always likes to feel one's better with age but how the hell can you tell?'

I told him he looked pretty trim for 60, and asked if he worked consciously at doing lots of exercise. 'No,' he said, 'I'm fit because I believe in running – to me movement is tranquillity, and as long as I'm doing something I'm happy. I run up and down stairs. I don't like walking so much, although one has to walk! I try to watch my diet a bit. I just drink wine – but only in the evening. I don't drink alcohol *per se*. I don't smoke. I lead a very ordinary life really. And enjoy it.'

His most memorable moment? 'On the winner's dais at Monte Carlo in the 1961 Monaco Grand Prix, I guess. It was probably my greatest race. Because for the whole three hours and 40 minutes – 100 laps – I had a very under-powered Lotus – 40 horsepower less than the three Ferraris, and yet the distance between me and the drivers who were second and third was from three to six seconds every lap. It really was a big fight.'

In the 2000 New Year's Honours list, Moss was knighted by the Prince of Wales, standing in for the Queen who was on an official visit to Australia. As Moss drove his Mercedes away from Buckingham Palace after the ceremony, it's said – and believe it, if you wish – that he was stopped by a palace guard who joked: 'Who do you think you are? Stirling Moss?' And that Moss smiled and replied: '*Sir* Stirling Moss, actually.'

Chapter 21
Skiing

I am a mad keen skier – even keener about skiing than astronomy. In 2010 I even spent a night in an observatory on top of the Pic du Midi above the Pyrenean ski resort of La Mongie and then skied down in the morning – a perfect combination of two excellent interests.

Apart from my broadcasting years, celebrity interviews were my main occupation; and skiing, once I got going at the age of 30, became my main hobby. All that changed in 1986 when, following the premature death of the *Financial Times* leisure editor, Arthur Sandles, in the Swiss resort of Saas-Fee, I took over as the paper's ski correspondent. From here on in, my roles reversed – even more so after I became editor of the Ski Club of Great Britain's magazine *Ski+board* in 2001. Skiing had well and truly become my life and livelihood, and diary stories my hobby. Luckily the two often feed off each other.

As I've mentioned in earlier chapters, I have been lucky and cheeky enough to meet many celebrities on the slopes as well as in restaurants, and skied with several Olympic and World Cup champions. One or two, like Franz Klammer – whose record of 25 World Cup triumphs has never been equalled – have ended up as good friends.

Even non-skiers remember him – the King, or, more appropriately, the Kaiser, of downhill racers.

In Austria, particularly in his native Carinthia, he is still a living legend. Autograph hunters mob him even though it is now – incredibly – 35 years since the world watched, hearts in their mouths and their mouths agape, as Klammer, arms windmilling, skiing beyond even his limits and getting away with it, skied the race of his life to win gold in the men's downhill at the 1976 Olympics in Innsbruck. Two decades later, he was still 'getting goosebumps' watching an action replay on a big video screen during celebrations in Telluride, Colorado to mark the anniversary of his epic victory.

'1973 was my very first downhill victory,' he reminded me. 'I went out of the starting gate to win the race – not just to ski the race, but to win the race. And this is a completely different approach. I had this approach when I won race after race.'

'They say you're not a true champion until you've won the Hahnenkamm,' I said, referring to the celebrated and fearsome downhill in the Austrian resort of Kitzbühel.

'I agree – because I won it four times!' he laughed.

I have also been lucky enough to ski more than once with Tommy Moe, the 1994 Olympic downhill champion, with Stein Eriksen, the celebrated giant slalom gold medallist in the 1952 Oslo Games, and have interviewed the great Austrian champion Hermann Maier in Portillo, Chile, and Vienna.

Then there were those unscheduled lunches with Clint Eastwood and Princess Caroline, and the interview – punctuated by some skiing – with my namesake, California's Governor Schwarzenegger.

I can't claim Robert Redford is a friend, although we did have lunch while he stood over us in the restaurant at Sundance, his ski resort in Utah, and he did send my wife Vivianne a signed photograph afterwards. But the only souvenir I have from him is a letter of reply to one I sent him hoping he hadn't been upset by a tongue-in-cheek 'ski wars' feature I'd written about him and the neighbouring ski area of Snowbird, run by a Texas oilman, Dick Bass. I cherish the letter except for one thing – it's addressed to *Annie* Wilson. But when you collect memorabilia, you can't have everything.

When I covered the now-defunct Aspen 24 Hours race (in which world-class racers skied through the night at breakneck speeds) for the BBC's *Ski Sunday* programme as both reporter and spare cameraman, the highlight for me was not filming interviews with the British team, Martin and Graham Bell, although they are heroic figures to me – it was chatting to Cindy Crawford on the stage at the end of the 24-hour endurance race. Even though her main concern was to steer me away from the back of the stage in case I toppled down the gap onto the snow…

It was also in Aspen that I skied with the tennis champion Chrissie Evert. She told me her then husband, Andy Mill – a former member of the US ski team who'd been to two Winter Olympics – had joked that if ever she dumped him, he would release a film of her first ungainly attempts to ski that he'd shot while he was teaching her. Although they eventually did part, as far as I know he never carried out this threat. However, by coincidence I had seen quite a lot of Adam Faith professionally in East Sussex when he was having his two year affair with her in the early 80s and I was 'doorstepping' him in the hope of getting the story. He never gave me a decent quote about their relationship but, to his credit, he was always unerringly polite and friendly.

I never saw Evert play at Wimbledon, but I did have tea there with Susan Hampshire once after the whole day's play had finally been rained off. I knew Susan through her brother John, who ran a wonderful hotel in Filzmoos, one of Austria's prettiest ski resorts. I often used to telephone her for quotes to go with some of my skiing features, but as an actress she was discouraged from skiing in case she broke something, or even got a skiing tan which could have caused problems for the make-up department.

Some of the saddest stories I heard from a skier were the reports of abuse suffered by Michael Edwards, rather better known as Eddie the Eagle, from members of the public – precisely the people who, you might think, would admire his pluck and his persistence, often against all odds. Long before he became famous, I had skied with him at a race training camp in Austria, and he was truly an excellent skier, even with pretensions of getting into the British team. But he was too old. We are talking here about alpine skiing, not ski jumping. Few people realise how good he was. He took up ski jumping as an alternative to downhill because so few British skiers had tried it.

Recently one tour operator offered clients a chance to ski in Alberta, with the suggestion that they could really go for it without the need to be 'wimps like Eddie the Eagle'. One thing Eddie was not, at the 1988 Calgary Winter Olympics, was a wimp, and I'd love to see the people who penned such a gormless, asinine remark having to stand at the top of any Olympic ski jump and to watch their faces at the prospect of having to jump off it on skis. Being treated like an amiable clown because of his brave but hardly successful performances in Calgary was all very well, and he took it on his jutting chin. But sometimes teasing a figure of fun can turn to jeers and abuse, as he told me back in 1990 when the wounds were still raw. He did stress, however, that most people treated him with affection. 'But there are a few vicious people out there who don't like the fact that I am so popular,' he said.

Edwards told me: 'For a time, I couldn't go to a pub, or anything like that, because you know when blokes get together, and they have a few pints, they can take the piss, and also take their anxieties and the personal pressures of their lives out on me, and they start saying: You're a c**t, you're a bastard, and everything else, and You're a bloody lousy skier, and all the rest of it. This was happening everywhere in the UK. I've had a few nasty phone calls, some really nasty letters – Why do people love you when you're such a prat, you're ugly, this kind of thing, they're horrible – and I had to hide them from my then girlfriend. I've even been abused by people when I fill up at petrol stations. One woman came up to my car in Bedford and started really shouting and blasting at me, saying: Who the hell do you think you are, you're nothing, you're a crap skier, and all this kind of thing. We drove off to my girlfriend's house and they almost drove into the drive and my girlfriend told them to get lost. It would never have happened in Canada or America. They're great over there. But the Brits are a certain sort of breed.'

So what sort of 'breed' does Edwards see himself as being? 'Fun-loving, likeable, very approachable,' he said. Anything else? 'Kind, considerate, affectionate, loving, very courageous. Oh yes, and very daft, and very stupid!'

John Dunn, the late 'gentle giant of broadcasting', and Gloria Hunniford, on both of whose Radio 2 shows I was a guest when various ski books of mine were published, each provided me with some nice diary tales. I first met Gloria in tricky circumstances. She and her first husband had just separated and, wearing my *Sunday People* hat. I was sent to 'doorstep' her at her home in Sevenoaks. While I was waiting for her I met her son Michael. Both would be part of my life later: Gloria forgave me and became a friend. And Michael ended up running a hugely successful company producing in-flight magazines, and commissioned me on a number of occasions to write for *easyJet* magazine about skiing. Strange how life turns out.

I often quote Gloria when I am writing about the Swiss ski resort of Wengen. She had hurt her shoulder playing tennis, and spent a week in Wengen unable to ski. Yet simply strolling around the village, having plenty of hot chocolate and watching the mountain railways come and go, she always maintained she had a wonderful time and was never bored.

I remember asking Dunn, a passionate skier who normally preferred the slopes of Flaine in France, how he got fit for skiing. Dunn, one of the best loved voices on radio, who presented a daily show on the network for more than 30 years, and was named Radio Personality of the Year three times, was an unusually tall (6ft 7in) man. But unlike the reporter and former newscaster Sandy Gall who used to tell me he was too tall to ski down hill (his excuse for preferring cross-country), Dunn never had a problem with alpine skiing. 'I do a few physical jerks to keep fit,' he said: 'an amalgam of various exercises I've tried over the years which I go through most days. Nothing really wildly strenuous at all. One is always told you should try to raise your heartbeat, and discretely and rather shame-facedly I try to do this – wearing out the sitting-room carpet in the process…

'You don't become addicted to it in the sense of how you can when you're jogging, but you feel that you've ratted on yourself if you don't. On the other hand it's a wonderful way of rewarding yourself – by not doing it. You say to yourself: Right, I have earned the right not to do them. But then you'd have terrible puritan feelings again afterwards, and then you'd have to get back on the straight and narrow again. I work in a system of rewards – you're only allowed to do this if you've done that. It's quite a good system. But to be absolutely honest about it, I wouldn't do these exercises at all if I didn't want to go skiing in the winter. There's nothing admirable about it.

'The curious thing about this particular sport is that it actually acts as a sort of lure, and I know that if I don't in fact keep my joints moving to a certain extent, it will be quite impossible to ski when the time comes round. So even in the middle of summer I'm conscious of the fact that the reason I'm going through this stupid routine is not actually to keep fit, it's to make sure that when February comes round I will be able to move the appropriate joints in order to propel myself down the slopes.'

As for the professionals, Konrad Bartelski, the only British male skier ever to stand on a World Cup podium, had a typically iconoclastic attitude to getting fit when I questioned him on the subject. 'I play golf. Tennis...'

Any exercises?

'Never. Never. Exercises are like homework from school. You know you've got to do it. You don't want to do it. And most of the time you don't do it. But you're thinking about it. And because you haven't done it, you depress yourself more than you would have done if you weren't doing any. I'd much rather take part in a game where your mind is being tested and your body is being tested which is more enjoyable than doing something that's just routine. If you enjoy it, you'll do more if it.

'Well of course I did take part in a specific training programme when I was racing. Skiing covers every muscle in your body and no matter how much training you did, you'd still find muscles you hadn't tweaked. So you had to be very versatile in what you were doing – you had to do a bit of everything. In some ways sport in itself, as long as you're pushing yourself to the maximum, is the best form of training. The other point is if you're just moving around, instead of taking the lift, just walk up the stairs. Instead of taking the escalator at airports or the underground, take the stairs, make yourself more mobile which you can do almost anywhere.

This is better than trying to do some exercise for 10 or 15 minutes at night.'

Bartelski's World Cup efforts were most vividly described by David Vine, the most authoritative voice of skiing of his generation – even though he'd never properly learnt to ski (he just sounded as though he knew what he was talking about, and actually he did). Even Graham Bell, an excellent replacement, and veteran of five Winter Olympics – now *he* can ski! – once admitted to me that he used to listen to tapes of Vine's commentary in order to brush up his own broadcasting technique. I used to be slightly scornful of Vine's lack of skiing experience until I met him one day on a flight back to London from Geneva. The poor chap, who must have been well over six feet tall, with the inevitable long legs that go with that kind of height, was wedged so tightly into his economy seat that he could scarcely move. We got chatting and I found him so self-effacing and charming that I became an instant fan.

There's a great Alpine story about David Gower, the former England cricket captain, and the rental car he 'lost' under the ice of the frozen lake at the celebrated Swiss winter resort of St Moritz. He certainly enjoyed something of a playboy reputation, as the *Observer* noted in a feature to mark his 50th birthday in 2007: 'He hurtled down the Cresta Run, wrote off a hire car on a frozen lake and – most notoriously – buzzed an England tour match against Queensland in a rented Tiger Moth biplane during the winter of 1990-91. This earned him a £1,000 fine and banishment from all the next summer's Tests against West Indies.'

(The Tiger Moth incident happened soon after the car-in-the-lake episode, so one assumes he hadn't yet abandoned his 'enfant terrible' reputation.)

Gower was a regular on the Cresta throughout the late 80s. The first time he announced plans to try it, in 1986, the former England captain Peter May was chairman of the England selectors, and he was questioned about Gower's intentions. He was asked: 'Is this what you think your captain and senior players should be doing a couple of weeks before the West Indies tour?'

Gower told me. '…And he, God bless him, told them: I'm sure they're going to be very sensible about it. He didn't actually say we must come home immediately. I was saying of course we won't do anything silly, and No, of course we won't go down the Cresta… So of course we did! '

Four years later, in 1990, it was once again the Cresta that indirectly triggered the car-in-the-lake drama. 'Perhaps you don't want to go into it?' I asked Gower slightly nervously. 'Well I can't go into it now,' he joked. Phew. He was happy to talk about it. 'I was bloody glad to get out of it – put it that way!

'There were three of us – and we'd come across to do the Cresta again. We'd hired a car in Zurich. It was a three-way split on the car. We'd driven up to St Moritz, no problem. Lambie [England team-mate Allan Lamb] and some of his friends had come by train a day later.

'He and I were having a private race between the two of us – a race within a race. The rules of racing at the club are that you should be out with your toboggan on the ice half an hour before the race. We arrived 15 minutes before the race. Unfortunately for Lambie he was spotted contravening the rules of racing – by arriving too late. So when it came to the race itself – announcement over the tannoy, Gower to the box please – off I went – did a 50 second-point-something – not particularly quick. And then about ten slots after me – Allan Lamb to the box please – arriving but not racing. So our man went down and recorded a 49-something-something. So he beat me on time. But when the official timesheets were printed up at the end of the race it said Lambie had been disqualified. It was a moral victory for him and I had to apologise when I took the trophy – a bottle of champagne.

'I said: Yes, I do appreciate that you raced extremely well today, Allan, but…. Unfortunately it turned into a huge night. Drank the champagne. Went out for dinner. Went down to the King's Club. Lambie and his party were leaving the following day by rail again. And unusually for him he had an early night. At about 3 o'clock in the morning we're still down at the King's Club and someone says: What about the car then?'

Gower and friends went back to the car, and for a while had fun ice-driving on the lake but eventually, before dawn, decided it was finally time for bed and started looking for a ramp to drive off the ice onto terra firma. 'But we got too close to the end of the lake,' said Gower. 'And when I saw the white of the ice turn to grey in the headlamps, I thought that wasn't a good sign. Brakes don't work too well on ice, and so we slid into the middle of the grey bit. Stopped. Opened a door or two. And thought – water! Basically there was water everywhere – let's get out of here before anything else happens! So we got out. Walked to the thicker ice – only five yards way, but there was a difference! And we looked at the car and said: What are we going to do now? You can see the situation. We've cracked the ice, and we've got however many hundredweight of Opal Vectra mid-range saloon from Zurich in about a foot of water. It doesn't seem to be going anywhere. Went back, turned the lights off, shut the doors, took a ski bag or two out of the boot, thought, save the chains for later... I thought, well I'm not going to reverse this out, am I? Not much traction in there for us. And I thought, only thing we can do is leg it. Can't do much now. AA aren't around at 4 o'clock in the morning!

'So we walked back to town, with the bottom of my cord trousers freezing up nicely – stand them up easily by the time we got back to the hotel room. The only people awake are some taxi drivers outside the Palace Hotel who are not speaking English, so I thought, oh sod it, I'll just go to bed. We'll sort this out in the morning.

'Woke up in the morning. Missed the early alarm call. Phone the hotel manager. I said: Heinz, do us a favour will you? I think I left my car on the lake last night. Can you send someone out to make sure it's still there please? Fifteen minutes later he gets back to me and says: Mr Gower, there is no car on the lake.

'Are you sure?'

'Yes'.

'Ah. Thanks Heinz. Then I think the car is at the bottom of the lake.

'They're very protective of their lakes – and their water. The gist of it was – there wasn't much I could do. The insurance wasn't going to cover it, because it wasn't the sort of place you're meant to be driving hire cars – you're meant to stick to roads, and stuff like that. Basically I had in effect to pay for the car, pay for the police divers to fish it out. As soon as there was a thaw in the lake they could get in there. And it became a very expensive long weekend. It was unfortunate. Car was valued at about 21,000 Swiss francs –and it came out of it valued at 1,000. The police probably took up about 5,000 Swiss francs. Wasn't very clever in the end. But the upshot was we were delighted to be alive and well and kicking. Every now and then I have the odd little nightmare about what could have been. By and large I'm grateful it remains a good story rather than anything more serious.'

I once helped Heston Blumenthal out after his glasses were smashed in a collision with a snowboarder when he and I were with a group of my fellow ski writers in Ischgl, Austria. Luckily I happened to have a very good spare pair, which I lent him for the last couple of days of our trip. I am still waiting for an invitation as his guest at his restaurant, the Fat Duck…

For the record, as it were, I should mention, I suppose, the achievement I am best known for. It would be strange, really, to leave it out. In 1994 I skied every day for the entire year, accompanied by my then French girlfriend, Lucy Dicker. All told, during the *Financial Times* Round The World Expedition, we visited 240 ski areas in 13 countries (including skiing in the Andes, the Himalayas, Australasia, Japan and more than 100 ski areas in North America) thus entering the *Guinness Book of Records* while writing about our adventures every Saturday in the *FT* that year.

Chapter 22
Calm down, dears

Like Barbara Cartland, the film director and bon viveur Michael Winner cut his writing teeth on the world of diary stories. He wrote a newspaper column, Michael Winner's Showbiz Gossip, in the *Kensington Post* when he was only 14.

But where did people like him, and later the likes of Nigel Dempster, Paul Callan, Bill Deedes or even me, get their stories from? As I mentioned in the opening chapters, 'diary' stories could come from all manner of sources. And strangely, though 'diaries' were sometimes referred to as gossip columns, idle gossip was rarely one of them – unless the gossip could be checked out and 'copper-bottomed', the Fleet Street term for ensuring a story's accuracy.

Of course some stories could be – and often were – if not completely fabricated, certainly embellished or enhanced. Quotes could certainly be made up, and attributed to 'sources' or 'close friends'. I recall one diary columnist who would sometimes invent quotes, and justify them by saying: 'Well, it's the kind of thing he would have said – or should have said!'

But to get back to sources: in my case I would telephone celebrities on a regular basis, and for that I needed a good contacts book. Winner obviously had one of those. Contacts I got to know best would allow themselves to be wined and dined and often, if not always, produced good stories during the meal. Unlike a phone call, they were unable to end the conversation by putting the phone down. They were, if you like, trapped, but usually happily so.

Other 'sources' included events, especially parties: book-launches were always worth going to, and often productive. Diary stories even walked into the newspapers. It was quite common at the old Express building in Fleet Street for people to walk in off the street and ask to speak to a reporter. These visitors – early versions of 'citizen journalists' if you like – were 'tipsters' who would hope to be paid for their efforts. Busy news desks would sometimes fob them off with diary writers rather than news reporters, since diarists were sometimes regarded as rather foppish second-class citizens by self-important news hounds. But sometimes a great news story might start in a diary column.

Some quite skilful diary tipsters would be journalists working from home, scouring local newspapers and magazines, scissors in hand, and cutting out bits and pieces in the hope that one or more of them 'offered exclusively' might make a diary paragraph or even hit the jackpot as a showbiz page lead.

Then there were the doormen, restaurant owners, hotel concierges and the club managers, either keen to gain publicity for their establishments or to make a little extra pin money by putting in a call to the diaries.

Fleet Street's finest often didn't bother to take the bait when they received 'celebrity alerts' from these 'professional' sources; their tip-offs often turned out to be wishful thinking on the management's part, especially if they emanated from place like the London Hippodrome and Stringfellows. In too many cases the 'big names' would turn out to be a permutation of people like Sue Pollard, a rather worse-for-wear Peter Cook or Tony Blackburn.

But on one occasion, following up such a call, young Winner hit the jackpot and turned up one of the funniest diary stories of the day.

Tipped off that 'some royals' were expected at a Mayfair nightclub, he strolled along fairly unenthusiastically. The resulting story has virtually become Fleet Street folklore, although few people realise that the reporter was Michael Winner. As he recalled when we spoke towards the end of 2010…

'Ex- King Constantine of Greece and ex-King Michael of Romania turned up. And the doorman said: "Are you members?" Whereupon the owner, Rico d'Ajou, rushed over, hit the doorman, and said: "Wha'd'ya mean, are they members? Get a table for these fucking kings immediately!"…'

I once wrote a limerick about him:

An overweight gourmet called Winner
Went to drastic extremes with his dinner
'It's just lettuce pie'
He said with a sigh,
'It's my desperate attempt to get thinner!'

Well of course Mr Winner has lost a lot of weight since I wrote that. 'I lost 52 pounds well before going down with a bacterial infection closely followed by picking up a hospital superbug,' he told me, making it quite clear that it was will power and not hospital that had shed the pounds. 'As a result I wrote a diet book – *Michael Winner's Fat Pig Diet* – which sold very well, and was chosen by *The Times* as one of the three best diet books on the market. It still sells well.'

Fortunately he also recovered from his life-threatening illness, and was spared for the nation. After the debacle of my attempted phone call to him (prompted by Harry Fowler) when he slammed the phone down after 20 seconds, I never expected to find myself in his palatial home in Holland Park, in west London. But here I was, on assignment with the *Daily Express*, to interview him about a subject the newspaper was keen to discuss: no, not food. Money. His money.

Late in 2010, Winner had allegedly (and by design) gone £9 million into the red, explaining: 'I have an opulent lifestyle and it goes on private planes, restaurants, chauffeurs, and I have quite a big staff'. It was quickly pointed out, however, that Winner was worth in excess of an estimated £35 million, 'and shouldn't have too much trouble paying it all back'.

Back in 1990, when I interviewed him at his London home, the financial landscape was rather different. Interest rates were high. And all the prices Winner refers to are obviously from around 20 years ago. On the tape I have of our interview, you can hear him lighting up cigars in mid-sentence and puffing away as he speaks.

Recalling his days in newspapers, he said: 'I never had any money at all, at first, because I was very badly paid... In newspapers in the '50s I remember very well I was earning £27 a week on the *Evening*

Standard, with rather generous expenses, and as you journalists know, the expenses [back then!] get you more than your salary, and I was getting about £40 a week expenses. When I was making my little documentary films I was getting about £30 a week or less – £20 a week. But I started getting a little money around the late '60s and from then on I had enough. I sort of struggled on and on and on, and eventually they gave films to younger people because these pop stars came into movies. And I had Billy Fury in *Play it Cool*, and Dick Lester had Helen Shapiro in *It's Trad Dad*. And that took me into feature films – fairly slowly. From the mid '60s I actually started to get salaries that meant something, and occasionally I got some profits. It wasn't really until *The Jokers*, which was quite a successful comedy I made, which did bring some profit, that the money started to go up a bit.

'I always laugh when people say I became a millionaire from the *Death Wish* films. I haven't had any profit from any of the *Death Wish* films because the bookkeeping has been so... extraordinary. I haven't actually had a penny, and I'm always slightly riled when I hear people say I've made all this money from them.

'There is a rather true saying, of course, that money can't buy you happiness. But it's much nicer to be unhappy in comfort. It's not so much that you rush out and spend it, but that you can if you want to. If you buy well, you can just have clothes altered. I used to buy suits for about £50 or £60, but when I got fat, and I hadn't bought any clothes for about 20 years, I was in shock when I went out and bought a single jacket that was £700 off the peg. I couldn't believe the prices. So I think it's nice to have money.'

He continued: 'I've never spent money on girls, and I have to say that's contrary to the myth that girls are after money. I have never found any girls in England or America or anywhere else who are after money. You offer to buy them something occasionally and they actually try to stop you. This idea that young beautiful girls are after men with money for their money I have never found to be true. Quite the contrary. They quite frequently buy me things, and I say please don't spend your money on me. You can't buy women, in my opinion. They just want to be entertained, in one way or another.

'Another thing I would strongly advise people to do is to spend money on enjoying themselves. There's nothing worse, I think, than people who deprive themselves to save for a rainy day. They should buy something that gives them pleasure. Then they're ahead of the game. The money has given them a memory of pleasure. I've never done it myself, to be honest, I've never spent enough money. I'm only just doing it now, putting in a swimming pool. I should have done it years ago. I only got myself a chauffeur after running thorough the rain for parking meters for years on end. I can never get those days back. I strongly advise people to spend money because if they enjoy it they've had benefit from it for sure. Nobody can take that away.

'It is always amusing, I think, that when you go with a bank, who make endless mistakes in your account, whether you have a great deal of money or a little, that the mistakes are always in their favour. I've never known a bank mistake in a client's favour. I have a file of bank errors going back 15 years or more, and the only reason I don't change the bank is I think they're all in it. But the funny thing is there is not one error in my favour. It's all in their favour. Having said that, people should mistrust financial advisers, and basically mistrust the stock market.

'I think the awful thing is that when you trust an expert with your money, you then go back and you say I've found this wonderful chap and he's going to do me well. But most of them don't do you well. If the stock market goes up, they do you well – if you sell at the right time. If it goes down they do you badly. None of their skills have very much to do with it.

'At the time I started to put my money with this beautifully dressed and beautifully officed group, I also started to buy paintings for one of my first apartments – I'm going back to 1964-65. And I stood in the auction rooms, trembling at the thought of wasting my money on these silly paintings when I had these wonderful financial advisers who were going to do so well with it. What happened of course is that the paintings quadrupled in value, went up ten-fold, twenty-fold and even thirty-fold and furthermore gave me great pleasure – because it gives you no pleasure to know that the bank has got your stocks and shares there, and may well lose them, whereas it gave me great pleasure to look at the paintings, most of which, if not all of which, I still have. And they have gone up greatly in value. And I do think that if I were a young person today, I would buy modest antiques if I couldn't afford great antiques, because there's a very true saying that if you buy cheap, you buy twice. That is a wonderful saying. If you go and buy a modern table from any multiple furniture shop, and try and sell it, you'll be lucky, if you paid £500 for it, if, a year later, you can get £20. You'll be very lucky if you can get anyone to take it away. If you buy an antique table, it will undoubtedly go up, and you can put it in any sale room in the country, and at least get your money back, or see it go up a bit. Although there are an enormous number of fake antiques about, and an enormous number of fake pictures about – many of them in the poshest galleries in London – many of them described at auction as one thing, but are in fact another.'

[The ITN newscaster Ivor Mills once admitted to me that he'd bought a fake – deliberately. He was sent to cover a London exhibition of the works of David Stein, the celebrated art forger who made a fortune by faking pictures in the styles of Picasso, Chagall, Matisse and Klee, and he ended up buying one. It was in the style of Picasso's *Les Femmes d'Alger*. 'It's probably the nearest I shall get to owning a Picasso,' he said. 'I certainly couldn't afford the real thing…']

'If you buy 10 or 20 things,' continued Winner, 'even with no knowledge, the chances are you'll do better, in my view, than going into the stock market, and you will have the pleasure of it and you can use it for ever. And thank God, in 1964 I bought rather good furniture which in those days you could buy in the low hundreds, and it will see me through life. And if I ever have to sell it because my career collapses, I will do awfully well out of it. In fact I am selling a table, in auction, which I paid £10,000 for which I have no doubt at all will fetch £30,000, and that's over a period of about six years.'

Winner lit another cigar, and said, through clenched teeth: 'I'm selling it because I'm building a swimming pool in the basement and I've got to re-arrange the furniture. I hate selling anything, actually. It's a wonderful table. A George III table. I don't need the money, but I've got nowhere to store it, nowhere to put it.

'My advice on the whole is to be quite cautious. I would advise people if they have a business on their own, to invest in themselves. At least they're in control of their money. Invest in yourself. Because you can trust yourself. And many people who start small, perhaps selling goods from a barrow, or selling goods from the market – become multi-millionaires. And I can think of many young girls, who could be described, quite incorrectly, as bimbos, who I've gone out with over the years, some of whom have done unbelievably well in business. I had one young actress here with very big bosoms who used to go around giggling a lot and everyone thought she was extremely silly, but she had a nose for business and by the age of 23 she was employing 600 people in factories in Miami. She was an English girl, making clothing. And she has an enormous business – and she did it entirely on her own. And there was another girl I went out with in America who was a very famous beauty queen. This girl, one would have thought, was only capable of choosing shoes or clothes, and she suddenly told me she was going to real estate school, aged about 30, and we all thought it would take her the first year to learn how to spell *house*. And I have to tell you that three years later she was one of the biggest real estate agents in Los Angeles, and is today a multi millionairess. I do think this is a good example where a lot of people, particularly women, think for some reason that the management of money or the management of business is beyond them because they are conditioned to think this by men. But they are marvellous businesswomen. A lot of these very pretty girls... I'd much rather trust them with my money than these men in three-piece suits.

'I have given a great deal of money away to people who are hard up, people I know. But if I don't know them that well and they ask to borrow £5,000 or £10,000, what I tend to do is say: Look, here's

£500, have it, it's a gift, but please don't aggravate me because I know you may not give it back. So I don't mind giving money away but I hate lending money because then you expect a return and I'd rather not do that.

'I wouldn't want to be broke. I think you'd have to find out the hard way and I'd rather not. I think people who haven't got there financially get a bit bitter and say Why are other people having all this and not me? I've never regretted anything I've spent money on because I'm rather good at my luxuries. I've sometimes spent rather a lot on a painting but it's always been very good. I've never thought I've made a ghastly mistake and it's actually very ugly. I must admit that occasionally I've bought film scripts and said Why did I spend money on that?

'People spend a lot of money on cars. I have four cars and most of them are 25 years old. [Remember: this was back in 1990.] I have a Rolls Royce Phantom 5 which everyone thinks looks incredible. I paid £8,000 for it. That car today is £350,000. I have a Mercedes – sports car – it goes perfectly well – it's 26 years old. I paid £4,000 for it. If you buy a really good car, second hand, check it out carefully, the chances are it will well outlast the family car that people are buying, and furthermore it will increase in value. I've also got a 1975 Bentley which I paid £8,000 for about three years ago, and that's doing me very well, and I've had nothing wrong with it at all. The only car I have had trouble with was a Ferrari I paid £33,000 for, which has been rusting in the garage for seven years and done about 17,000 miles. That's the only new car I've bought in donkey's years – probably 26 years – and it's taught me a lesson.

'I had a mother who as you may know lost £3million pounds at the Cannes casino during the '70s and that, in today's money (1990), is £10million. And she used to sell all the paintings and furniture left to me by my father to pay for the previous night's debts. And she was, all her life, an inveterate gambler. I only resent it because when she sold these paintings, they were paintings that I particularly liked which my father had bought saying One day these will be yours.... I can see the paintings clearly now, and I resent the loss of beauty, not the loss of something worth money

194

because I would never have sold them anyway – I would have died first. But it made me very cautious. I've never managed to buy any of them back. They were all sold in the south of France and sold to dealers. In a way I don't resent it because it made her happy. She enjoyed herself at the casinos, she was a big shot in the casinos, so somewhat on the principle that it at least gave her happiness, I don't resent it. In a way I'm rather glad.

'But it's made me quite cautious with money. I actually don't spend very much other than on paintings and furniture, general living, food and drink. I don't take holidays because I don't have time. So actually I don't spend that much. I had a plate of muesli for lunch today and so my lunch probably cost about 30p. I'd rather be healthy.'

Healthy that is, apart from the cigars?

'Well cigars are very erratic. I sometimes smoke a lot and I sometimes don't smoke at all because I had some heart problems some years ago and they told me to stop. Today is a bad day. I've probably smoked six or seven. But I also have a number of weeks when I smoke none at all. But I do smoke far too much, and spend far too much and it's a stupid exercise. The cigar I'm smoking now is about £15 of cigar and that is really stupid because it's damaging to your health and quite useless and I'm on the verge of stopping which will distress the press greatly because they like to say I'm a cigar-chewing moron…'

Thank you Michael. That was certainly a longer interview than the one we had on the phone!

Chapter 23
Old friends

Somehow or other a few VIP contacts become friends and never go away. Over the years the original link or raison d'être for the relationship is gradually forgotten. I can name these people on the fingers of two hands.

As I've mentioned, Col John Blashford-Snell and I have been chums for more than 30 years. Likewise the brilliant ski racer Franz Klammer (20 years). Ken Bruce – the most delightful and skilful of broadcasters – and I still have lunch in London at least once a year (always in the same Turkish restaurant near Broadcasting House) having first met in the 1980s. Many years ago I 'did a Crawford' with Ken and wrote about the break up of his first marriage as details were bound to come out eventually, and he was happy for me to get the story right when it was first published. I also had the bright idea – many years ago – of enlisting Terry Wogan's support for Ken when it seemed (quite wrongly) that Ken's slot on Radio 2 might be under threat. Wogan was happy to oblige.

What was much happier was breaking the news of Ken's third marriage when he 'fell for the porcelain complexion and high-cheek bones of Kerith Coldham', an attractive researcher on Jimmy Young's programme. 'Oddly enough, we didn't meet at Broadcasting House,' he told me. 'We met at the Eurovision Song Contest in Birmingham [he was the regular Radio 2 presenter of the contest]. We needed an extra pair of hands and Kerith volunteered. We got on rather well, and went on holiday together to Hong Kong. We found we had a great deal in common: we both laugh a lot and enjoy the theatre, opera, the cinema, chocolates and champagne, even though we can't afford them all at once.'

Amusingly, Ken always maintained that even though Wogan earned more than him, he (Bruce) was 'more expensive to run.' The Irish chatter went on for so long when Wogan was broadcasting his daily radio programme that there was hardly any time left for records. Bruce, on the other hand, reckoned he cost the BBC far more in record rights fees. 'When I started, I was trying to work my way in gently and unobtrusively, so I didn't say very much in between records. It cost the BBC a fortune in needle-time. Terry's programme was very much cheaper...'

What's remarkable about Ken is the way he is able to 'chat' by email in between records. I sometimes email him when he's on the air, thinking he'll get back to me some time after the show. But almost invariably, back comes a reply there and then. And you'd never guess from his seamless performance that he's replied.

One of my favourite stories (indirectly) involving Ken concerns a bizarre incident in 1979 in which a young BBC announcer was 'tested' to see whether he could be tricked into telling listeners (erroneously, of course) that the Queen was dead. Bruce was then working on Radio Scotland's *Night Beat in Glasgow* when a new, inexperienced announcer, Robert Sproul-Cran, took a call on the hot-line from the head of Radio Scotland in Edinburgh. He was told the Queen was dead.

'Robert was no fool,' Ken told me, 'and immediately thought he was being set some kind of trap. Are you genuinely telling me the Queen has died? he asked. The reply, once more was: I am telling you the Queen is dead. Now you tell me what you are going to do about it.'

Bruce relates that Sproul-Cran was now convinced it was a set-up.

'He said to me later that he could have put the phone down and gone into full Royal Death scenario. Robert said he had continued the conversation for a little while... but likened his approach to humouring a bore in the pub. Needless to say, he had not taken the station off the air to begin playing funeral music.

'The likelihood was that our esteemed bosses would not remember the conversation in the morning, but to protect himself I suggested Robert ought to write a full report in his log. Within hours, the ordure had hit the air-conditioning. Resignations were required. The Head of Radio Scotland went, as did his deputy.'

Another long serving chum who was close to both me and my wife Vivianne was John Gardner, the thriller writer who penned some 14 James Bond books after Ian Fleming died. He was never completely happy doing the 'bloody Bond' books. 'It was a job I shouldn't really have taken on,' he told me. 'On the other hand I couldn't really turn it down. There was even a clause in my contract not to reveal who my favourite Bond actor was.' It was Connery, of course.

'It always struck me as being strange that Bond conformed so much to habit – the last thing someone in that job would do. He drove a Bullnose Bentley, which is rather drawing attention to yourself, and wherever he went in the world he knew the barman – Ah Mr Bond, how nice to see you again – I kind of changed that.' As the official Bond author, he used to have a Bentley Mulsanne Turbo on permanent loan.

Gardner, who died in 2007, was a workaholic and recovered alcoholic who even in his 81st year was still writing at all hours. He worked every day – even a little on Christmas Day. 'I work because I am scared stiff of losing the ability to put words together,' he said. 'Touch wood, it's never happened, but I have nightmares that it might.'

His fictional characters included the cowardly secret agent Boysie Oakes (introduced in *The Liquidator* in 1964, the first of a series Gardner described as 'born in the hope of being an amusing counter-irritant to the excesses of the many imitators of 007') and Big Herbie Kruger (who first appeared in *The Nostradamus Traitor* in 1979). He also expanded and developed Arthur Conan Doyle's Moriarty in *The Return of Moriarty* in 1974, followed by two other Moriarty books.

Gardner took over the Bond books in 1981 (Kingsley Amis had written one after Ian Fleming's death in 1964). 'What I wanted to do,' he told me, 'was bring Fleming's Bond into the eighties.'

In an extraordinarily varied early career, Gardner had started out as an Anglican priest, but after five years had a crisis over his faith, which contributed to serious drink problems and a brief career as a Marine commando. 'I must have been the worst commando in the world,' he reported. 'I bent an aeroplane I was learning to fly. They say a Tiger Moth's undercarriage will stay intact no matter how hard it bounces, but I am the living proof that it doesn't.'

Gardner's first – and only non-fiction – book, *Spin the Bottle* (1964), chronicled the agonies he went through with his habit of two bottles of gin a day. A member of the Magic Circle, he said: 'If I were still a magician I'd now be playing the northern clubs and I'd be down-at-heel, seedy and a chronic alcoholic.'

Instead he became a drama critic, covering the Royal Shakespeare Company for the *Stratford-upon-Avon Herald*, for which he worked in the late 1950s and early 1960s. He would often get a lift to work from Peter Hall, then director of the fledgling RSC. During his time at the *Herald*, Gardner visited Moscow with the RSC with Peter Brook and Paul Scofield.

In 1989 Gardner moved to the United States, where he lived in opulent style near Charlottesville, Virginia, but then a series of medical crises left him 'financially drained'.

[In a *Financial Times* interview, I had described these as a 'fearsome litany of life-threatening illnesses'. Starting with prostate cancer, 'they came thick and fast, with barely enough time between each to recover before the next assault: a minor heart attack, temporary blindness in one eye caused by problems with a carotid artery, pneumonia, and then what appeared to be terminal cancer.']

Gardner described some of his treatment thus: 'They said 'Ah, swallow this camera' which I did. When they told me I had oesophageal cancer, I remember saying 'I'd better go and make my peace with God, hadn't I?' Fortunately I was no longer an agnostic, which I had been after giving up the priesthood. But they said: 'Oh no, we can do something about that. And they did. But by then the medical bills had wiped out half a million dollars – our entire life savings. I spent a fortune on staying alive.'

On return to the UK in 1997, Gardner's wife, Margaret (with tragic irony), unexpectedly died herself, leaving him living alone in reduced circumstances and faced with the prospect of re-establishing his career in Britain. 'Short of funds and temporarily without a British publisher,' he recalled, 'I withdrew to a cottage in

Basingstoke, administered by a charity, and went about re-igniting my career. At first nobody was really interested. I went from huge success to John Who? in zero seconds flat.' But a publisher was finally found. Refusing to remain in the dumps, Gardner even chose an uplifting email address, JollyJG.

Apart from being fuelled by a chronic shortage of funds, Gardner's stubborn determination to keep writing was also partly inspired by a new character, Suzie Mountford, a World War 2 detective sergeant who was the heroine of a five-novel saga. Mountford just happened to be the surname of a teenage sweetheart who had 'dumped' him for no apparent reason some 50 years earlier

This produced an extraordinary and poignant real-life sequel which I offered to Richard Kay on the *Daily Mail*. It was the column's main story, under the headline 'Bond that never died'.

'By including the surname of an old sweetheart as the romantic lead in his latest yarn, *Bottled Spider*' the story ran, 'Gardner... has reignited a passion from 50 years ago. It all came about because his old flame picked up a copy of the saga and was intrigued enough about the appearance of her name to contact the publishers.'

Gardner, a widower, had confided in me: 'I told a few people that the character was based on memories of a lovely girl, Patricia Mountford, to whom I was engaged – then dumped by – in 1948-49 Cambridge.' He and Patricia (who went on to be a nurse and never married) met when he went up to Cambridge in 1947. 'We realised very quickly that we were deeply and passionately in love,' he said. 'We became engaged, but in October 1949, she broke it off. Nobody else was involved but I was devastated. I learnt that when a woman doesn't want you, there's little you can do but walk away.

'Then a few months ago I received a letter from her and we met again after all these years. I think it took about five minutes, maybe less, to realise that little had changed.' Our meeting again was like rolling back the years, feeling like teenagers in 70-plus year old bodies.'

The couple dated until Gardner's death. Vivianne and I have a large and very beautiful print of Venice on our wall in Haywards Heath to remember John by – left to us in his will.

Occasionally one meets a celebrity by chance, through friends or family, and establishes a relationship before starting to write about them. The thriller writer and sometime film producer Peter James is such a chum. His Swedish partner Helen is one of my wife's oldest friends. He has become so successful now that he hardly needs me as an unofficial publicist – which is nice in a way because friendship rather than PR is what binds us together. But I like to think that, for the first ten years of our friendship, stories I wrote about him helped keep him in the public eye. And his series about Roy Grace, a Brighton police superintendent, have gradually proved a huge hit, not only in Britain, but France and Germany, where he is an award-winning writer. As I was writing this, his latest Roy Grace novel, *Dead Like You*, was at number one in the UK's best selling fiction. Peter and I see as much of each other as time allows and we also enjoy skiing together.

I would hate to think that, after all the years of interviews, none of the celebrities I have met – and continue to meet – had ended up as friends. Luckily for me, this handful of chums – plus dear departed friends like Paddy Milligan, Reggie Bosanquet, H E Bates and Bill Deedes – have ensured that this didn't happen.

Chapter 24
Mentors acknowledged

I learnt my trade of diary writing – a considerable improvement on earlier teenage jobs such as washing up in a fish and chip restaurant, working as a railway dock porter in Folkestone, as a steward on a molasses tanker, and as a night porter in a seaside hotel – from four journalists to whom I will always be most grateful.

Bob Friend introduced me to the concept, but it was Paul Callan who provided me with a regular income on Londoner's Diary in the *Evening Standard* once I had fled the Bob Friend nest.

Michael Hellicar, who for some reason employed me on the *Daily Mirror* Inside Page in the early 70s, was a tremendous inspiration. Even in the days when long lunches were almost *de rigeur* in Fleet Street, I can't remember him leaving the office during working hours. Often I would return from an interview or lunch (usually both) to find him alone at his desk. Without his looking up, I would know that behind his owlish but fashionable glasses, he had noted my return. Nothing much evaded his gaze, even when he was seemingly pre-occupied with his typewriter.

From Hellicar I learnt that diaries could and should be intellectually stimulating and intriguing instead of merely social chit-chat. He inspired people who worked for him to produce quirky copy. Going to work when he was in charge was always an adventure. This proved equally true of working for Peter Tory. All this appealed to the news and current affairs flair I had somehow acquired from working on various news desks in between writing for gossip columns. I think diary skills are enhanced by having had some hard news experience. My time with Mike was regrettably limited, however, and within a few months he'd moved on to become the *Mirror* features editor. I too moved on soon afterwards to rejoin Southern Television.

Fast forward a decade or so, and I was approached to see whether I'd like to work on Peter Tory's version of the *Mirror* diary. It was the start of an unexpectedly warm and mutually beneficial relationship. At that stage I didn't really know him, except for offering him material when he was running the William Hickey column at the *Daily Express*. It wasn't long before I joined Tory and another writer, Neil Mackwood, on a new column Peter would be writing on the *Star*. It was an unlikely vehicle for Tory's talents, and it's tempting to suggest that his subtle skills were wasted there. Indeed, the columnist Peter McKay, a friend of Tory's, described him as a 'piccolo player in a Rastafarian band'. Nevertheless, it was an exhilarating column to work for and I think along with Jeanette Bishop, the 'office manager', we made a great, tight-knit team.

I feel Tory has something of Kenneth Branagh's TV character as *Wallender* on a good day about him (just the look – but not the unkempt, unshaven aspect, doom-laden, world-weary aspect of the Swedish detective. Oh, and with some humour. A lot of humour.)

Tory has an unusual background. His father Sir Geofroy was a career diplomat. Peter himself was a former actor with the Royal Shakespeare Company. He was also a passionate airman, with his own Chipmunk aeroplane. He was and is a master of whimsy, often writing about the ducks and swans on the trout lake at his former home in Oxfordshire, and a mythical grandmother he called Granny Barclay. We had regular spots in the column devoted to 'Loony Lords' (the antics of eccentric dukes, marquesses, earls, viscounts and barons) and 'One for the Tower' which focused on people guilty of distinctly unpatriotic or reprehensible deeds (sometimes including the self-same loony lords).

Mackwood and I soon realised there was little point in trying to write any stories before lunch. It had to be the afternoon, when Tory had given the day's proceedings a little more thought. Thus occasionally we would remember that after a long lunch, the cupboard was bare. On one occasion, after a particularly good feast, Tory climbed into one of the huge metal waste bins newspaper offices used to have, and dug deep into the debris. After a few moments he triumphantly produced – Neville Chamberlain-like – a piece of paper. 'I think,' he said, 'I have thought of a way of turning this press release into a very good lead story.'

After four fun-filled and usually hilarious years on the *Star* (interrupted only by my skiing exploits in the winter), I followed Tory to our final Fleet Street partnership: the *Sunday Express* diary. There were just the two of us now, and teamwork was even more essential. 'Let's write this together' was Tory's habitual and flattering *leitmotif*. We were the Ravitz and Landauer of the *Sunday Express*, with Peter now more of a mellow cello than a piccolo. We usually knew we were on to a winner if we giggled like schoolboys while were writing a story together. (Although there was always room for doubt – 'we'll be the judge of that, dear' was a familiar Tory response when I claimed to have brought 'a good story' into the office).

One of our favourites was the discovery that a sculptor, Nigel Boonham, commissioned to fashion a bust in bronze of the then Archbishop of Canterbury, Robert Runcie, had taken a dislike to Runcie whom he decided was in some ways a flawed archbishop. To this end, he mischievously built an extra dimension into the bust which was hidden from any observer. With great glee he inserted a tiny fiendish figurine of an imp (a child of the Devil) inside Runcie's head. 'It was a light-hearted thing,' claimed Boonham later, 'and not meant as serious comment. In retrospect I can see it might lead to misunderstandings, but it was not really meant as a reflection on the Archbishop.'

Methinks Boonham was perhaps protesting too much. In any case, he claimed that Runcie, when told of this mischief, simply smiled. It is rumoured that if you pick up that celebrated bust you can still hear a tiny metallic rattle.

One of Tory's greatest wheezes, while editing the William Hickey column (the most famous gossip page of Fleet Street – a position of grandeur disputed by the late Nigel Dempster) was to send an expedition, with himself Lawrence-like on the lead dromedary, to discover Basingstoke in darkest Hampshire.

Says Tory today: 'Basingstoke council had built a new ring road, and the good citizens immediately found themselves cut off from the outside world. They were trapped. Motorists, once caught on the system, could not find their way out of it. It was like that famous song, *Charlie and the MBTA*, a musical account of the underground-overground railway circle that surrounded Boston (Mass). Charlie went round and round and his relatives had to throw sandwiches through the window as it whizzed by. So it was in Basingstoke; food was thrown into passing family cars; pantechnicons, bread vans and milk floats simply disappeared.'

Tory claims he read a story that a parachutist had drifted into the vicinity and was never seen again. He also said strange clouds had been seen over the area and that rain had fallen upwards. And he disputed the belief that the tall building at the centre of Basingstoke, often poking through the ground mist, was the headquarters of the Automobile Association, the AA. He firmly believed that the structure was in fact the HQ of the AyAas, a tribe almost certainly of extra-terrestrial origins. It was the duty of the Fourth Estate, he insisted, to get to the bottom of the mystery. No authorities were taking the matter seriously.

Tory/Hickey decided to lead an expedition. It was, in style, to be turn-of-the 19th century, rather than high-tech. Camels – actually, racing dromedaries borrowed from the Marquis of Bath – were to be the transport, and a team drawn from the *Daily Express*, including a bearer, a black employee from the accounts department who agreed to strip to the waist (wouldn't be allowed today) and to carry Tory's air rifle, was assembled. It included the art critic of the *Daily Express*, John Rydon, and John Roberts, a hard-nosed reporter, who would walk ahead holding a union jack. Pith helmets and other appropriate gear were to be worn for the occasion. Tory, protected from the fierce sun with a parasol, led the expedition.

All of this, Tory reminded me over one of our recent lunches, was regarded with horror by the *Daily Express* editor, Arthur Firth. 'He was a gentle figure of conventional newspaper thinking who didn't even begin to understand it and believed his career to be at stake,' he said. However, Tory had an ally on the 'back bench' – the 'cabinet' of a national newspaper – in Lloyd Turner, the night editor, an Australian, and Tory's flatmate and future boss at the *Star*. Firth's protestations were overridden. Turner explained to the editor– 'not a man of iron in the Beaverbrook tradition' – that it was the 'Silly Season', that period of the year, August, when all proper news stopped. Significant events ceased, so papers had to make things up or write about solar eclipses and Morris dancing championships. Why not an expedition to discover Basingstoke? It could project the mood, if not the historically pressing endeavour, of the Relief of Mafeking.

It went ahead. For days before the arrival at the old city walls of Basingstoke, Hickey (Tory) – with staged pictures to illustrate the developments – reported in his column the day-to-day progress of the expedition. Finally, at the end of the week, Tory was seen squinting through his binoculars, from the fringe of a Hampshire wood, at the distant tower of the AyAas.

There had been much excitement in Basingstoke. Billboards had daily announced the approach of Hickey. A TV crew appeared. Finally the 'camels' and brave explorers arrived in the old town. Police held back the crowds. Children perched on their fathers' shoulders. Hickey/Tory dismounted and strode towards the mayor, a grey-haired and delighted figure, who was overjoyed at seeing Basingstoke finally 'discovered' and placed on the map. The pair shook hands. The huge headline on the *Daily Express* showed the picture across two pages under the headline 'BAYSINGSTOKE, I PRESUME.'

Basingstoke was relieved. 'Arthur Firth was hiding a cupboard,' says Tory, tongue-in-cheek. 'Dempster was enraged. He didn't understand it either, of course. He would shout in El Vino [the Fleet Street wine bar much frequented by diarists], 'Does anybody find Tory's Basingstoke stuff funny?'

But even Peter was once out-Tory-ed, as it were, in the most surreal way by his celebrated friend and colleague Keith Waterhouse.

One night, in a Blackpool restaurant during a Conservative party conference, Waterhouse inveigled Tory into a bet which resulted in

Tory losing his trousers. Waterhouse made off into the night with them, and Tory had to borrow a pair of chef's trousers.

Back at the bar of the Imperial Hotel, Waterhouse made himself busy introducing Tory's trousers to various Conservative party grandees, insisting they shake a proffered leg by way of greeting. In later weeks, Tory, by now wearing his own trousers again – but of course, not the missing pair – would receive sinister, late-night calls, claiming to be from his missing garment, relating, in a falsetto, northern accent, the various risqué adventures the trousers were enjoying with their new master.

Anyone who has worked on diaries may also be amused by the following example of my old boss Bob Friend's chutzpah in his dealings one night with Peter. Bearing in mind that Friend had started me off on the diary trail, and that Tory, many years later, had made a pretty good job (I like to think) of polishing my skills, I found it a fascinating story when I heard it. In one sense it was a case of the biter bit. In another it was a far more impertinent act than my habit of gate-crashing celebrities' restaurant meal-times.

One evening Friend was a guest at Tory's mother's home in Kent, along with Tory's sister and assorted party friends. 'I was regaling the assembly with anecdotes, some about my father,' says Tory. (Sir Geofroy, now retired peacefully in Ireland, is the former British ambassador to Dublin and High Commissioner in Malaya and Malta.) Half way through dinner, Bob asked permission to use the phone (a landline of course, in those days). Although Friend had closed the door behind him, Tory could hear snatches of conversation in the hall and recognised that Friend – the cheek of the fellow – was actually, there and then, filing a story about the dinner conversation. The story Bob had 'skulked out of the room to file' (Peter's own words!) concerned Sir Geofroy's diplomatic attempts to heal a rift between Duncan Sandys, the then Minister for Commonwealth Relations, who negotiated the independence of Malaysia in 1963, and Tunku Abdul Rahman, who became Malaysia's first prime minister. It involved an exchange of letters between the two men which in fact had been drafted by Sir Geofroy. 'My father was effectively writing letters to himself,' said

Tory. 'Bob couldn't wait to sell the story. He went to the front hall and closed the hall door. I heard urgent secretive murmurings to a copy-taker including the names of Sir Geofroy Tory and Duncan Sandys.' Needless to say, Tory was not amused.

Another great travelling companion in the diary world was Garth Gibbs, a South-African chum (still ruggedly good looking in that way that 'colonials' tend to enjoy) in spite of the passing years. I worked with Gibbs and for him on various diaries. He tells this story about the Queen and Paul Callan. [Callan was once a near neighbour of Tory's in Oxfordshire: Tory describes him as 'an Oscar Wildean figure, who drinks vats of fine wine, and has wit and mischief in equal parts. He is hugely larger than life. Always has been. Callan is the very last of old Fleet Street. There are no more like him.']

Says Gibbs 'Callan is a genius at getting the right person to say what he wants to be said. Take the story of the Baked Bean (cockney rhyming slang for you know who).

'The Queen once stepped off her yacht in Hong Kong and, like so many women, decided to go shopping for a bargain or two. Word leaked back to the *Daily Mirror* that 'Brenda' (as she was affectionately known in security circles) had popped in to a tailor's called Mr Soong.

'I was assigned to track the tailor down and eventually did so by phoning every Mr Soong in the Hong Kong telephone directory. After a lot of attempted Mandarin and gobbledegook, I finally got through to a Mr W W Soong. It turned out to be the right one.

'Asked about his dealings with the Queen, he said: I gave Her Majesty a very reasonable rate. Callan asked: What exactly did you make for her?'

'Mr Soong gave him detailed information about the outfits, the fabrics and even the cottons. Callan knew that the Queen's dress designer back in Britain was Norman Hartnell and she was wearing his designs when she arrived in Hong Kong,' says Gibbs. 'So he asked Mr Soong whether the Queen had asked him to make copies of the Hartnell outfits she was wearing.

'Mr Soong said she had. And added: But I gave her a very reasonable rate. Minutes later Callan was on the line to Norman Hartnell, and said: We want to quote you as saying nervously that you guess imitation is the best form of flattery.

'Hartnell agreed to the quote at once,' says Gibbs.

A couple of hours later, one of the Queen's aides was on the line. 'Brenda wants to know what you are writing,' he said.

And Callan replied: 'Tell her to buy tomorrow's newspaper.'

One of the joys of working in Fleet Street was that the very nature of the work often put writers in bizarre situations. Here, to end with, is one of the strangest it-happened-to-me anecdotes – although this one happened to my friend and former boss Mike Hellicar.

When he was writing for the *Daily Mirror* he was on an assignment in Hollywood and he was invited to a lavish birthday dinner for an old-time show business agent called Seymour Heller.

They were all standing around in a private room having a pre-dinner drink at the Beverly Hills Hotel, when the big double doors were flung open and there stood Frank Sinatra. Hellicar knew Sinatra had been invited but hadn't really believed he'd be there.

Says Mike: 'To my surprise, Sinatra gave a start of recognition when he saw me – a surprise to me because I had never met him – and he strode over with his hand outstretched. At that moment I sensed that there was trouble ahead because people drifted away and regrouped well away from us.'

Sinatra said: 'Been a long time, doc... I'd been thinking I should make an appointment to see you about a bit of a problem I've got.'

The rest of the room held its breath. Hellicar had been warned that if Sinatra showed up he wasn't to say he was a journalist – he regarded the press as his sworn enemy. However, it appeared he thought Mike was a doctor, so no introductions or obfuscations were necessary.

Dinner was called and Old Blue Eyes insisted on sitting next to Mike. Over the soup, he came to the point. 'I got trouble with the waterworks,' he said, waving his spoon towards his lap.' But all

Hellicar could think of was Ava Gardner's often-quoted description of the said area: King Donkey and then some.

Fumbling for his zip, Sinatra whispered: 'It don't feel right... It don't look right... Mike told me: 'I realised that I was going to be asked to give an expert medical opinion on the spot, so I put down a restraining hand and suggested we had a proper consultation next day. I told him I need the latest equipment, everything to hand, plus X-rays, tests, samples, so it could be sorted out for once and for all.'

By this time no-one in the room was even pretending to hold a conversation. They were all agog. 'You're right, doc', said Sinatra, just stopping short of producing the offending organ. 'Tomorrow, then.'

In the time honoured tradition of his profession, Hellicar made a quick excuse and left before the main course was served. 'My night was sleepless,' he said. 'If Sinatra discovered I wasn't really his doctor, I thought I could expect a visit from the Mafia...'

Next morning, his host called him. 'Don't worry about all that,' he said. 'Sinatra's a bit, well, gaga, these days as well as being a notorious hypochondriac and he always thinks everyone's his doctor. He'll have forgotten all about his waterworks troubles today and he'll be convinced he's got something else wrong with him.'

That's the problem with celebrities...

Chapter 25
Last, but...

Many years ago I chanced upon a poignant newspaper story that made me re-evaluate the benefits – or otherwise – of the newspaper coverage sometimes so eagerly sought by thespians. The following duly appeared in Peter Tory's *Star* Diary:

> On a yellowing wall deep in the vaults of the reference library of this newspaper, there has been glued for some time an ageing newspaper clipping which tells the sad tale of an elderly actress, one Miss Eleanor Barry. It records that Miss Berry was crushed to death at the age of 70 when she was buried under an avalanche of her own press cuttings. (They had fallen on her from on top of a wardrobe.)

Well, I suppose hers may hopefully be a unique and sad case.

If you add up 40 years – on and off – of interviewing celebrities, that's an awful lot of hours of chat. And an awful lot of murdered trees. One way or another, simply doing my job brought me into contact with literally hundreds of men and women celebrities. Although I can take absolutely no credit for it, I was lucky enough to interview many of the leading actors, authors, politicians and TV presenters of the age – not all of whom are in this book, partly because sometimes I kept no record of what was said. If I could recall everything we discussed, I could probably write a second book like this one. Fortunately I have at least kept many if not all of the newspaper cuttings and tape recordings from these encounters. And there are many cuttings I have not re-visited. One has to draw the line somewhere. But in this chapter I would like to mop up, as it were, a few random highlights.

One of my great discoveries, in terms of unexpected personalities, came after Peter Tory came up with a typically nutty idea. Would I take the train to the Highlands and cover Scotland's premier Bagpipe Championships: the Glenfiddich Solo Piping Championship at the castle home in Perthshire of the Duke of Athol? Tory thought it was a fairly hilarious notion. I wondered what I could do to justify the train fare. I soon had my answer in the shape of Major General Frank Richardson, a former honorary surgeon to the Queen. Richardson was the senior judge at the event. And I couldn't help but notice that whenever any contestant started blasting away on the pipes (an instrument I actually like, by the way), he turned his hearing aid off. He was, as we reported later, 'as deaf as a crofter's doorpost.'

What we didn't know, but should have, was that he was also a war hero, as his obituary in the *Independent* in 1996 made very clear:

In the fiercely fought Battle of Keren during the Eritrean campaign of 1941, while Richardson was busy organising recovery of casualties, he realised that one of the Scottish battalions had lost their momentum. Grabbing hold of his bagpipes, which he always carried with him, he moved among them and with complete disregard for danger he played them forward. This brave and inspired action raised the spirit of the men and they overran the Italian positions. Rightly, Richardson was awarded a DSO: many thought he deserved the Victoria Cross.

At the time we were unaware of this, and we shouldn't have mocked him, of course, but we did try to do it gently. 'How can you judge the pipes if you're deaf,' I bellowed, rather unkindly, into the then 83-year-old's fragile ear. 'Hear them better that way,' he replied. It turned out that he could pick up the sound more easily at close quarters through the bones of his inner ear. Well, he was a doctor, so I guess he knew what he was talking about. So each time the skirls and squawks gathered force and power, he discretely lifted his hand to his ear and removed his hearing aid.

The Duke of Athol wasn't much better. 'Tone deaf' he admitted. 'Got thrown out of the choir at Eton.' Meanwhile Tory recorded that 'Wilson, the silly chump, could not even spot the difference between a soloist's warm up and the real tune.'

After this piece appeared, General Richardson contacted us from his home in Edinburgh to say, in full agreement with Tory's verdict on me: 'Any fool knows that a hearing aid distorts the sound of the pipes. One thing's for sure – your man knows the square root of eff-all about bagpipes.'

Well in spite of such a (deserved) reprimand, we kept in touch with the delightful former soldier. Not that he was too keen, and luckily (and rather predictably) didn't appear to read the *Star*. It turned out that his many talents included literature. He had written many books about – of all things – homosexual generals. His first book, in 1972, was entitled, *Napoleon, Bisexual Emperor*. Frederick the Great, Alexander the Great, Kitchener and Gordon of Khartoum were among his subjects in *Mars with Venus; a study of some homosexual generals* (1981). Richardson's take on them was that if they were gay, they were better soldiers in that they had no wives at home to worry about them or compromise their military preoccupations. 'Homosexuals make wonderful generals,' he said. 'There's not much point in going home to their wives, is there? So they spend all their time soldiering – if you get my drift. I was an army doctor, you know, and I always wanted to help them.'

Richardson went on to write an extraordinary book claiming that Florence Nightingale was a lesbian. Much to my incredulity, he told me: 'Florence Nightingale was a rip-roaring old lesbian who tried to have an affair with my great aunt Helen. But she didn't succeed. My great aunt wasn't like that. My book includes six very long unpublished letters from Florence. The letters show a tortured soul. She was born in the wrong time, you see. Her feelings were insufferable to her. She should have been able to take her problem to a medical officer.' This was unhappy news, of course, for the nation, and we were anxious to inform our fellow countrymen (and women) about it in the *Star*.

As a result, we received a letter of complaint from Edinburgh, typed on an ancient machine by Richardson, and I must admit reading it again after a quarter of a century it does make me feel a touch guilty. It was accompanied by a hand-written letter which said: 'I believe that Mr Wilson will agree that I do not lack a sense of humour and I certainly believe that he also possesses one, but I am inclined to agree with two or three of my advisors who consider that he stepped over the mark in the article.'

His letter to the editor began: 'My views on Miss Nightingale are grossly travestied. I have the greatest reverence for Florence Nightingale, and gratitude for all she did for the British soldier and those who care for him. My book about her will be seen to be motivated by profound sympathy. Not by iconoclasm. Intelligent readers of recent books about the great lady should have little difficulty in divining the source of her agonised belief that she had sinned against the Holy Ghost. She wrote: My enemy is too strong for me. She did in fact get a little help from one doctor, Sir John MacNeill, but I believe that if she had been born half, or even a quarter of a century later, she could have had a happier life, though probably not such an immensely useful one. As for Mr Wilson's cracks about my hearing aid – a disagreement with a German Teller mine during the battle of Alamein has finally led me to be dependent on this for hearing the human voice – especially girls' voices – but I believe it distorts music. My chief surviving pleasure is listening to classical music, including that of the Highland Bagpipe, for which I prefer to remove the hearing aid, which is, in any case, quite unnecessary for the clear sounds of the pipe chanter. If your roving reporter should encounter me again and should see my right hand, having removed the hearing aid, moving down towards the top of my stocking, he had better watch out for the *sgian dubh* (the ceremonial knife worn as part of the modern Scottish highland dress, and worn tucked into the kilt sock with only the pommel visible) in his gizzard…'

So we were right about Florence Nightingale (for all his protestations) and probably wrong to make fun of his hearing aid, though really the whole point of drawing attention to the aid was not because he had one, but because as a senior bagpipe judge he intriguingly turned it off when listening to the instrument. Taken at face value, it seemed to me, it was undeniably funny.

Perhaps the general should have stuck to writing books about bagpipes. He was in fact also the co-author of *MacNeill Piobaireachd and its Interpretation* (1987): a classic work on piping. Indeed, he told us: 'I'm a bagpipe man. Don't give me a big build-up in this Nightingale business. I'm practically extinct. I'm just an old spent match.' And sadly the valiant and intriguing Major General did finally expire in August 1996.

But he'd given us the excuse for another limerick…

> A bagpipe judge, deaf in one ear
> Claimed a number of generals were queer
> Adding 'Flo of the Lamp
> Was hopelessly camp' –
> No wonder she hated Crimea!

One of the nicest – and I suppose most vain – souvenirs of friendships with celebrated artists is the gift of a painting, perhaps even a sketch or portrait. I have a very colourful and really brilliant cartoon of myself by Bill Papas, the wonderfully talented and delightful chief *Guardian* political cartoonist throughout the 1960s. He lived near me just outside Canterbury, and for reasons I no longer remember, agreed to portray me in glorious watercolours.

Born in South Africa to Greek immigrants, Papas had been the only artist allowed to cover Nelson Mandela's treason trials in Pretoria, and the syndication of these drawings landed him the job at the *Guardian*. His work appeared in *Punch*, the *Sunday Times* and was syndicated to more than 100 newspapers around the world.

By the early 1970s he tired of politics and moved to a Greek fishing village with his wife Tessa. 'I've always wanted to paint rather than just do cartoons,' he told me before he left. 'At the same time I don't want to be shoved in jail. Wherever we decide to go in Europe, I'm bound to get called a bloody foreigner.' He'd got his first break as an artist in England – having tried working as a travelling fish filleter and wine factory worker in Germany, a dishwasher and children's nanny in Sweden, and a riveter in England. He was working at a Lyons' Corner House when he got a job illustrating children's books for Collins. 'While I was negotiating with them, I used to dash out of Lyons, borrow a friend's suit, and then carefully adopt the kind of airs and graces I thought were needed for the job. Then I'd dash back to Lyons and change back into my working clothes. You can imagine my horror when the editor who'd given me the job turned up in the soup queue at the Corner House. She never referred to the incident until I met her recently and we had a good chuckle about it.' Papas spent the next 14 years sailing around the Eastern Mediterranean, writing and painting. During this time he had exhibitions in Athens, Jerusalem and London. He regarded himself as an artist-reporter, 'a recorder of people, places and events'… 'A sketchbook commands respect, a degree of awe and instant communication in a way a camera cannot. It is a passport to people.'

As well as my cherished portrait by Papas, I also have a portrait of me in pencil by John Ward (another near neighbour), the establishment artist who quit the Royal Academy in a row over modern 'ghastly muck'. He didn't paint many hacks like me – more often it was cabinet ministers, college principals, businessmen and city dignitaries. When he died in 2007 aged 89, The *Guardian* said of him: 'He particularly prized his connections with royalty, and Diana, Princess of Wales, in her wedding dress, Princess Anne, the Princess Royal (for a portrait now in the National Portrait Gallery), and the Duchess of Gloucester each sat for him. He also painted the christenings of Princes William and Harry, made drawings of Balmoral for the Queen and gave sketching lessons to Prince Charles in Ward's beloved Venice. When his work earned him the CBE in 1984, he admitted, 'I love medals and orders and dingle-dangles and I shall certainly wear mine all the time'.

…'In 1997 he was one of four artists who resigned from the Royal Academy on account of the 'Sensation' exhibition of young British artists, including Damien Hirst and Tracey Emin: "They've been invited into Burlington House," he said, "and what have they done? I'll tell you. They've taken advantage of us and written Bum on our walls, and they call it art.'"

Ward's picture of me was the result of a short film I did with him for Southern Television. He didn't want to give me the drawing as he didn't think it was good enough. He even wrote this at the side of my portrait: 'I don't think this does justice at all to the noble visage – but he will have it. Dress him up one day and bring him over and I'll do a better one!'

Ward told me an amusing story about the perils of sitting for a portrait. It concerned his friend, the celebrated fellow portrait painter Henry Carr. 'Henry was painting an elderly gentleman one afternoon,' he said, 'when he suddenly noticed that his subject had turned an odd sort of colour – and that his jaw had fallen open. Henry, keen to finish a final detail or two, quickly located a strong elastic band and put it round his subject's face in order to keep the chap's chin up, as it were. He put the finishing touches to his canvas, and then picked up the telephone to call the fellow's widow!'

The author H E Bates was another near-neighbour, and used to bounce my twins Amber and Lara on his knee when we went to visit him at his long-time Kent home at Little Chart Forstal – just by the village green where he used to organise friendly cricket matches I would occasionally take part in. Bates kindly autographed some of his books for me. After he died, I was still able to get his books autographed! Many were illustrated by John Ward, so he did the honours instead. (Ward also illustrated some of Laurie Lee's books. Using this rather tenuous link, I once rang Lee and he said: 'Didn't anyone tell you I'm always stoned on Saturday? Why don't you call me next week?')

Getting books or records autographed by proxy was also how I got John Lennon to sign the *Pussy Cats* album he had produced for the mellifluous singer Harry Nilsson. He signed the record sleeve 'Love from Harry and John Lennon'.

When I interviewed the amiable Nilsson in London after a performance of his musical *The Point* at the old Mermaid Theatre I discovered, among other things, that he watched between 80 and 90 hours of television a week – 'the equivalent of two full-time jobs!' – and that the TV stayed on all night long, whether he was awake or asleep.

When I was skiing correspondent of *Esquire*, edited by Rosie Boycott in the early '90s, she invited me to a literary evening in

London's Knightsbridge, at which various awards were being given to authors. It was black-tie do and I arrived late, with just five minutes to struggle into my bow-tie. I feverishly popped into the loo to get to a mirror. But my fumbling fingers were getting nowhere. In desperation I asked the only other man present if he'd mind helping me. He was having a pee at the time, but said: 'Give me a moment, and then I'd better wash my hands.' Cool as you like, he helped me get the dreaded bow-tie on and we both hurried into the hall with minutes to spare. The main award went to Howard Jacobson. I had never met him – or so I thought – until I recognised him as the good Samaritan in the gents. I'm sure he knew he was up for an award, and yet he'd graciously risked making himself late to come to my rescue. What a nice man. And he thoroughly deserved the Booker prize he won in October 2010.

Dame Barbara Cartland, step grandmother to Diana, Princess of Wales, had been a gossip columnist on the *Daily Express* before writing 723 books which sold a record-breaking billion copies. As the so called 'Queen of Romance' she, more than anyone, personified the original Mills & Boon genre (romance but no sex please). No wonder she always took my phone calls and babbled on at breakneck speed about almost any subject under the sun. I once interviewed her for *Healthy Eating* magazine for a feature about whether celebrities ever raid the fridge during the night. As usual she was polite to a fault, and in the end I could hardly get her off the phone.

'I've written five cookery books for my chef,' she said in a Mach 1 rush of words,' but he's so grand that I wouldn't think of walking into the kitchen and helping myself in the middle of the night. He'd be simply livid, having arranged all these things for you, do you see? So you wouldn't dare do it even if you wanted to. Anyway your metabolism runs down when you're asleep, therefore you shouldn't be hungry.'

So you wouldn't send anyone else to raid the fridge for you? Either of your two husbands, for example?

'Certainly not!' she said. 'They certainly wouldn't have, and the children would not have been allowed to.'

Was that because you were such a good cook they didn't need to?

'I don't cook. Oh no, no, no! I used to cook scrambled eggs very well for the children. But I have a chef, and I understand cooking. I could go out and have a very good dinner with you and then tell the chef what I'd had.

'But if you're healthy you sleep peacefully and anyhow older people don't sleep as much as young people. And these damn doctors keep giving you the same endless infernal sleeping pills which is absolute nonsense. You shouldn't get hungry in the night you see – it shouldn't happen. I have never ever raided the fridge. What I've always done when I have guest is I have biscuits always by the bed in a tin, you know, if they feel hungry in the night. But my own family never wanted to eat things in the night because they were properly fed. If they're stuffing themselves at night that's bad feeding. It upsets the organisation of your stomach, you see. If you have a proper breakfast, proper lunch and proper supper, you won't want other food. This is the point – all these little things you keep giving people are bad for them. You see it's very important that you shouldn't give them the wrong things.

'And the most important thing, if your children are young, is to give them something with honey at night. Honey makes you sleep, you see. That's very very good for them. All that eating little things in between, especially chocolate, puts weight on you. My chef makes the most marvellous chocolates which are freshly made in the house and they really are good, but I only allow myself to eat them on Friday and Saturday night

'People often feel hungry if they've been out late at night and had a lot to drink. What they need to do is to take evening primrose pills which will sober them up completely and when you wake up in the morning you wouldn't know you'd been drunk the night before. You won't have got a headache – no hangover at all.

'I don't drink myself – I'm practically teetotal, but evening primrose oil pills are very good for men. Tell the men to take four or five of those and a glass of milk before they drive and if you do that you ought to be all right. It's the new thing. It saves you taking taxis, which are very expensive. I did know a doctor who always carried milk in his car, and something to eat like a bun or something, so if he'd been drinking before he drove home, he drank his milk and ate his bun and he was all right if he was breathalysed. Milk is terribly important as it absorbs the alcohol...'

I have interviewed Greta Scacchi only once – after a star-studded poetry reading at Jeremy's Restaurant, in Haywards Heath, run by my friend Jeremy Ashpool. And it got off to a dismal start. The first thing Greta said to me – after I'd called her Miss 'Skatchy' (because that's how Scacchi looks as if it should be pronounced) – was 'but you have called me by the wrong name'. It is of course pronounced 'Skacky'.

After I'd recovered from that (and been forgiven) Scacchi admitted that there was a time when a romantic Shakespeare sonnet was just the sort of mournful companion she needed to comfort her over problems of romance. 'I don't really have a favourite poem – it depends on my mood. When I was lovesick, I adored Shakespeare's sonnets. They suited me perfectly. I felt an empathy with someone being sorry for himself by the light of a burning candle; but later when my mood changed I felt he was going on a bit. It's a moody thing. Now, when I'm waking up in the early hours with a baby to look after, Sylvia Plath's *Morning Song* seems much more appropriate. It's difficult to realise how much poetry you still retain until you do a reading like this. I can still remember most of the poetry I learnt as a little girl. I wish it was as easy to remember my lines as an actress. I studied French poetry in Perth, Australia, and I find it exceptionally delicious. I love Victor Hugo, Baudelaire and especially Jacques Prévert – he's a sort of Charlie Chaplin of poetry, and there's often a twist in the tail of his poems.'

After the interview, I sent her a limerick in place of a sonnet.

> At a poetry reading, Miss Scacchi
> Packed a punch like a tumbler of sake
> Was that magical voice
> (Like a purring Rolls Royce)
> Enhanced by a quick drag of baccy?

To my delight, she actually sent me an excellent limerick back, written specially in response to mine. To my great chagrin, though I've searched high and low in order to reproduce it here, I seem to have mislaid it – doubtlessly in a 'safe' place where it will turn up too late to grace these pages.

There's nothing for it now but to end my hunt for big names, at least temporarily:

> So that's all, up to date, of this story,
> Meeting folk who've achieved erstwhile glory
> And we've now reached the end
> From a start with Bob Friend
> Then with Hellicar, Callan, and Tory.

Forgive Us Our Press Passes

By Ian Skidmore

Journalist, broadcaster and author Ian Skidmore collects rare books and fine wines by choice and unlikely anecdotes and engaging eccentrics almost by accident.

His first, hilarious, account of such encounters was celebrated a quarter of a century ago in the first edition of this book.

The Liverpool *Daily Post* said its publication identified him as 'the successor to Tom Sharpe' and actor Ian Carmichael described it as 'a comic masterpiece'.

Wales on Sunday said it would be a 'hard act to follow'.

It was chosen as BBC *Book of the Year*, had the highest listening figures on Radio Four, and was read twice on the BBC Overseas Service.

Now, revisited, revised, and expanded to more than twice its original length it is being published in this special edition.

The *Daily Post* described Ian Skidmore as Wales' funniest columnist, and the *Western Mail* as 'a great eccentric'.

UK: £9.95
ISBN: 978-0-9558238-0-0
A Revel Barker Publication
revelbarker@gmail.com

Man Bites Talking Dog

By Colin Dunne

From a modest start on a country weekly in the Yorkshire Dales Colin Dunne staggered, via Leeds and Halifax, London, Leamington Spa, Newcastle upon Tyne and Manchester to Fleet Street in its heyday.

For the best part of half a century he delighted readers of local, regional and national newspapers and magazines with his canny ability to spot – and more importantly to report – the strange, the odd, the unlikely and the just plain daft elements of human life.

Whether interviewing film star Brigitte Bardot, poet Basil Bunting, or even Corky the Talking Dog… discovering the nightlife of Hamburg, the ice maidens of Reykjavik, sharing life on a beach with the models for a Pirelli calendar, or watching Antiques Roadshow being filmed in Jamaica, Colin Dunne was the man for any assignment that was identifiably barmy.

And always back in the office were the reckless and the feckless, outrageous, disgraceful, immoral, completely unreliable, but also the richly talented, wildly inventive and, above all, endlessly amusing.

UK: £9.95
ISBN: 978-0-9563686-2-1
A Revel Barker Publication
revelbarker@gmail.com

www.ingramcontent.com/pod-product-compliance
Lightning Source LLC
Chambersburg PA
CBHW051823090426

42736CB00011B/1627